I0820255

Praise for *Retirement Bites*

"We survived dial-up internet, latchkey afternoons, drinking from the hose, and every breakup ever set to a Cure song—but retirement? That's a whole new beast. *Retirement Bites* is the brutally honest, occasionally hilarious, and totally essential guide for Gen Xers who never thought they'd grow up, let alone plan for life after work. Rock on, retirement."

—Bradley Schurman, author of *The Super Age*

"If you feel like it's the end of the world as you know it when it comes to retirement, this book is exactly what you need to get closer to fine. It is an easy-to-read, optimistic, and thorough blueprint for getting on track for retirement. Plus, it is loaded with data, real-life stories, and pop culture references that my fellow Gen Xers will love. In short, other retirement books can't touch this."

—Matt Schulz, author of *Ask Questions, Save Money, Make More*

"With longer life expectancies, financial security is as important as your long-term health. *Retirement Bites* is the roadmap for people of all ages who want to get ready for a better future."

—Michael Clinton, author of *Roar*

"Many Gen-Xers find themselves hurtling toward retirement with a deep sense of insecurity about whether they'll ever have the financial wherewithal to quit working. Chock-full of reassurance and practical strategies, *Retirement Bites* is like having a savvy financial planner at your disposal, one who understands where you've been and where you want to go."

—Christine Benz, author of *How to Retire*

"Most Gen Xers don't want to live, work, or retire the way their parents did. In *Retirement Bites,* Kerry Hannon and Janna Herron provide an honest and insightful look at how this cohort has been shaped by unique economic, cultural, and technological shifts during their working lives and provides a hopeful and even fun road map forward as they revolutionize retirement and take steps to create a financially and emotionally secure future."

—Ken Dychtwald, PhD, author of *The Power Years*

"*Retirement Bites* has been needed for a long time as too many Gen Xers are unprepared for their financial futures. Authors Kerry Hannon and Janna Herron point the way to solving the challenges and nail the useful steps and actions that this generation can take. As your guides, they provide the knowledge and information that Gen Xers need to protect their future and innovative strategies to ensure that this generation can preserve their lifestyle and build financial independence."

—Cindy Hounsell, founder, Women's Institute for a Secure Retirement (WISER)

"Generation X will soon be coming of age—retirement age. The oldest Gen Xers are turning 60 and the youngest are now in their mid- to late 40s. Many are feeling behind on their finances, but if they take action now, their retirement reality doesn't have to bite. Whether you're on track or looking for ways to catch up, *Retirement Bites* offers a step-by-step road map for strengthening your situation. Authors Hannon and Herron provide expert guidance and oodles of practical tips, fun pop culture references, and inspiring real-life stories for achieving a meaningful, purposeful, and secure retirement."

—Catherine Collinson, founding CEO and president, Transamerica Institute and Transamerica Center for Retirement Studies

RETIREMENT BITES

ALSO BY KERRY HANNON

In Control at 50+: How to Succeed in the New World of Work

Getting the Job You Want After 50 For Dummies

Great Jobs for Everyone 50+, Updated Edition: Finding Work That Keeps You Happy and Healthy... and Pays the Bills

What's Next? Updated: Finding Your Passion and Your Dream Job in Your Forties, Fifties, and Beyond

Great Pajama Jobs: Your Complete Guide to Working from Home

Never Too Old to Get Rich: The Entrepreneur's Guide to Starting a Business Mid-Life

Love Your Job: The New Rules for Career Happiness

Money Confidence: Really Smart Financial Moves for Newly Single Women

Suddenly Single: Money Skills for Divorcées and Widows

Getting Started in Estate Planning

10 Minute Guide to Retirement for Women

RETIREMENT BITES

A GEN X GUIDE TO SECURING YOUR FINANCIAL FUTURE

KERRY HANNON

JANNA HERRON

NEW YORK

Cover design by Ann Kirchner
Cover images © Mentalmind/Shutterstock.com; © MM_photos/Shutterstock.com; © Bazzier/Shutterstock.com; © Hand Draw/Shutterstock.com; © Nikkytok/Shutterstock.com

Basic Venture
Hachette Book Group
1290 Avenue of the Americas, New York, NY 10104
www.basic-venture.com

Printed in the United States of America

First Edition: September 2025

Published by Basic Venture, an imprint of Hachette Book Group, Inc. The Basic Venture name and logo is a registered trademark of the Hachette Book Group.

Library of Congress Control Number: 2025935297
ISBNs: 9781541705845 (hardcover), 9781541705852 (ebook)

LSC-C

Printing 1, 2025

KERRY HANNON:

For teaching me to read and always providing love and clarity—Patrica Hannon Bonney

JANNA HERRON:

For my father-in-law, John Herron, one of my biggest cheerleaders, and who I hope is beaming from heaven because I wrote a book

CONTENTS

INTRODUCTION

Retirement Bites

But the question remains: What are we going to do now? How can we repair all the damage we inherited? Fellow graduates, the answer is simple. The answer is...
[The wind blows away Lelaina's speech cards]
The answer is, I don't know.

—Lelaina Pierce
Reality Bites, 1994

Are you freaking out about retirement?

That's what many Gen Xers may be feeling. The oldest of the generation have reached that magical age of 59½, which is when you can dip into retirement accounts such as 401(k)s and IRAs (individual retirement accounts) without getting dinged by an early withdrawal penalty. The youngest have another 20 years to go before they turn 65 and become eligible for Medicare. That's not as far away as you might think. But you're probably still busy thinking about all the other responsibilities coming down the pike, like paying for your kids' college or caring for your aging parents. Maybe saving enough for a comfortable retirement of your own has taken a back seat for now. Maybe you feel like you're only slightly behind—there's still time, right? Or maybe, just maybe, you're up late with a calculator and a 401(k) statement, not sure how to make it all make sense.

That's okay. Seriously. First of all, you're not alone. We're thinking about this, too. And just look at these sobering stats:

- One in four Gen Xers don't have a retirement account at all, while the typical household for the generation has just $40,000 in retirement savings, according to the National Institute on Retirement Security.[1]
- More than three in five Gen Xers are not confident in their ability to achieve a dream retirement,[2] while nearly half believe they could outlive their savings.[3]
- The majority of the 64 million Americans born between 1965 and 1980 expect to postpone their retirement.[4]

"Gen Xers have far less confidence in their financial futures than other generations," Kelly LaVigne, vice president of Consumer Insights at Allianz Life, told us.

No kidding. But here's the thing. Despite being tagged as slackers growing up, that's not why many of us are behind on retirement readiness. Actually, there were some pretty big forces working against us—namely vanishing company pensions and the slow evolution of the 401(k) into "the" retirement savings vehicle. We're not entirely to blame. Let's go over how we got here, starting with pensions.

VANISHING PENSIONS AND THE SLOW RISE OF 401(K)S

While pensions are still commonplace for public-sector state and municipal employers, they have all but vanished in the private sector. Today, just 15 percent of private-sector employees have a pension,[5] compared with 32 percent in the early '90s.[6] More than half of private-sector employees participate in a 401(k) plan, according to the Bureau of Labor Statistics.[7] But about 48 percent of Americans don't have access to either a pension or 401(k)-type plan at work.[8]

Just 25 percent of our generation reported in 2012 that we would have income from traditional employer pension plans when we retired, while 39 percent of the oldest Baby Boomers and 49 percent of the youngest of the Silent Generation—our parental units—said they would.[9] That older estimate for Gen Xers may have been generous. A 2021 report found that only 14 percent of us have a pension plan, as more companies continued the trend of closing these plans to new employees.[10]

"The retirement landscape shifted dramatically for this generation, and they're at risk of falling through the cracks," Catherine Collinson, CEO of Transamerica Institute and Transamerica Center for Retirement Studies, told us.

Pensions, or defined benefit retirement plans, really began to phase out in the mid-1980s when Gen X was just entering the workforce. At the same time, more employers were adding 401(k)s after new regulations in 1981 allowed contributions to these plans to be made from a worker's wages and salary, not just from a profit-sharing bonus. Still, these 401(k)s were not the robust savings vehicles they are today. For a long time, they were largely viewed as supplemental to pensions, and Congress, for whatever reasons, did not foster the growth of these plans from their inception through the mid-1990s, right when the earliest Gen Xers needed to start saving. Congress was needed to enact reforms because of the tax-avoidance structure of 401(k)s and its predecessors.

In the '80s and '90s, the government did nothing to support the 401(k) system. For instance, in 1983, the maximum annual contribution limit to 401(k)s from both employees and employers was reduced to $30,000 from $45,475 and was frozen there for 17 key years.[11] And under a 1986 provision, an employee could contribute no more than $7,000 in pretax dollars to 401(k) plans. That was hardly enough to get you where you needed to go to fund your own retirement without a pension.

It wasn't until the oldest of us were 36—in 2001—when Congress increased the total maximum contribution to 401(k)s and loosened rules around the pretax cap for employee contributions. That year also saw more options for rollovers between plans and created the Roth 401(k). Five years later—when the youngest of us hit our mid-20s and the oldest were over 40!—Congress finally passed legislation that encouraged employers to automatically enroll workers into 401(k) plans and allowed employers to provide default investments, two efforts to increase participation as it became more obvious that the 401(k) was a main pillar for a comfy retirement.

Those efforts, and the education around saving, have worked—but were maybe too late for us. Think about this: The average Gen Xer started saving for retirement at 31, while Millennials and Gen Z got the savings message much earlier.[12] They started saving at 24 and 18, respectively. And they are saving to the max: Millennials contribute 12 percent of their annual pay to their retirement, while Gen Z socks away 20 percent. Gen X puts just 10 percent away.[13]

"The American Dream of retirement is going to be challenging for most Gen Xers," Dan Doonan, executive director of the National Institute on Retirement Security, told us. "This really isn't surprising given the terrible retirement hand that has been dealt to Gen Xers: Most don't have a pension plan, they've lived through multiple economic crises, wages haven't been keeping up with inflation, and costs are rising."

DISAPPEARING HEALTH BENEFITS IN RETIREMENT

As if our meager savings weren't bad enough, Gen X can also look forward to much lamer health benefits than the Baby Boomer generation. The number of employers who provide supplemental health care insurance in retirement is fast approaching nada. The share of large companies—defined as those with 200 or more employees—offering retiree health care insurance coverage was 21 percent in 2023, down from 29 percent in 2020 and way down from 66 percent in 1988, according to KFF, a nonprofit health policy research organization.[14]

Why is this important? Health care spending becomes a huge expense in retirement, especially in the latter years. And while Medicare is awesome, it doesn't cover every penny. There's no monthly premium for Medicare Part A, the hospital insurance, but there is a premium for Medicare Part B, the medical insurance part. There's also a deductible, copays, and co-insurance, where you typically pay 20 percent of the cost for a service. Some retirees now purchase a Medigap plan to pay for these out-of-pocket costs, but it used to be that some employers offered supplemental insurance that covered these instead. Not much anymore.

There are two big reasons for this. Employers are tapping out from providing this benefit because health care costs keep going up. Unions, which often kept pressure on employers to offer this benefit, are also on the decline. Medicare has also improved some during that time, with the prescription drug benefit added in 2006 and Medicare Advantage plans offering extra benefits, so that the incentive for employers to provide supplemental coverage has waned.

"There's just a whole shift that kind of caught up with Gen X and I think that they don't realize," said Judith Brown, a fellow Gen Xer and a certified financial planner. (Judith drove a 1984 Buick Skyhawk back in the day, blasting the Eagles on the radio.)

CONCERNS OVER SOCIAL SECURITY'S FUTURE

Not to continue to pile on, but add to all that the growing, unaddressed concerns over Social Security. The reserves for the social program that retirees depend on are expected to run out sometime in the early to mid-2030s—estimates change year to year—at which time benefits to seniors will be cut by around 20 percent.[15] That's such heinous timing. The oldest of Gen X will be turning 70.

No wonder 55 percent of us are unconvinced that Social Security will be there to support us when we need it.[16] Lawmakers likely will address that shortfall, but the longer it takes for a solution, the harder it is to plan accurately. Tellingly, the financial planners we interview regularly model out what a client's retirement would look like if Social Security benefits are cut. You know, just in case.

"Being able to project what you're going to receive is an important piece that will potentially dictate someone's lifestyle in retirement," Brian Ellenbecker, a certified financial planner and financial adviser at Shakespeare Wealth Management in Pewaukee, Wisconsin, told us. "When planning, making an adjustment for reduced future benefits is prudent."

OTHER OBLIGATIONS

But it's so hard to plan for any of this when there are big things in the way. We get that. Did you know that Gen X carries the most credit card and student loan debt of all generations? The average credit card debt for us is over $9,200—almost 40 percent more than Boomers and Millennials and 175 percent more than the Silent Generation and Gen Z![17] Some of us also hold a huge amount of the nation's student loan debt, averaging over $44,000 in loans—the most of everyone. (Even more than Millennials!)[18] And we have to deal with not just our student loans, but maybe even a Direct PLUS loan we took out for our kid's education if we couldn't save up enough in the meantime to pay for tuition. No wonder our hard-earned dollars are going toward whittling down those ugly balances rather than beefing up our retirement savings.

And even if Brenda and Brandon leave the nest, that doesn't mean they aren't depending somewhat on our wallet and credit cards. That leaves many of us sandwiched between our children and our aging parents, who require more of our time and financial resources. More than seven in 10 Americans between 35 and 60 have caregiving duties for both their children and parents.[19] These same people said they are struggling financially because of it, with three-quarters saying it's difficult to save for retirement and almost two-thirds reporting they're living paycheck to paycheck.[20] And similar to many of our friends, you may feel like time is running out, especially if the economy falters again.

But we're here to say it's not time to give up. Quite the opposite. Gen Xers, the answer is simple. The answer is not "I don't know," as Lelaina said in *Reality Bites*. The answer is to rise to the challenge.

"They're starting to reach that critical window in preparing for retirement, which is usually about 10 years before leaving the workforce," said Kelly LaVigne, vice president of Consumer Insights at Allianz Life. "This is the time when many people can really start buckling down."

Our generation is nothing but resilient and undaunted, traits borne from our earliest years as latchkey kids who weathered divorces, rode bikes—without helmets!—in search of pirate booty and dead bodies, and who subsisted on Spam, Pop-Tarts, and Stouffer's microwavable mac and cheese at home alone. We ushered in a music revolution. We jump-started the computer age. We raged against the machine.

In fact, we've already bounced back from one major whammy—the Great Recession. While Gen X lost the most wealth of all ages in the years after 2008, we also were the first generation to recover it all 10 years later, especially in housing equity.[21] That's propped up a bunch of us. That equity has only grown since housing's go-go years during and after the pandemic. That's great news for the 72 percent of Gen Xers who owned their homes in 2023.[22] Overall, total home equity in the United States has recently hit new highs, and housing values are expected to grow until Baby Boomers move to a nice golf community or move on completely.

We're also not a monolith. Depending on where you fall in the Gen X spectrum, your retirement outlook may differ. For instance, older Gen Xers are more likely to have pension plans than younger ones. But those born in the mid-1970s and later may have missed the brunt of the economic headwinds those born in the mid- to late 1960s faced. Later Gen Xers didn't feel the pain of the tech bust in the early 2000s because many were either in school or had very little money invested in the stock market.

"With Gen X, you've got to split us right down the middle. You've got young Gen X and older Gen X. And they hit things very differently," Bradley Schurman, author of *The Super Age*, who was born in 1977, told us. (By the way, *The Goonies* was and remains his favorite movie today, although *Footloose* came with his family's first VHS player, so it got a lot of rotation as well, he told us.) "Many Gen Xers my age really weren't knocked back financially by some of those forces in the way those ahead of us were."

Plus, if you're in the younger Gen X set, your retirement vision may get a boost from the Great Wealth Transfer. Between now and 2045, an estimated $84 trillion will be passed down to heirs. The bulk of those assets, more than $53 trillion, will be transferred from Baby Boomers to their children.[23]

"The Boomers really have created more wealth than any other generation in US history," Schurman said. "And younger Gen Xers and early Millennials are going to be the ones that get the first wave of this from their parents."

The other big plus is that most of us are in our prime earning years. In fact, we're pulling in almost $127,000 on average before taxes.[24] Sure, a lot of that is going to those obligations we talked about earlier, but that's still a lot. With some finagling here and adjustments there to your budget, priorities, and mindset, you can get on track to a better retirement outlook—no matter what bumpy road lies ahead. And that's where we come in. We're stoked to help you find your way.

Kerry Hannon (who just missed the Gen X cutoff but is an honorary member of the generation for our purposes) is an authority on retirement, jobs, career transitions, entrepreneurship, leadership, and personal finance. She's an award-winning author of 14 books on retirement, working, and personal finances. She's also a senior columnist at Yahoo Finance where Janna Herron, the other coauthor of this book, also worked before. You may have seen Kerry or Janna on TV or radio, or read one of their articles or columns.

For Janna, this book is really personal. She's at the tail end of Gen X—born in 1979. Her inner circle are all part of the MTV generation. Her son is in high school and the empty nest years loom large—as do college costs. She's talking to her parents and her in-laws about their future care and needs. And she and her husband are dreaming of buying a teardrop camper and road-tripping across the US. Her friends, siblings, and colleagues are facing similar circumstances and having those same kinds of conversations. All of it takes money and she's right there with you, hoping, planning, strategizing for those golden years. Janna is not only writing this book for you, but she's also writing it for herself.

And then there's Yahoo Finance, spawned from Yahoo—the brainchild of fellow Gen Xers and now billionaires Jerry Yang and David Filo. Yahoo is basically the garage band of search engines. While at Stanford University in a campus trailer in 1994, Yang and Filo created the site to keep track of their favorite interests on the internet. As it grew more popular among their classmates and beyond, it morphed from "Jerry and David's Guide to the World Wide Web" to an acronym for "Yet Another Hierarchical Officious Oracle," according to an archived Yahoo press release.[25] But the dudes insist that the actual dictionary definition of *Yahoos*, characters in *Gulliver's Travels* who were rude, unsophisticated, and uncouth, was the real reason they chose the name.

"David and my titles were Chief Yahoos...and after a while, David, because he was running a lot of our expenses, he became the cheap yahoo," Yang told Yahoo Finance during a 30th Yahoo anniversary interview. "We really tried to create an environment where hierarchy is not really the key that makes everything run. It's really this idea of teamwork and trust, and building a great brand and great product being the most important thing."

And a byproduct of that business counterculture was Yahoo Finance, born in 1997. It has been there with you during the boom and bust of the dot-com era, during the long slog of the Great Recession's aftermath, and during the double whammy of a generational pandemic and meteoric rise in inflation. Yahoo Finance is in it for the long haul and wants to see you through to retirement.

Here's what to expect from our book and how to use it.

Retirement Bites lays out a blueprint for Gen Xers to take control of their assets and financial future in a manageable, realistic way. We go over the retirement challenges our generation faces combined with straightforward action steps you can take now. You'll find insightful contributions from leading workplace experts, economists, and financial advisers, as well as voices of everyday Gen Xers at different stages of their retirement savings journey. Our ultimate goal is to get you to where you can visualize a comfortable retirement—even as new challenges may arise—but not be overwhelmed by the steps you need to take to get there.

The book is organized in four parts:

"Part One: Getting Started" should motivate you. It should first get you focused, so you can fight inertia, fear, and other factors that hold you back from acting and building wealth. Then, get set to envision your dream retirement and feel excited about this journey rather than dreading it. After you know what you want for your golden years, we'll help you figure out how much you need to save to make that dream a reality and provide the road map to get there.

"Part Two: Saving and Investing" goes over the nuts and bolts of retirement accounts and how best to allocate your investments so you reach your retirement goals.

"Part Three: Increasing Your Cash Flow" provides the different ways Gen Xers can up their income before retirement. That includes tips on how to stay in the workforce longer, ways to get the most out of Social Security, and advice on how to tap other assets for retirement income.

"Part Four: More Than Money" addresses a host of money-adjacent considerations when preparing for retirement, including how to juggle saving for your children's education while also socking away for your own retirement and caring for your aging parents. We'll dive into how to plan for your health needs, the financial and lifestyle factors at play if you consider relocating, how to find the right financial professional to help you achieve your financial goals, as well as how to plan for what happens to your wealth after you're gone. Last, we provide tailored advice for business owners facing retirement.

We promise you'll be so much chiller about your retirement prospects after reading this book and following the advice we lay out. Taking control of your finances now allows you to build a rewarding future. You can finally look forward to the years to come instead of covering your eyes. Let's get ready to tackle your financial future.

PART ONE

Getting Started

1

YOUR MONEY MINDSET

The Psychology of Money and Retirement

> *Close eye. Trust. Concentrate. Think only tree. Make a perfect picture down to last pine needle. Wipe your mind clean, everything but tree. Nothing exists whole world. Only tree.*
>
> —Mr. Miyagi
> *The Karate Kid*, 1984

Thinking about money issues can make you an emotional mess and stir up all kinds of emotions, positive and negative. It can make you feel anxious. It can make you feel confident. It can make you feel generous.

Our guess is that one big reason you might be desperately seeking retirement savings salvation right now is that the whole concept of managing your money—regardless of whether it is spending or saving—just turns you inside out and upside down. But this is not a yada-yada situation to gloss over.

Saving for retirement can ratchet up that fear of facing your finances a notch or two, or ten, for plenty of reasons. That's because the bucket of dough that you ideally should set aside must potentially see you through three decades of life post-career. That amount can easily glide over the million dollar mark. That sum honestly seems daunting. It's pretty tough to believe you can actually accumulate that much, especially if you got a late start.

Even though making decisions about retirement savings can feel overwhelming, your attitude is something you can control. In finance, most people do not make decisions in a spreadsheet. So says Morgan Housel, author of *Same as Ever: A Guide to What Never Changes*, and *The Psychology of Money*: "They make them at the dinner table. They make them in the conference room with their coworkers. It's not just numbers and charts. It's this whole collision of emotions and psychology and hormones and your past experiences all colliding against each other."

So let's talk about your mindset when it comes to saving for retirement. We'll start with a general discussion of the psychology of money and why it's important for you to understand what might be holding you back. Then we'll explore the general vibe around retirement savings among Gen X. This context will help set the table for the chapters that follow.

YOUR EARLIEST MEMORY OF MONEY

Aja Evans, a board-certified therapist specializing in financial therapy, likes to kick off her sessions with her clients with the question: What's your earliest money memory? "The reason why I ask that is because a lot of people don't think about how important childhood was to formulating their money beliefs," she said.

Studies show that between the ages of seven and nine is when we start to formulate our money beliefs. The little tidbits that you pick up from people around you, from your parents and relatives and friends and schoolteachers, all add up. That's when you're starting to formulate the foundation of your money beliefs that will go on to carry you through adulthood. Maybe your parents fought about money, and, as a result, you do everything in your power to avoid conflicts about money, to the point where you won't talk about it with your spouse or partner or even your financial adviser. You instantly get a flash of fear and shut down the conversation. You walk away.

Perhaps one of your parents struggled with a dependence on alcohol, and while money had nothing to do with it, there was a sense of instability in your home and concern that they might die, or lose their job, or go away. As a result, maybe you hoard your money. Fear of spending can stem from the sense of worry that something may be taken away from you without warning. That the other shoe will drop.

Getting to the root of a negative money mindset can be liberating. Once you see where it's coming from, you can work to change it. Being aware of your money personality is a key stepping stone toward financial health and wealth.

Brad Klontz, a financial psychologist, and his research partner, Sonya Britt, have determined that core money beliefs fall into these categories:

- Money Avoidance: Ignoring—money is a source of fear and anxiety
- Money Worship: Happiness—money means happiness
- Money Status: Self-worth—net worth equals self-worth
- Money Vigilance: Hoarding—saving money is the key to peace of mind

In fact, many of us fall into more than one of these categories. But finding your place in these categories can help you start to unravel your inner relationship with money. Once you understand what money represents to you, you can determine how that plays out in your life.

NAMASTE

Stephanie McCullough, one of our fave Gen X financial planners and founder of Sofia Financial, meets her mostly Gen X clients exactly where they are, she told us: "Don't think you have enough saved for retirement? It's okay. Built up some credit card debt? You're not alone. Feel that you don't have a mind for money? Let's look at it together. I work with what someone has and focus on what they can control to move forward toward their goals." (McCullough's favorite movie of all time is *The Princess Bride*, and she whiled away her teen Saturday nights watching *The Love Boat* and *Fantasy Island*.)

She likes to compare her yoga practice to how she works with her clients. "The goal of a yoga practice is physical, mental, and spiritual well-being," McCullough said. "If one segment of our lives is off-kilter, it will impact the others. Similarly, money is interconnected with all parts of our lives—our relationships, security, and sense of self-worth. It gets emotional—and that's perfectly fine."

According to McCullough, when you bring the money stuff into alignment with your deepest-held values and priorities, it will help you determine a goal to achieve harmony and balance.

To get more adept at a practice such as yoga or a sport of any kind, you must do it regularly, whether you feel like it or not. Success in financial management is much the same. The best financial advice is simple but not necessarily easy. Wins are earned through disciplined, sustained behaviors, McCullough said. "The first step is to show up, to start to pay attention, to make time to focus on it."

Your Money Makeup

Here's an exercise to get the juices flowing. Take a few minutes and jot down answers to these questions:

- What's your age?
- Are you self-employed?
- What's your individual income right now?
- What money role do you play in your relationship with your

partner, if you're married? Are you the bill payer, the investor, the budgeteer?

- Do you still have children to raise and educate?
- What are your future financial goals? Some possibilities: You want to be able to travel, stay in your home, buy a new car.
- Do you have any health issues that require an ongoing cost for medication or therapy?
- Will you have to support your parents one day, or do you already?
- What's your greatest fear about finances?
- What's your top concern about your current money situation?
- Are you a saver or a spender?
- How important is it to you to spend money on things like clothes, or experiences such as vacations?
- How important is it to give to causes that matter to you?
- What kind of lifestyle do you have today? Would it be difficult for you to scale back if you needed to?
- Are you likely to inherit money one day? How much and how soon?
- Do you view yourself as a financially independent person or a dependent one?
- Are you a savvy investor and do you typically do your own research and execute your investment choices all by yourself, or do you tend to take other people's advice about investing?
- Are you a conservative or an aggressive investor?
- If you're working, how many years until you plan to retire?
- What are your skills? Would you need to go back to school or add skills if you plan to start a second act?

While these questions cast a wide net, your answers allow you to let the light in and begin to see your relationship with money. That, in turn, will help you begin the work that's necessary to build a rich retirement life.

KEYS TO A POSITIVE MONEY MINDSET

- **Lay out audacious financial goals:** Money may not buy you happiness, but it does buy you freedom. The goal is to have enough money so that you can spend your life the way you want. That might mean prioritizing time with family and friends. Or soaking up sweet moments like vacations. Or having the ability to pursue hobbies and things you're passionate about without being anxious about money.
- **Give yourself permission to dream:** For us, setting a dollar amount for our goals doesn't motivate us as much as envisioning what it is we're saving and investing for. This changes as you roll through the years, so be nimble and ready to let go of some things to make room for ones you can't even imagine right now.

  Kerry's dad always said, "You have to dream to get there." Design a vision board with photos, either a virtual one or one with actual photos you can place on your desk, that shows places you'd like to go, where you hope to live one day, or even a cause you want to be able to support.

  For her motivation to save for things she wants in her life, Kerry keeps a photo of a beautiful farm in Virginia with views of the Blue Ridge Mountains in the background and another photo of a beach in St. Barths.
- **Make an actionable plan:** Do you have a budget? If not, now is a great time to start recording your expenses so you can get a sense for how much you spend on different categories like housing, utilities, groceries, transportation, loans, and fun stuff. How much are you able to save? When you are saving for a particular goal, take a look at your budget and make a specific plan for where the money will come from. Will you earmark some of the money you are already

saving for this particular dream? Or will you need to cut back on spending in order to finance your goal? If so, where will you make this cut?

- **Steer clear of the "I'll pay it back tomorrow" mentality:** Debt is a dream killer and is the biggest roadblock to building a life filled with possibilities and options. Half of Americans who hold a credit card carry balances from month to month,[1] and that adds up. Savings or investment accounts accrue interest or dividends, but the opposite is true for debt: It keeps piling up and you end up paying more to service that debt. Once you have established a budget, stick to it and know that eventually you'll get where you want to be.
- **Ramp up your investment knowledge:** Take the time to learn how the stock and bond markets function. This will help you stay the course when the market gets rattled.

Money aside, perhaps our biggest piece of advice is to pause from time to time and savor where you are right now. Be present for the conversation, the moonrise, the laughter. There is so much pressure to succeed and build wealth that we often forget to appreciate what's happening now.

GEN XERS' "GLOOMY OUTLOOK"

The FINRA Investor Education Foundation—a not-for-profit established by the Financial Industry Regulatory Authority (FINRA) to support investor education—studied the financial behaviors and perceptions of Gen Xers, comparing them to those of Gen Zers, Millennials, and Baby Boomers. The survey focused on Gen Xers' behaviors related to retirement savings and debt, and perceptions about their financial situations, including financial satisfaction, financial anxiety, and financial well-being.

"Our overarching goal was not to assess Gen X's retirement prospects per se, but rather to gain a sense of their general financial health, including retirement-related decisions, relative to generations that came before (Boomers) and after (Millennials, Gen Z). Through this lens, the news about retirement savings is generally good for Gen X," Gerri Walsh, president of the FINRA Investor Education Foundation, told us.

"Few Gen Xers have positive feelings about their financial situation," Walsh said. And according to the FINRA research, their views are much more negative than those of Baby Boomers. There are a few explanations of why Gen X may have a somewhat gloomy outlook, Walsh said. "For one, Gen X is the first generation to do worse than their parents, so perhaps their expectations about where they would be financially at this point in their lives have fallen short of reality. It's also likely that many Gen Xers are currently in a financially demanding and stress-inducing life stage—with many caught in the sandwich generation—balancing the competing responsibilities of raising children and caring for aging parents. They also report high levels of anxiety about debt, particularly student debt."

About one in four Gen Xers reported having student loan debt, and 60 percent are concerned that they won't be able to pay off those loans, according to the data.[2] Interestingly, one in five Gen Xers with student loan debt hold it for someone else, like a child or a grandchild. And unlike Boomers, most Gen Xers are not yet retired, so they are not yet receiving Social Security and Medicare benefits, which can help alleviate financial stress. (And indeed, some Gen Xers may wonder if Social Security will even be available in retirement.)

Fidelity Investment's "2025 State of Retirement Planning" found that Gen Xers hold the most negative retirement outlook among all generations, with just over half confident that they will be able to retire on their own terms. One-third say they will continue to work in retirement to supplement their income.

"Many Gen Xers have watched their parents' generation age into retirement and experience long-term care events," Rebecca Bast, a wealth management adviser at Northwestern Mutual, told us. That creates anxiety, she added. "They understand the real risk that a long-term event could create in their financial lives, and yet relatively few have acted to help prevent it." This is mostly because we've been focused on other present-day matters.

Even when we reach a point in our lives when we have been successful financially, having the confidence to start to enjoy it can be tough. "I'm 57, born in 1968, and I'm finally spending," Cary Carbonaro, a certified financial planner and author of *Women and Wealth*, told us. "There's no reason not to spend at this point in my life, [and] now I have to turn the spending spigot on which is really, really hard for me because fear has kept me from spending all these years. Now I can actually enjoy the money, but it's very, very difficult. And I do this with my Gen X clients, too. If they have turned off the spending spigot for all these years, when I tell them they can turn it on, they're like, what? I don't even know how to do that." (Madonna was—and is—her fan-girl fave.)

And yet, despite this gloomy outlook, Gen X is actually in better financial shape than attitudes suggest.

Bank of America's research[3] shows that there has been slight year-over-year growth in the share of Gen X 401(k) participants who increased their contribution rates in their retirement plans. Bank of America internal payments data suggests that some Gen X households are investing relatively large quantities of their paychecks after-tax to fund additional investment accounts. In fact, the average amount invested by Gen X from after-tax earnings is over 40 percent higher than the overall population, and higher than all other generations, according to that data.

Meanwhile, FINRA Investor Education Foundation research found that, overall, Gen Xers reported good financial health given their life stage—that is, they are generally more likely to report healthy financial behaviors than the younger generations (Gen Z and Millennials) but less likely than Baby Boomers.

Gen Xers are now investing and setting funds aside for retirement at the highest rates ever. Six in 10 Gen X respondents reported owning a retirement savings account. Within this group, over 80 percent are actively contributing to these accounts. And, with a small percentage of Gen Xers reporting they took a loan (10 percent) or hardship withdrawal (9 percent) from their retirement accounts in the last 12 months, Gen X appears to be mostly contributing to and not withdrawing from their retirement savings.

We are, in fact, increasing the amount from our paychecks that we set aside in our 401(k) accounts and in outside investment accounts. And those of us who are 50 and over are saving an additional catch-up contribution without blinking an eye.

"Generation X is at a financial crossroads," Gerri Walsh told us. "Despite having experienced numerous challenges through the years, from the dot-com boom and bust to most recently the coronavirus pandemic, Gen Xers report relatively good financial health overall."

What was curious about what FINRA teased out in their research is this: Even though we are saving more than before, only one-quarter of us report high financial satisfaction.

Here's what's interesting. It turns out that people who are optimistic tend to have a better handle on their finances.

OPTIMISM = HIGHER INVESTMENT RETURNS

In a report, Goldman Sachs Asset Management and Behave Technologies, a behavioral economics firm, surveyed nearly 5,000 US workers and retirees and teased out psychological factors that can slash the gap between your retirement savings goals and your future reality.[4] These findings help us understand how we make choices and handle our financial lives.

Folks who are upbeat about what lies ahead are generally the ones who tackle a budget for today, live below their means, and are willing to get lean and mean with an eye to the potential rewards that come from a focused savings effort for the future, according to the Goldman Sachs data. Moreover, the majority of highly optimistic people have a personalized retirement plan. These optimists don't sit on the side with rose-colored glasses. They step it up to actively manage their finances when there's high inflation or when there's considerable market twitching, according to the research. In fact, they're inclined to tweak their investment allocation, hire a financial adviser, and contribute to their emergency savings accounts during those hand-wringing times.

Having a broad perspective beyond saving for retirement can help you through rough patches. Author Morgan Housel weighs in here: "If someone asks me, 'Morgan, what are you saving for? Are you saving to buy a new house, buy a new car, or retire?' I'd say, 'No, I'm saving for a world in which unpredictable things get thrown in your way all the time.'"

Don't discard those visual cues, though. We both believe in the oomph of having a picture of button-down goals you're saving for to spur you in real time to get excited about saving. The possibilities are the energy that can drive you.

In essence, we need to shift our mindsets to become proactive optimists. That might not happen overnight, but once you become aware of your outlook, you can begin to look for the bright spots. And based on that Goldman Sachs research, who wouldn't want to give that a try?

THE H.O.V.E.R. METHOD

Here's a clever reminder of the ingredients it takes to create a positive mindset for your money and for your retirement years: H.O.V.E.R. It stands for hope, optimism, value, enthusiasm, and resilience.

Hope is trusting that you can realize your goals. Where there is a will, there's a way, so to speak. When you take the time to appreciate the concept of believing in your own gifts, you can step into your power.

Optimism is a fundamental feature in loving what you do every day. It helps you jump over obstacles and pessimists and financial setbacks. When you're optimistic, you have a feeling of excitement that you can push into, that motivates you to act and to see scenarios and solutions to problems. It keeps you reaching out and asking for help and advice when you are tentative on what to do. It keeps you from shutting down when it seems impossible to imagine you will have enough money saved to retire securely or embrace your life in your next chapter.

This can-do approach quiets the urge to throw in the towel and back away from the challenge of getting your financial world on track. It also opens your eyes to see how "you can" bring about change, and not focus on how "you can't."

One way to foster optimism is to pay attention to what's going right in your life, and stop obsessing on what's going wrong—or supposedly might go wrong. It can be as easy as running a mental recap in your head each night of three good things that went right that day. These things might be as sweet as the look on your dog's face, or as common as a neighbor's tree bursting with orange and red leaves in fall, or as simple as a phone call with a childhood friend.

Optimism also comes from gratitude. Routinely taking stock of the tangible things you like the most about your life can build gratitude, and in turn optimism. Give yourself a moment or two to be thankful for whatever those things are, day by day.

Value means having the internal awareness that if you make the effort, you'll progress. It means you value the significance of your own skills and talents. This comes from the heart.

It's empowering when you have that self-confidence and self-awareness—one that doesn't rely on how someone else views you. One way to build value is to continually learn and improve your knowledge. To deal effectively with change and to create transformation in your financial life, keep developing yourself.

Enthusiasm is the zing that boosts your energy and supports you through changes—both internal and external. It's a superpower. An eagerness to try new things, take a risk, and see the upside of taking control of your retirement and financial planning will pay off.

Resilience, or the ability to recover from a setback—say, a job loss, a divorce, or a health care scare—is essential to joy in your retirement. When you're resilient, you're hardwired to ride out stock market instability, or a layoff. Resiliency gives you the inner strength to pivot and turn the downswings into prospects.

Resilient people aren't "stuck in a moment," as U2's Bono sings. They're curious. They keep learning, keep asking questions, and stay nimble. Resilience is something you can develop. One way is by regularly learning new things. Here's why: When you learn new things, you're a novice again, but then you get it. It clicks, and you're off. And that pattern repeats again and again with each new undertaking. It doesn't have to be learning about investing. It can be learning to play pickleball or building a wooden boat or taking an acting class.

Is there a hobby or sport that you can pull lessons from to help you manage your financial life?

For example, when Kerry takes riding lessons, she constantly needs to remember to be patient, not to rush, and always communicate with her horse. She reminds herself to step out of her head and into her body to be present, to focus on her breath and the natural rhythm of riding. Her coach is there to support her, to advise her ahead of time, to tell her to have a good time, but when it's showtime, she and her horse enter the gate together and canter into their zone. Their practice and preparation and trust in one another have set the stage.

YOUR TO-DO LIST

- Journal about how your memories of money impact your money mindset today.
- Find a few times each day to reframe negative money thoughts into positive ones. Record these in your journal.
- Enroll in a class or course to learn something either in the arena of personal finance or in an area that you are curious

to learn more about. The act of learning is a key to building optimism and resilience.

In the next chapter, we'll discuss the key factors to creating your unique retirement vision.

2

DESIGNING YOUR RETIREMENT VISION

I had worked for this old man and once he told me that he had spent his whole life thinking about his career and his work. And he was fifty-two and it suddenly struck him that... his life was for no one and nothing. He was almost crying saying that.

—Celine
Before Sunrise, 1995

For this chapter, we're going to set aside the financial factor and focus on the view from the balcony. Spinning out your retirement vision is a process you'll own. And it's a fun thing to do. It begins with a dream—a vision of what might be. No one can whip this up for you—not even the greatest financial adviser on the planet, and you wouldn't want them to anyway.

To get psyched about saving, you need a reason why you care, an end game. This is not a time for "Oh well, whatever, never mind."

Skip Kurt Cobain's funeral dirge. It's time for the upbeat tempo dynamic to kick in. Think about it like you are saving for life, not saving for retirement. We're not talking about a dream for your retirement that conjures up episodes of *Lifestyles of the Rich and Famous*, but one a bit more grounded.

"Money can't really be the end-all goal," Dr. Jordan Grumet, a Gen X author of *The Purpose Code: How to Unlock Meaning, Maximize Happiness, and Leave a Lasting Legacy* and *Taking Stock: A Hospice Doctor's Advice on Financial Independence, Building Wealth, and Living a Regret-Free Life*, told us. (Grumet's favorite teen movie was *Can't Buy Me Love* and his favorite TV show was *Cheers*. For tunes, it was Squeeze or Public Enemy, LL Cool J, and Run-DMC rotating on his playlist when he got home from school.)

As a hospice doctor working with people who have terminal illnesses and are dying, Grumet was treating people who were pondering their lives. "They were looking at their lives as they were getting closer and closer to death and starting to answer some of those bigger life questions such as what was my purpose in life? What was meaningful to me?"

When people find out that they're dying, all of a sudden they become very clear on what is important to them, Grumet said. "Almost no one regrets that they didn't make enough money and they don't regret that they didn't spend more hours working."

You might ask yourself questions about the meaning and purpose of your life as you start to envision your retirement years. As Grumet said: "We really focus on a certain net worth and our retirement age and the problem with that is it's a very fear-based calculation."

What is our money supposed to do for us? Making money and saving money is the goal for feeling okay about stepping out of the workforce. But what you do with that money is at the heart of it. And what you do depends on finding an idea that pulls you forward and keeps you on track.

Give yourself permission to daydream with a healthy dollop of imagination. Don't be the old man Celine tells Jesse about in *Before Sunrise*.

Right now, you might be feeling a little jumpy about how much money is enough to retire. You may wonder if it's even possible for you to retire. Now is not the time to check out and avoid this. Study after study has rolled out in the past two years about the financial quake that awaits members of Gen X who have drastically undersaved for retirement. Of course, it's impossible to say that every person in our age cohort shares this situation across the board.

But we do know that now is not the time to care *less*, but rather to care *more*.

The design we are going to dig into here will encourage you to look at *living* in retirement, not how you pay for it. What habits or behaviors do you need to change today for tomorrow? Chip Conley, author of the book *Learning to Love Midlife: 12 Reasons Why Life Gets Better with Age*, told us that a massive transition happens for most people when they approach their 50s. "A drizzle of disappointments—parents passing away, kids leaving home, financial reckonings, changing jobs, changing spouses, hormonal wackiness, scary health diagnoses, addictive behaviors becoming unwieldy, and the stirring of a growing curiosity about the meaning of life."

Oh boy. Then Conley turns that around. What you might not realize is that for many people from 50 on, the U-curve of happiness starts going up, Conley said. (Some researchers have argued that theory may be a tad too robust and generalized.)[1] But let's go with it. People are often happier in their 50s, 60s, 70s, and sometimes 80s, than they were at half that age. And this happiness can actually lead you to living longer. Becca Levy, a researcher at Yale, found in her studies that if you shift your mindset about aging from negative to positive, you get seven and a half years of additional life.[2] Now that's a significant impact on your longevity and something worth saving for.

To Conley, the ultimate middle-age skill is knowing what you want in life. We agree. When you get clear on what you want and what you don't want—the things that aren't serving you anymore—the future looks brighter. Now let's get you ready.

WHAT'S THE FREQUENCY, KENNETH?

Your vision will be your touchstone. And it will morph as you move into the middle stage of life... and through it. The hardest part about this process for many folks is getting started. But it begins with reconnecting with your own frequency.

"We're built not to see the future," author Bradley Schurman told us. "So cut yourself some slack. It's a rare portion of the population that can look 5, 10, 15, 20 years out and say, 'This is where my life is going to be. This is where it needs to be.' And then take those actions accordingly that get them there."

Schurman continued: "It's not so simple as just to snap your fingers and say, 'Hey, let's go, let's get excited about retirement.' I don't think people get excited about retirement. It's not sexy. It's a traumatic period for most people—getting there, and then living through it, because it's a disruption in what has been their norm for the entirety of their life."

Schurman is spot-on there. Retirement feels like something that is out of sight, out of mind. It's natural to be skeptical about the process of pulling back the covers and getting all touchy-feely, but retiring is all about retiring *to*, not retiring *from*. There's no living in the past.

WHAT'S YOUR VISION?

One way to jump-start this journey is to create a vision board. You can put one together on a poster board, or you can create one on your computer with an app like Canva. It's made up of myriad images of what your goals are, what a successful retirement means and looks like to you, and what inspires and motivates you. This could be snaps of snowcapped mountains, a wakeskater, a hiker, a beach house, a person teaching a class, someone grooming a horse, an older adult reading a book to a young child, someone volunteering at a food bank, and so on.

Add catchphrases to it, as well. Sure, they can be simplistic, but there's no need to be bashful or embarrassed; this is for your eyes only. Some of Kerry's are:

Do it with passion or not at all.
These are great days.
Those who don't believe in magic will never find it.
Life isn't about finding yourself. Life is about creating yourself.

Your vision board is a work in progress. If you use an app, make a habit of pulling it up on your computer from time to time and moving things around. If it's poster board, prop it up on a wall or in a corner of a room where you see it on a regular basis, and add new images to it, or pull some off.

Have fun creating your board. This is playtime with a serious spine ultimately, but for now, let it all hang out. Seriously. It's an imaginative art project that reveals your life, who you are, and who you will be. It's a personal, aspirational, and practical statement all wrapped up in one package.

There's truly a joy in doing something that's fun and creative and wildly optimistic that reaches for the stars. Make this one of those things.

We know that money is the keystone of ramping up for retirement—cash flow, taxes, insurance, investments, estate planning—but it means nothing if you don't know why you are saving and for what.

The end goal is to integrate your values, vision, and wealth for a life without regrets.

Your vision could be that you live in a rustic log home with lots of windows, high ceilings, exposed beams, and a stone fireplace that sits in the living room. From your porch, you have spectacular water views or mountain vistas, and fields of wildflowers surround your home. You spend time with friends and family. You wander the trails and fields with your Labrador retriever.

You travel to places you love, or have always imagined visiting. You play with your grandchildren, build new friendships. You continue to learn to do new things, joyfully return to a hobby you set aside, or perhaps you imagine creating a microbusiness as a passion project, say, a chocolatier. This is what Deborah Langsam did when she retired from her position as a botany professor at the University of North Carolina.

Is there an old passion, hobby, or sport that you want to dive back into? Perhaps it's sewing. Marilyn Arnold won sewing contests as a kid. When she retired from her insurance executive position, she started a side gig making pillows from old wedding dresses and then expanded to create more personalized items, like quilts from ribbons won in competitions or from old T-shirts from memorable rock concerts.

It could be painting. Tim Carrington retired from his work as a journalist and started painting landscapes at his home in Rappahannock County, Virginia. Now he sells his paintings in local galleries.

Joyce Harman shifted from her veterinary practice to chasing a dream of creating beautiful, often abstract, photography. One exhibition of Harman's photographs relives a five-state tour of dangerous storms, rural mountain scenes, soaring trees, and eclipses. "The magic of the work I do now is in the creativity it spurs," Harman said.

"After years of the emotional rollercoaster and critical attention to detail involved in saving lives of horses and dogs and inevitably losing some along the way, it's liberating to be free to experience the world without life and death and pain as guardrails," she said.

Don Covington loved the circus and when he retired from the Navy, he ran away with the Big Apple Circus as the company manager.

You might want to get involved with projects that connect you with younger generations through mentoring or coaching. The real fountain of youth is the fountain *with youth*, according to Marc Freedman, founder of CoGenerate, a nonprofit social impact organization that works to bridge generational divides, bringing older and younger people together to solve problems.

As you do this self-exploration, allow yourself time to run a self-assessment that honestly explores your values, what you're good at, your skills, and zone in on your goals, hopes, and dreams. We call this a soul search. Write down all the things you have not had time for, things you love to do, events you would like to go to, places you want to travel to. How might you incorporate these things into your retirement?

How would your days look in retirement? These activities can include volunteering, part-time work, starting a microbusiness, or turning on your inner artist. Would you want to get involved in a group activity like a travel or hiking club? Or maybe you could start an activity group, one that takes regular dog walks or bike rides, for example.

MAPPING THE BIG PICTURE

When you're thinking about making a major shift, it's easy to feel daunted by a confusing mass of questions. But a complex challenge becomes more manageable if you can step back and see the bigger picture. For some people the perfect way to scope out a complicated dilemma or opportunity is to create a mind map, according to executive career coach Beverly Jones of Clearways Consulting.

A mind map is a branching diagram used to describe a concept, project, or situation. Each map roughly resembles the hub and spokes of a wheel. The hub at the center represents the theme you want to explore. The spokes that branch from the hub represent the main aspects of your topic. Those branches are further divided into subtopics, with the process continuing for as long as you have room.

Mind maps are one way to organize information and visualize an opportunity or problem. They can help you understand and describe a confusing situation. "Maps move us from the trap of linear thinking, encouraging us to become creative," Jones told us. As your map evolves, you might spot connections or new directions that you could have otherwise missed. Beyond that, the visual nature of maps is said to stimulate the creative part of our brains, per Jones.

For some people, mapping feels more natural if they physically draw it. But some people use mind-mapping software that makes the map easy to edit.

TIPS ON DRAWING A MIND MAP

Start by picking one goal or problem you want to explore. Choose an image or a word to represent your key issue and place it in the center of the page. From that center, draw branches representing major thoughts or categories related to your central theme. Expand upon your main thoughts with smaller branches representing subtopics.

Be brief. Use only one word to label each branch. A single-word label not only saves space but it also seems to be the most effective way to capture ideas and trigger connections.

Create icons. A picture can be worth a thousand words, and imagery is a powerful element of mapping. Simple pictures can symbolize multifaceted situations. Consider how a religious icon—like a cross or a crescent and star—might remind you of deep values and experiences.

Color code. You can use colors or shapes to represent moods or categories of ideas.

Connect. Use arrows, dotted lines, or background shading to show relationships among various categories.

Work quickly. To get started, draw swiftly and don't worry about perfection. Don't bother to edit and don't make judgments about your work. You'll have time for refinements later. The goal of a quick start is to help you to make connections and spot relationships that you haven't already considered.

Have fun. Don't be afraid to be silly while you're creating your map. A benefit of mapping is that it can help you break out of your same old ways of thinking. If you play with cartoons or invent emojis, you might find it easier to think outside the box.

The mind map presented here is from Beverly Jones. It maps out her "career" after she retired in her 50s with an early retirement package from her position as a corporate lawyer.

THE ROLE LEARNING PLAYS IN YOUR VISION

More learning, or lifelong learning, as we call it, should be an important element of your vision. We both had to set aside so many educational opportunities as we focused on our careers. The good news is that these days a growing number of educational outlets are available for adults.

When you begin to learn new things, your mind shifts. It's energizing. You begin to look at the world differently. And you build resilience.

You're a beginner and then you become knowledgeable; then you are a greenhorn again and then you gain wisdom. It's a rhythm of beginning and accomplishment and beginning again. Learning strengthens the muscle that prepares you for a retirement, one that builds and grows and takes you places you can only dream of now.

Learning new things as you near retirement can help you pursue an encore career or create a business at midlife, or it can simply provide you with mental engagement. The classwork can be as basic as participating in a free online class or something more demanding, such as an immersion in a grade-free educational experience on a university campus or a fellowship.

WORK IN RETIREMENT

A pause here for a word on the role of work in retirement. We will dig into this deeper in Chapter 6. But let's throw this into the mix here, because this is likely to be part of your retirement vision.

Working in some fashion is part of retirement for most of us, at least in the early years. It's not something to dread, or a proverbial four-letter word. It's a way to shape your life in many ways to feel relevant and part of the human experience.

"Longevity and working longer for our generation have been baked in from day one," Schurman said. "Gen X, at least the younger Gen Xers, have heard from day one—'Social Security isn't going to be there for you. Don't expect it. There's not enough money there.' We just know working longer than our parents did is going to happen."

Yet it's not likely to be pedal-to-the-metal work but potentially a mash-up of part-time, contract, or freelance projects. It could be seasonal work. Or you might find yourself launching a start-up side by side with a Gen Zer.

"As someone who's been working since I was 14, I can't imagine a traditional retirement," Barbara Brooks, now in her late 50s, told us. "I consider myself a ReWiree—rewiring the way I think about retirement to align with my life's passion and purpose. I don't really see myself ever fully stepping away from my career because I love what I do and my mission of advocating for middlescent women through my company, SecondActWomen (secondactwomen.com). But I'd be lying if I said I'm not concerned about having enough socked away. I'm creating a path where my work will continue and remain fulfilling, fun, not something I have to walk away from. Fingers crossed!" (Brooks's favorite TV shows as a kid were *The Carol Burnett Show*, *The Love Boat*, *Happy Days*, and *Laverne & Shirley*.)

Paid work in some form just makes sense even if you have saved adequately for retirement. It's a safety net. It might be enough to allow you to stave off dipping into tax-deferred retirement accounts so they can continue to grow, or potentially you might even continue to set savings aside. The cash flow may also enable you to push back taking your Social Security benefit until you're 70, so you get that extra 8 percent a year bump in your benefit between your full retirement age and 70 and score a heftier monthly check for the rest of your life. Work might even provide you with health care insurance until you reach age 65, when you are eligible for coverage through Medicare.

But to us, the biggest advantage of reflecting on what kind of work you might do is the psychological payback it gives of feeling relevant, valued, and the hard-to-quantify human connection that can bubble up from keeping a hand in the game. It's about participating in a community, and although it is super hard to imagine today what your world might look like in the future, the reality of loneliness and isolation are huge issues for adults as they age.

PICTURE A "SEQUENCE OF PSYCHOLOGICAL SHIFTS"

While some of you may already be fantasizing about the opportunities of retirement, some of you may be experiencing quite negative emotions when thinking about the future.

All too often, we are left to our own devices when it comes to finding a new sense of purpose in a postretirement period. "For most of the changes in our lives there is both ritual and widespread supportive services," Ken Dychtwald, founder and chief executive of Age Wave, a consulting and research company, told us. "In high school, when you contemplated college, you visited campuses. There's counseling, and numerous supportive websites. However, when it comes to retirement, people are basically told 'good luck, have a good time.'"

Add in the underlying awareness for many that there are fewer days ahead than behind, and this emotional shift becomes even more weighted, Marc Freedman, cofounder of CoGenerate and author of *How to Live Forever*, told us: "Time is more precious. Questions of purpose and legacy are more prominent. That can sound depressing, but for many people it is a powerful source of motivation for making the most of this period."

Part of the psychological fear of retirement stems from the loss of identity people feel when they no longer work, according to Dorian Mintzer, a psychologist and retirement transition coach. Whether you appreciate it or not, our work life forges and fine-tunes our identity. This identity is an important way we define ourselves, so much so that it's often how we introduce ourselves to strangers.

"Often people don't recognize the role that work has played in their life—the structure it provided, the reason to get up in the morning, self-esteem, community, camaraderie," Mintzer said. "That's the emotional piece that catches people unaware."

Compounding that can be an underlying expectation that when we hit retirement we are supposed to feel joyful. "Some people aren't prepared that there is some grieving to do, and that's why they're feeling sad and depressed when, hey, this is supposed to be their time to kick up their heels," she told us.

To help overcome this, spend some time looking ahead at least five years before you officially retire. "Since I've been coaching, I've coached a bunch of people who are approaching retirement," Jones told us. "I've also had lots of friends who've moved to retirement recently, and I don't know anybody who has been satisfied. I know a lot of people who thought, 'Well, I'll think about that when I retire.' And at the beginning of retirement, people who haven't thought ahead, who think of retirement as doing nothing, have been kind of depressed in some lingering way. That's a very common reaction because if you've had a career, whether you love it or you hate it, you've been really engaged. You've had a reason to get up; you've had a reason to keep learning all kinds of things. If you think of retirement as the end, it's a very negative thing."

Think about the things you love in your job that you often don't notice, Jones said. "Do you like being a vice president and having people look up to you? Do you like being a leader and helping people grow? Do you like being a mentor? Notice those kinds of interpersonal interactions that you really like."

Meanwhile, start engaging in other kinds of activities that can give you the same feedback in retirement. Are there nonprofits, or clubs, or alumni groups you can get involved in now? Notice what makes you feel good. The goal is to continue receiving that positive feedback the day you retire. It's this sort of engagement that does wonders for your mindset.

What new retirees miss most about work are the relationships, Dychtwald said: "They didn't realize how much they would miss the person whose desk was next to theirs, or who they chatted with every morning asking about their kids and all of those things."

Jones suggests that you start working on building your post-career social life before retirement: "You want to reach out to people who are older and people who are younger to see if there's a potential connection because you share an interest or values or something."

So often, Dychtwald said, the focus for retirement is on finances, which we applaud. But, he added, "I think the successful transition to retirement really requires a psychological metamorphosis. During this transitional period, some people still feel unsettled, anxious, or bored, but eventually they realize that 'I can be fresh. I can be new.'"

"People have traditionally thought of retirement as an on-off switch," Dychtwald said. "You're working and then you're retired. I have come to see it as a series of four stages. There's the pre-retirement 'anticipation' period—which spans the five or so years before retirement—when folks are imagining what they'll do and who they'll be when they no longer work. Then the immediate period of retirement is like a 'liberation,' a honeymoon period where people are usually exhilarated."

That only lasts a year or so, per Dychtwald, and then there is another shift toward "reorientation" where people explore those big questions such as, "What am I going to do all day long?" and "What will matter to me?" Then, further downstream there is another shift toward "reconciliation," when folks piece together what their life was—to make sense of it and turn it into wisdom, and get ready to leave their legacy.

START TO THINK OF OPTIONS YOU MIGHT PURSUE

Give yourself permission to consider a few options, or to try something to see if it's right before you commit. Understand that even as you're envisioning what retirement could look like now, you have the power to change the vision when the time comes to actually retire.

Give yourself some breathing space in your vision of retirement. Ideally, you allow yourself a year to get the kinks out. No big decisions, no set-in-stone new roles to take up. This is the time for some freedom to try things out and see if you enjoy them, whether it is a volunteer project or an RV road trip to see your favorite bands in concert.

In other words, give yourself the space to just be. Allow your new chapter to unfold and bubble up without trying too hard. Say yes to lots of invitations but keep your boundaries. No long-term commitments. This year is your year to decompress and discover.

When Jeff Hutchinson retired from Dominion Energy in Richmond, Virginia, he took a gap year to figure out what he wanted to do. "I was emotionally ready to go," said Hutchinson, who has adjusted well to life after work. But he didn't want any specific must-do things that first year. His days now are full. His activities include getting together with former coworkers for lunch and tackling the pile of "when I retire projects" that were stored in his garage over the years. And he enjoys helping around the barn with the half-dozen horses he and his wife, Mary Beth Donnelly, tend to, along with maintaining the fields and fencing of their 56-acre farm in Beaverdam, Virginia.

Hutchinson knows he's lucky to have a lot on his plate. "I tell my friends, 'Don't let retirement scare you.' So many people are so worried that they're not going to have anything to do. You need to plan a little."

Jennifer Jacobs, now in her early 50s, a nuclear engineer and former nuclear operations officer for the US Army Reserve, started her retirement pivot more than a decade ago when she read an article about foster care and the difficulty of finding a child's family.

In her work life, she focused on nuclear nonproliferation. Her efforts crisscrossed with the intelligence community, whose analysts often track and find terrorist networks. As unlikely as it sounds, that experience helped Jacobs discover how similar technologies could be used to help foster care professionals find the families of foster children.

It didn't happen quickly, but in 2011, she cofounded Connect Our Kids, a technology nonprofit based in Falls Church, Virginia, which helps social workers, lawyers, and volunteers to do just that, while also providing support to both children and their families. These tools are now being used by 2,000 foster care professionals in more than 40 states and Canada.

"Hearing the stories of reconnection and reunion made possible by our tools gives us a daily sense of profound purpose," Jacobs told us. "There's no greater reward."

The problem is that many retirees don't seriously set aside the time to plan a vision like you're doing right now. For those who encounter retirement earlier than expected because of a health crisis or downsizing, facing the new reality can be rocky.

There is no cookie-cutter solution to what will make a perfect retirement for you. There's no "one-size-fits-all." It's your own recipe. It's your playbook to write.

CONSIDER THESE SOUL-SEARCHING QUESTIONS

No one is grading or judging you on your answers. That's the beauty of this exercise. Take as long as you want to answer these—days even. The only wrong responses are the ones you opt to ignore. Write out your answers. There's something about the process of actively writing, or typing, that makes it real, tangible, meaningful.

- What's my purpose?
- What's important to me?
- What kind of work—paid or unpaid—do I want to do when it is time to retire?
- What am I curious about pursuing when I retire?

"Start with a list of 20 or so things you're curious about," Robert Laura, a retirement coach, told us. "When you're curious, it fosters motivation. Tape that list to your refrigerator door." (Laura, born in 1972, lights up when tossing out that *Ferris Bueller's Day Off* was his fave movie, and for listening vibes—AC/DC and Van Halen topped his chart.)

THE BEST OF ALL WORLDS EXERCISE

Now we want you to imagine that you're financially set, that you have enough money to take care of your needs now and in the future. In that light, consider these points:

- How would you live your life?
- Would you change anything? Let yourself go. Don't hold back on your dreams.
- Describe a life that's complete and richly yours.

Next scenario: You visit your doctor, who tells you that you have only five to 10 years left to live. The good news is that you won't ever feel sick. The bad news is that you will have no notice of the moment of your death. Given that reality:

- What will you do in the time you have remaining to live?
- Will you change your life? If so, how will you do it?

Final take: This time, your doc shocks you with the news you have one day left to live. Ask yourself:

- What did I miss?
- What did I not get to be?
- What did I not get to do?

YOUR IDEAL WEEK

This exercise is designed to help you envision your dream retirement. Try to be as specific as possible as you complete these entries. This is your opportunity to be brutally candid about your goals, who you are, and the things you love.

- Describe hour by hour how you would spend your ideal day—if you had all the resources you need to live exactly as you like.
- Describe how you would spend your ideal week—if you had all the resources you need to live exactly as you like.

Another twist on this is to silo it down into categories. Ask yourself:

- What must you do?
- What could you do?
- What would be fun to do?

This exercise is meant to provide you with an outline of immediately actionable steps you can follow, with room to add others as you go. When we describe our ambitions, dreams, and goals, or at least put them down on paper in black and white, they become real. And once they are real we can begin to gradually find ways to incorporate them into our daily lives and our future reality. You should also note the cons, or things you want to be certain not to do in your next stage of life. Along the way, we can discover ways to trim back the roadblocks for getting there, and add new things to boost our chances of getting to our dream retirement.

HOW CAN I?

Now that you've begun to formulate a picture of your retirement and what matters to you from a broad perspective, it's time to whittle it down to reality. Doing so will help you tease out precisely what it is about planning for retirement that makes you freeze.

The best way to go about this process is to spend a week or two tracking your feelings and observations from the time you get up until the time you turn out the lights for the night. In a journal, make note of what happens each day, how you feel at different times, what makes you smile, and what makes you anxious. Jot down those moments when you feel confident and those when you feel bored or stressed or overwhelmed.

When you read back over your journal entries, you might find your sticky spots. Think about them. And then, instead of saying, "I hate this," ask yourself: "How can I change this? What do I want to replace it with? What's my goal?"

Kerry learned this lesson from her dad. Whenever she asked his counsel about a goal she had, he would always ask, "How *can* you?" He would ask her this even when others were telling her she couldn't do it. The lesson is this: Surround yourself with people who bring that kind of attitude.

Once you understand what motivates you and where your blockers are, you'll be better equipped to make a practical plan for retirement.

Finally, remember that designing your retirement vision is not a chore. Creating your vision board and journaling can become a fun part of your daily routine, and with them you can begin to envision your own personal retirement-plan possibilities. That sense of taking control gives you power, and having dreams can provide a dose of adrenaline.

Sure, money and wealth are part of helping us be able to do the things that bring us joy, but it's so deeply important to remember that happiness is often found in the simplest things in our lives. So hold that concept dear as you spin up the view of your future.

Ours is a culture that often determines our worth as human beings by how much money we make or have socked away. We encourage you to take time to ponder moments of wonder and delight that you want to include in your retirement vision.

These are often the things that really make life worth living. As author Annie Dillard memorably put it, "How we spend our days is, of course, how we spend our lives."

In the end, however, after all the list-making, self-evaluation, and dreaming, you must *choose* to envision your happiness in retirement.

One of the biggest mistakes retirees make is to dream far too small. That's why it's key for you to put in some time right now to really allow yourself to visualize what retirement might look like for you.

YOUR TO-DO LIST

- Create a "pros and cons" list of your current life and what you'd look forward to creating in the future.
- Build a tangible vision board.
- Reframe retirement goals from "I can't" to "How can I?"

Now that your vision for retirement is beginning to gel, your next step is to figure out what it will take financially for you to achieve it. In the next chapter we'll help you calculate your magic retirement number—the amount of money you need to save to ensure you achieve the retirement you've got in mind.

3

CREATING YOUR FINANCIAL PLAN

RACHEL: I'm so sorry, you guys. I didn't mean to bring you down.
MONICA: No, you were right. I don't have a plan. Phoebe, do you have a plan?
PHOEBE: I don't even have a pla.

—*FRIENDS,* SEASON 1, EPISODE 4, 1994

It's understandable that many of us didn't have a financial plan in our 20s when we were just figuring everything out. Decades later, it's time to get one together if you want to make those retirement dreams come true. To start, you need to calculate your magic retirement number—the amount of money you need to save to ensure you can live the retirement you've imagined. Once you've got that key figure, your next move is to calculate how much more you need to sock away between now and then to hit that final goal. We're gonna be straight with you: Depending on how much you've been saving or not saving, the gap might be alarming. But trust us, we'll help you put together that financial plan to get you closer to your goal.

Chuck Hansberry is an attorney in Montana (he is also Janna's brother-in-law). For the longest time, he worked for a large law firm and every year put money into his 401(k) like he was supposed to. "But it was just a big black box. I never really paid much attention to it," Chuck, a bona fide Gen Xer born in 1969, told us.

It wasn't until around 2017, when listening to financial podcasts while mall walking during Missoula's winters, that Chuck realized he hadn't been taking his financial future seriously enough. By then, he had his own practice with a partner. From those podcasts, he learned about the benefits of 401(k) profit sharing, a feature available to small business owners, as well as the investment advantages of health savings accounts, or HSAs. (We'll get into both later.) He figured out the magic number he needed to retire and fired his financial planner who was charging too much. He and Janna's sister Dawn also reexamined their spending and their financial priorities, including putting two kids through school. (This chapter covers all of these exercises.)

"I've been completely do-it-yourself since and that's when everything kinda went on steroids," Chuck said. He's now semiretired at age 55, working about a quarter of the year on his schedule and traveling stateside in a converted van he renovated himself or by bike abroad. (In the mid-90s, Dawn and Chuck crisscrossed the country in Gertie 1, a 1972 VW camper. Thirty years later, it's Gertie 2, a RAM ProMaster cargo van.)

It's time for you to take the same plunge. Let's start with finding that magical retirement number.

MAGIC RETIREMENT NUMBER

How much money do you need to retire how you want? Wouldn't it be awesome if there was just one answer. The median amount that Gen X thinks they will need for retirement is $700,000, while nearly a quarter of them say they will need at least $2 million.[1] That's a huge range and, to be frank, an ill-informed one, because about half of the people surveyed just guessed. We can do better than that.

It's pretty easy to find a calculator online to do this magic retirement number calculation for you. It's not like you need a TI-84 for this.

Just do a Yahoo search (see what we did there?) or a Google search (or search with Ask Jeeves, if that's still your jam) for "AARP Retirement Nest Egg Calculator," "Prudential Retirement Income Calculator," or "Schwab Retirement Calculator." The search results provide links to some of our favorite calculators.

The rad thing about these calculators is that they do most of the heavy lifting for you. Not only will these estimate how much you need to save for retirement, they also will calculate how much you're falling short. Some may even suggest ways to get back on track, like extending your working years or increasing your annual retirement savings.

But the estimates that these calculators spit out are only as good as the inputs you provide. So this is where you need to get down to business and get the most accurate figures possible. If you're married or planning with a partner, be sure to do this together. Fire up those laptops and, heck, grab a wine cooler for old time's sake.

This is a short list of what information you may need, and where to find it:

- Your age (You should know this by heart.)
- The age you plan to retire (Remember: You don't qualify for your full retirement benefits from Social Security until 67.)
- Total household income (Use last year's tax return as a guide, line 9 on Form 1040, or annualize your gross pay on your most recent paycheck and add in any other income from side gigs, bonuses, or rental properties.)
- Expected pension income, if you have any (Use last year's annual pension statement.)
- Your total retirement savings (Total what you have saved in 401(k) or similar plans, IRAs or Roth IRAs, and any other brokerage accounts.)
- Annual retirement contributions (Check your paystub for pretax retirement contributions into a workplace retirement plan. Add any additional retirement savings here.)

The next batch of values may require you to guesstimate. A piece of advice here: Play it conservative. This is not Chapter 2. It's not an aspirational exercise. It's not like New Year's Day and you're convinced you can lose 40 pounds this year. It's more like February 1 and you've resigned yourself to just not gain 10 more pounds. The risk of being too optimistic could leave you short of the savings you need in retirement. So channel your inner cynic. That's what Gen X is known for. Here's what you might encounter.

Average annual return on investments: This return is how much your current retirement savings are expected to increase each year until you retire. Some historical perspective: Over the last 50 years, the S&P 500 has returned on average 11.5 percent per year. That, of course, includes the whiplash we experienced going from a go-go year like 2021, which returned 27 percent, to an oh-crap year like 2022, when the index returned negative 19 percent, and then back to a thumbs-up 2023 when the S&P 500 returned 24 percent. Your retirement portfolio won't be made up of just stocks, except maybe when you're younger. It will be mixed with safer investments like bonds, which typically offer smaller, though more reliable, returns. Generally, you'll have larger shares of bonds in your portfolio when you're closer to or in retirement. We'd suggest fiddling around with a range from 4 percent to 7 percent.

Annual increase in your household income: We believe that you're a totally excellent employee and you're on track for five more promotions. But the best way to find this number is to average out the changes in your income over the last five years. Use your past tax returns as a guide. Calculate the percent increase by using a percent change calculator online. Then average those increases.

Annual income you'll need in retirement: The general rule of thumb here is that you'll need 80 percent of your preretirement income for retirement because certain major expenses disappear after you retire, such as commuting and retirement-plan contributions. Fidelity offers a good breakdown, using where your income lands now.

- If your annual income is less than $50,000, then you'll need 80 percent of that for retirement.
- If your annual income is between $50,000 and $80,000, then you'd need 75 percent of that for retirement.
- If your annual income is between $80,000 and $120,000, then you'd need 70 percent of that for retirement.
- If your annual income is more than $120,000, then you'll need 55 percent to 65 percent of that for retirement.[2]

Revise this up or down based on how aspirational your retirement is expected to be, given the exercises you completed in Chapter 2. If you plan to be a globe-trotter, up that percentage. If you plan to babysit the grandkids in your spare time, dial it down.

Expected Social Security benefits: The federal government offers a tool to calculate your benefits based on your actual earnings in your My Social Security account. It will allow you to see what your monthly benefit will be if you file at 62—the earliest age you can collect benefits—or at your full retirement age of 67, and at 70, when you get the biggest benefit check because you waited longer to collect. Signing up takes about 10 minutes, and requires a strong password and multiple-factor authentication.

How long you expect to live: Just 35 percent of Americans know the average lifespan of retirees.[3] But knowing this information is key to making sure you don't outlive your savings. In fact, the majority of people who knew the following six US statistics—indicating they have a strong grasp on the details regarding longevity—were more confident they would be financially comfortable throughout retirement versus those who didn't:

- On average, a 65-year-old man will live about 19 more years to age 84.
- On average, a 65-year-old woman will live about 22 more years to age 87.
- The likelihood that a 65-year-old man will live until at least age 90 is 30 percent.

- The likelihood that a 65-year-old woman will live until at least age 90 is 40 percent.
- The likelihood that a 65-year-old man will not live beyond age 70 is between 5 percent and 10 percent.
- The likelihood that a 65-year-old woman will not live beyond age 70 is under 5 percent.

Many of the financial planners we spoke to generally model out to age 95 to cover their bases.

Bridget Grimes, a certified financial planner in Coronado, California, who specializes in advising breadwinner women—mostly Gen Xers—models out until age 100 for her clients. Women, as we saw in the preceding list, live longer on average and wind up single later in life.

"There's all sorts of crummy things associated with that. You file single, get a tax hit. Their health care is more expensive. You have less money, the whole nine yards," Grimes, who missed the front edge of the Gen X age cutoff by two years, told us. "There is this fabulous longevity, but then there's this tremendous cost that's associated with it. And how do you prepare for that?"

Your genes and current health also play a huge role. If your granny or paw-paw was still kicking it into their late 90s, you may want to put in 100. Or if you're in poor health with chronic conditions—and the members of your family tend to die younger—you could stand to take a few years off. Morbid, we know, but it is what it is.

Now you've got all your needed inputs. Type those suckers in and let the calculators run to reveal your magic number. We'll wait...

...

You there? Are you okay? There's a good chance—since you picked up this book in the first place—that you've got a little, or a lot, of catching up to do. Reality definitely bites, but it's better to know than keeping your head in the sand. Anyway, that was a lot of work. Take 10. Enjoy the rest of that Zima before moving on.

GETTING FROM HERE TO THERE

The good news here is that you're no longer in the dark. You can make a plan to get your retirement savings back on track so that you can actually have that dream retirement that you imagined while working through the exercises in Chapter 2. Getting your current savings from here to the number those retirement calculators spit out starts with understanding where your money is going today. If we were in class, that equation would look something like this:

Total Cash Inflows – Total Cash Outflows =
Net Cash Flow

Makes sense, right? "Bueller? Bueller? Bueller?" We're joking. Let's rewrite that equation like this:

Total Money Coming In – Total Money You Spend =
Money You Have Left Over That Can Go to Retirement

MONEY ROLLING IN

Let's tackle Total Money Coming In, or your income. Right now, you're either close to or smack dab in the middle of your peak earning years, which is usually from your late 40s to late 50s.[4] Women typically peak earlier, between 35 and 54, while men peak later, between 45 and 64. After that, incomes generally level off. Right now, householders ages 45 to 54—encompassing much of Gen X—are pulling in $101,500 annually from their nine-to-fives, the highest median income of all ages. Those households between ages 55 to 64 are earning a median of $81,240.[5]

Gen X households get a big boost from the ladies, who are more educated than their mothers. In fact, Gen X was the first generation where the share of women with bachelor's degrees exceeded the share of men who obtained one. By 2001, 31 percent of Gen X women had four-year degrees, compared with 28 percent of men.[6] The number of two-income households swelled with our generation. But even more interesting, the number of high-earning women has also jumped. Nearly a third of Gen X women bring in the biggest paycheck in a household, twice the rate of previous generations.[7] That's created a more self-reliant mentality among Gen X households, because the income coming in is more diversified and not dependent on one person.

So let's see how all this plays out in your household.

The fastest way to get a grip on what you have coming in is to gather the most recent paystubs for everyone in your household. But that probably tells only part of the income story. Pull out your most recent tax return again, which includes 1099 income from side gigs and dividends from investments. Your 1040 also will reveal income sources like tips and alimony, things reported above line 9 on the tax form.

While the goal is to calculate your monthly net cash flow, you might need to start with yearly numbers since the figures on your 1040 are annual. Use your paystubs to get an accurate reflection of your take-home wages now. They'll account for any raises you received this year that last year's tax return won't reflect. If you get paid twice a month—such as on the first and 15th of every month—multiply your after-tax salary by 24 to get the yearly figure. If you get paid every two weeks, multiply that by 26. Now fill out the yearly amount for each of the following income sources that you reliably receive every month:

- Wages, salary, and tips
- Interest on savings accounts, CDs, and so on
- Dividends from stocks, etc.
- Social security benefits
- Pensions
- Alimony, child support
- Other income

Add those all up. The calculator on your phone or an Excel spreadsheet is good enough. Divide the total figure by 12 to get a monthly figure. Boom! That's your income. Take a minute to pat yourself on the back. You may be an old yuppie now, but at least you're rollin' in the dough.

DOUGH ROLLING OUT

Now let's tackle Total Money You Spend. Remember The Notorious B.I.G.'s song "Mo Money, Mo Problems"? It's kinda apropos here. What often happens is, as we get raises, we up our standard of living—maybe to the point where we end up spending more than we make. This next part of the exercise will illuminate exactly how much of that hard-earned dough is rolling out the door. It will also help you to figure out where you can make some changes so that you can increase your investments for your future self.

"I think having the discipline to avoid that lifestyle creep as income grows is one of the most valuable skills that any Gen Xer can learn," said Judson Meinhart, a certified financial planner in Winston-Salem, North Carolina, who is also one of the youngest Xers. (One of Judson's fond memories of his childhood is the original TGIF lineup of *Full House* and "that show with the nerdy guy... Urkel!" He was talking about *Family Matters*.)

It took Janna's brother-in-law and sister, Chuck and Dawn Hansberry, some years to learn that about lifestyle creep, they told us. "Many times I look back on some of the choices and financial decisions that we made and I'm like, 'You're an idiot, Hansberry,'" Chuck said.

The best way to get a snapshot of your average spending is to pull out last month's bank and credit card statements. Personally, we like to document our spending over a three-month span to get a good average and to smooth out any weird one-off spending spikes. We'll leave that extra credit work up to you.

It's also good to split up those expenses into two categories: needs and discretionary. Needs are the expenses you really have to pay, or else you'll face major consequences such as hunger, delinquency, or risking the lights getting turned off. Remember: Some expenses may be a cost that you pay on an annual or semiannual basis, such as HOA dues or auto insurance. So divide accordingly to get the monthly figure. Here's a short list of needs to help you out:

- Mortgage payment or rent
- Property taxes, if not included in your mortgage payment
- Homeowners (renters) insurance, if not included in your mortgage payment
- HOA dues
- Life insurance premiums
- Auto insurance
- Medical, dental, and disability insurances
- Food
- Childcare
- Auto loan(s)
- Other transportation expenses
- Personal loan(s)
- Outstanding credit card debt (not including new monthly charges)
- Utilities: gas, electricity, trash, water, cellphone bills
- Child support
- Alimony

Discretionary expenses are the ones that you can adjust from month to month or even eliminate without any real immediate consequences. Put down the values for each discretionary expense. Here's another quick list:

- Household repairs and maintenance
- Clothing and laundry
- Educational expenses
- Automobile expenses (gas, repairs, and so forth)
- Entertainment and dining

- Recreation and travel
- Club dues
- Hobbies
- Gifts
- Major home improvements and furnishings
- Professional services
- Other and miscellaneous expenses
- Charitable/church donations

Last, add up any regular amount of money that you divert to any kind of savings, after tax. This doesn't count your pretax contributions to 401(k)s. So we're talking about any contributions to a savings account, 529 education savings plan, a traditional or Roth IRA, or an investment brokerage account.

Combine all of these tallies, and add up your total expenses and after-tax savings. The result will be the average amount you spend each month.

DOUGH LEFT OVER

Finally, it's time to tackle Money You Have Left Over That Can Go to Retirement. To begin, you need to figure out your net cash flow. To determine that, simply subtract your monthly expenses from your monthly net income.

If your net cash flow number is negative, your expenses are too high relative to the money you have coming in. If it's positive, but not by much, you still have some reductions in spending to make so that more can go toward your retirement savings. If you have a good amount left over, pat yourself on the back; that extra cash can help you boost your retirement savings.

Overall, you want your cash flow to roughly follow the 50/30/20 rule, said Jon Ulin, a certified financial planner in Boca Raton, Florida, "to keep things simple." The rule is intended as a "starting point," said

Ulin. (An older Gen Xer, Ulin finds himself always playing "I Won't Back Down," released by Tom Petty in 1989, while on the treadmill.)

What is the 50/30/20 rule? It means 50 percent of your take-home pay should be going to your needs, 30 percent to your discretionary items, and 20 percent to your savings. If your ratio is off, zero in on the items that are putting you over those parameters, especially in the discretionary category. The idea is to figure out where it's easiest to cut back and find more money that can go toward your retirement. But you may need to use that extra cash to achieve other financial goals. To get a sense of what those goals are, let's do a net worth exercise. This exercise will show you what other financial obligations you must address in addition to saving for retirement. It also will reveal the assets you have, besides your retirement savings, that you can use to finance your golden years.

WHAT ARE YOU WORTH?

While the cash flow exercise gives you a snapshot of your monthly money coming in and out, a net worth exercise gives you a holistic view of your total finances. It also gives us another fun little equation.

Assets – Liabilities = Net Worth

Overall, as of the end of the second quarter of 2024, Generation X has $39.62 trillion in wealth,[8] holding $46.66 trillion in total assets and $7.04 trillion in debt. To break that down by family, we can turn to the Federal Reserve's triennial cross-sectional survey. As of 2022, the median family net worth with adults ages 45 to 54 was $247,200, while the average was $975,800.[9] Of course, there's a wide variation there. The median often provides a clearer picture because it is the midpoint; half of families hold more than the median and half hold less. The average can be skewed if there are major extremes at either end. That's what we see here. Those on the top of the wealth and income spectrum hold way more wealth than those at the bottom, which is skewing the average so much higher than the median.

One thing is interesting, though. At age 30, Gen X was doing better in terms of net worth than the humongous generations that sandwich it—Boomers and Millennials. That's despite our generation having to weather such crappy events like the dot-com bust and the Great Recession during our working years. Don't believe us? Check out the table.

Assets, Debt, and Net Worth at Age 30

Generation	Total Assets	Total Debt	Average Net Worth
Baby Boomers	$135,273	$46,230	$89,043
Generation X	$201,344	$86,606	$114,737
Millennials	$190,267	$90,104	$100,163

Source: Federal Reserve Bank of St. Louis[10]

A big reason Gen Xers hold more asset value is because of their home value. Their home value was 7 percent more than Millennials' and 75 percent more than Boomers'. Their homes were also the source of their biggest debts versus the other generations, with the average Gen Xer carrying $63,302 in mortgage debt versus $34,646 for Baby Boomers and $59,861 for Millennials. Gen X also had more than twice as much retirement savings as the Baby Boom generation at 30, since Boomers were more likely relying on pensions and therefore had less saved for retirement. And so the little bit Gen X was able to put away was huge in comparison. And the MTV Generation carried almost half the educational debt as Millennials at 30, though now their education debt load is larger for a variety of reasons. Some have taken on loans for their children. Others were in repayment plans that didn't cover the interest and their balances grew over time.[11]

But averages don't tell us about you. What is *your* net worth? Let's start with assets, which is any property or item owned by an individual that has value and could be liquidated into cash if needed. Cash is also included in this calculation. The biggest asset most Americans own are usually their homes. Other assets include cars, investments, and other valuable personal property like boats and collectibles. (Exclude items like regular household furniture, which largely would sell for yard sale prices and wouldn't increase your net worth very much.) Add together the following assets:

- **Real estate:** Estimate the current value of your house and other real estate you may hold. Zillow provides a free home value estimator tool online. Check that against any recent sales of homes in your neighborhood to get an accurate estimate.
- **Total amount in checking accounts**
- **Total amount in other deposit accounts:** This includes savings accounts, certificates of deposit (CDs), and money market accounts.
- **Retirement and investment accounts:** Make sure to include money you have in 401(k)s, 403(b)s, IRAs, other retirement accounts, brokerage accounts, and any investments in T-bills, savings bonds, and I bonds.
- **Cars:** To get a good estimate of the value of the cars in your household, turn to the free online estimators provided by Edmunds or Kelley Blue Book.
- **Other assets:** Other assets may include business interests, life insurance proceeds, antiques, collectibles, fine jewelry, and cash.

Next, move on to liabilities, which is something that an individual generally owes. Put down the total amount still outstanding—in other words, the amount that needs to be paid off—not the amount of the original debt. Add together the following liabilities:

- **Mortgage debt:** Enter the total amount of your mortgage that you still must pay off.
- **Credit card debt:** Put in the total amount of outstanding debt that you owe across your credit and charge cards. Do not enter an amount if you consistently pay off your entire balances in full every month. Be honest!
- **Personal loans:** These include personal loans, payday loans, and any official loans you owe family or friends.
- **Student loans:** Input the total amount you owe, not your monthly payment amount.
- **Car loans:** Again, provide the total amount owed for all the cars in your household, not the monthly payments.
- **Other debt:** Include any other outstanding debts such as medical bills, business loans that you have personally guaranteed, home equity lines of credit (HELOCs), or home equity loans.

Now subtract your liabilities from your assets. That's your net worth, or your wealth. Knowing your net worth helps you with your retirement journey because it can provide you with options to fund your retirement. For example, selling your home and downsizing to a smaller, more affordable home will release some of the equity locked in your house that can be later used for your retirement. You also get a good handle on the obstacles you need to overcome, such as paying off credit card debt or student loans, on your way to a sunnier horizon.

YOUR TO-DO LIST

- Figure out your magic retirement number and subtract that from what you've saved so far.
- Calculate your net cash flow. Find out how much money is coming in and where it's going now.

- Get a handle on your total net worth by tallying up your assets and debts.

You've armed yourself with the knowledge you need to make important changes. Like G.I. Joe says: "Now you know. And knowing is half the battle." Keep all your findings in a handy place. We'll refer back to them and this chapter a lot.

Next up: the basics of saving directly for retirement.

PART TWO

Saving and Investing

4

NUTS AND BOLTS OF RETIREMENT ACCOUNTS

JACK: Tell me again Harry, why did I take this job?
HARRY: Oh come on, thirty more years of this, you get a tiny pension and a cheap gold watch.

—*SPEED*, 1994

Once you have a handle on your total net worth, you can begin to make some smart moves to increase your wealth. Your biggest asset, aside from your home, is likely to be your retirement savings accounts—money you have in 401(k)s, 403(b)s, and IRAs.

Whether you are saving with gusto or haven't given it much thought, let's take a look at your options for saving for the retirement you want.

In this chapter, we'll go deeper into how retirement accounts work and why you really do need to take a look under the hood of the accounts you're invested in. You may have some of this information stored on your mental hard drive already. But it never hurts to shine a spotlight on all the options available to you, what's changed since you last took a look, and check off the pros and cons of how you can use these accounts to ramp up your wealth.

In this chapter, we also review advice for job switchers and for those who are self-employed. And we discuss new options for those of you who have enrolled in an employer-provided 401(k) plan that uses your student loan debt payments as qualifying contributions, and for creating emergency savings through an employer-provided retirement plan. We also dig into an option to roll over 529 college savings funds into an IRA account. The end goal is for you to know in your heart that you took advantage of everything that was available to you to get to *your* ideal number.

YOU AND YOUR RETIREMENT ASSETS

Here are some of the types of retirement accounts you might hold. For more details, check the IRS website (irs.gov).

Defined benefit plan: This is a traditional pension plan in which an employer uses a formula based on salary and years of employment with the firm to devise an income to be paid to the employee or beneficiary on a regular basis at retirement.

Mention a Packard or Studebaker to classic car buffs and eyes glisten. These sleek wheels were once the epitome of luxury. In 1954, the two companies merged, but the new company lost its traction and US production came to a screeching halt in 1963. When the company went kaput, thousands of the company's workers discovered that their traditional defined benefit pensions guaranteeing an income stream for life were terminated, too.

The outrage caught the attention of lawmakers, and although it took more than a decade, federal legislation to protect workers' retirement savings was signed into law in 1974: the Employee Retirement Income Security Act, or ERISA. That law is the spine of much of today's retirement benefit landscape for American workers, but it's having a midlife crisis.

Employers have slashed traditional pension plans over the years, partly because of those stricter ERISA rules and the costs associated with those plans.

The gist of it: ERISA was created to protect workers by overseeing retirement accounts like traditional pension plans and, eventually, 401(k) and most 403(b) plans, but it only safeguards some of us.

ERISA fortified retirement savings to a more stable system, ensuring that plan participants receive their benefits and that the Studebaker-Packard pension collapse doesn't happen again. The law imposes funding requirements for companies, rules for employee eligibility, and fiduciary standards requiring employer plan sponsors to act solely in the interest of participants. It does not, however, require any employer to establish a retirement plan.

The law also shortened eligibility and vesting periods, making retirement benefits more portable, accommodating today's mobile workforce. And reporting and disclosure requirements under ERISA have reduced retirement plan fees for participants.

Importantly, the law established the Pension Benefit Guaranty Corporation, a federally sponsored insurance fund that safeguards workers when pension plans go up in smoke.

"In essence, it's an insurance company that says if your employer's pension plan goes belly up, there is at least an insurance company there that will pay you some percent of what your scheduled benefits were," Robert Powell, a retirement expert, said.

ERISA also protects 401(k) and many 403(b) plans since they're employer-sponsored retirement accounts. As the world of work has turned, ERISA has mostly kept its promises, but it's increasingly clear that the law needs some sharpening to make retirement savings safer for workers today.

There has been a price to pay for ERISA's guardrails. Employers gradually stopped offering traditional pension plans, partly because of those rigorous rules. In 1970, more than half of full-time workers were covered by a traditional pension, according to the US Bureau of Labor Statistics. Today, just 11 percent of private employees participate in traditional, or defined benefit, pensions, compared with around 35 percent in the early '90s.

Moreover, many small business owners contend offering a retirement plan to employees is simply too costly and complicated to manage under the law. ERISA turned 50 in September 2024. The job market, the state of the middle class, and the nature of work have all evolved in that half-century.

Here are some factors that ERISA doesn't account for: Five decades since the law was created, it only applies to about half of private-sector US workers—those who are covered by an employer retirement plan. The rest either work for a small business that doesn't have a plan or are contract workers. Only one-third of employees at small businesses have access to an employer-sponsored retirement plan.

The number of gig workers, contractors, and freelancers has also blown up. If you have earned income, you can save for retirement in a tax-advantaged saving option, like an Individual Retirement Account (IRA). But ERISA doesn't apply to IRAs, because they didn't exist when it was enacted. Because there's no fiduciary rule on these accounts, that potentially exposes participants, especially seniors, to financial exploitation during rollovers.

401(k) plan: A retirement plan in which the employee makes regular, tax-deferred contributions from a salary each pay period. Often, the employer matches a percentage of the contribution. The employee then selects from a menu of investment choices into which the funds are divided. Vesting is the employee's right to receive the employer-contributed funds after a set number of years of employment. Many small businesses steer clear of these plans; owners claim they are too costly and complex to navigate.

There is an extra amount of money people 50 and older can contribute annually in tax-advantaged plans such as 401(k)s, 403(b)s, 457 plans, and the federal government's Thrift Savings Plan.

403(b) plan: Similar to a 401(k), these plans are offered to public employees and people who work for nonprofit organizations.

Traditional individual retirement account (IRA): A tax-deferred pension plan that currently allows many people to invest a few thousand dollars annually if under age 50, with the amount bumped up a hair when they are 50 and older. Contributions are typically tax-deductible.

The account is tax-free until you withdraw the money at retirement. Usually there is a penalty for removing the funds before age 59½, and you must start withdrawing the money at age 73 if you are a Gen Xer.

Roth IRA: Unlike traditional IRAs, you pay tax up front on your contribution, but withdrawals are tax-free. (Normally, you must have held the account for five years and be 59½ or older.) Roth IRAs have income limits. A backdoor Roth IRA is a strategy used by high-income earners—those who exceed Roth IRA income limits for making contributions—to contribute indirectly (through the back door) by converting a traditional IRA (which does not have income limits) to a Roth IRA.

SEP-IRA (simplified employee pension): A retirement plan for people who are self-employed. There are limits, but contributions are tax-deferred until retirement. You can typically contribute up to 25 percent of your compensation. There is a catch-up contribution for those 50 or older. This plan can be either a pretax or Roth (posttax) arrangement.

Solo 401(k): A one-participant or solo 401(k) is a retirement plan for self-employed people without employees (a spouse is an exception). You can usually sock away pretax, up to 25 percent of your pay, with a cutoff contribution limit that fluctuates annually. This can be either a pretax or Roth arrangement.

You can open any of these retirement accounts through your local credit union or bank. Mutual fund companies and brokerage firms are also good places to do so. An IRA is easy to set up online: Enter your bank details, how frequently you want to invest, and the amount you want to transfer into your IRA.

Also, some states offer IRA programs that are open for those of you without an employer-sponsored retirement plan. These include Oregon, Colorado, Connecticut, Maryland, Illinois, California, and Virginia.

Social Security: These are retirement funds paid by the federal government, provided the person has been employed for at least 40 quarters.

Veterans benefits: These are funds paid by the federal government through the Veterans Administration to individuals who served in the US military.

Annuity: This investment is one in which you or your partner, as policyholders, make payments to an insurance company. The money grows tax-free until you withdraw it at retirement. It earns interest and assures you a steady income as long as you live, or for a set time frame.

Health savings account (HSA): This account must be paired with an eligible high-deductible health insurance plan. The money you put into the account is tax-free. It grows tax-free and is tax-free when used for health-related qualified medical expenses for you, your partner, or a qualified dependent. Your HSA balance rolls over from year to year, so the earlier you start, the better, because you can give your money more time to grow tax-free. HSAs can be invested in mutual funds, stocks, and other investments.

THE 401(K) PLAYBOOK

Let's start with your employer-provided plan, such as a 401(k). If you have access to a workplace retirement plan, increase your contribution rate by just 1 percentage point (from, say, 8 percent to 9 percent) and try to add another percentage point in successive years. If you're 50 or over, you can contribute more to a 401(k) than if you're younger.

Although Generation X workers began saving for retirement at age 30 (median), according to Transamerica Institute data, nearly two in 10 Generation X workers don't have access to saving for retirement in an employer-sponsored 401(k) or similar plan.[1]

Sigh.

If you do, hurray. One dramatic shift in the last decade for those of us lucky to have such an employer-provided plan is automatic enrollment, which is surely one reason our numbers are looking better.

In 2006, 11 percent of plans offered automatic enrollment. Now most 401(k) plans—6 in 10—automatically enroll employees into the retirement plan, giving them the option to opt out rather than having to opt in.

For our generation, almost all of us participate in our plans thanks to automatic enrollment, and we're deferring 8 percent of our salaries before our employer kicks in their contribution, according to a Vanguard report.[2] That prevails over many of the behavioral challenges that keep us from enrolling in our 401(k) plan and getting started with investing for retirement.

New 401(k) and 403(b) plans established after the passing of the SECURE 2.0 Act on December 29, 2022, now must automatically enroll all eligible employees at a default contribution rate between 3 and 10 percent of their salary, unless an alternative rate is selected by the employee.

And most employers automatically increase retirement savings by 1 percent per year, until the contribution reaches between 10 percent and 15 percent of eligible wages. These perks didn't exist a decade ago, but let's not whine over the past. This is a good thing.

TARGET-DATE FUNDS ROCK

More than eight in 10 of all 401(k) participants use target-date funds, and 70 percent of target-date investors had their entire account invested in a single target-date fund.[3] Target-date strategies are a "set-it-and-forget-it" way to invest savings based on the date of retirement, say, 2035 or 2045. At that point, the fund will shift an account's investments from stocks to more fixed-income and less volatile choices, such as cash and bonds, as you age. Participants who are pure target-date fund investors not only benefit from continuous rebalancing but are also far less likely to trade. That stability is crucial because each time you buy and sell investments you can trigger fees that over time can eat away at your total savings.

Before target-date funds and managed account advice became common, it was frequent for young workers to have equity, or stock, allocations well below recommended levels, causing them to potentially miss out on growth, according to experts we've interviewed. It was also more common to have extreme equity portfolios, defined as a portfolio with no equity exposure or 100 percent equity. Now, only 5 percent of participants hold those extreme equity portfolios and 3 percent hold extreme no-equity portfolios, thanks in large part to the rise of target-date investing, according to Vanguard data.[4]

SUPER SAVERS MEET GEN X

Super savers are workers who participate in a 401(k) or similar retirement plan and contribute more than 10 percent of their salaries into the plan. Per research from the Transamerica Center for Retirement Studies, 44 percent of workers participating in a 401(k) or similar retirement plan are super savers—15 percent contributing 11 percent to 15 percent, and 29 percent contributing more than 15 percent of their annual pay. And these so-called super savers are found across generations: a whopping 53 percent of Generation Z, and 44 percent of Millennials and Boomers.[5]

The disappointing news here, gang, is that only four in 10 of our age group are currently in this elite group.

But hold on. When we looked closer at the charts we saw something that made us smile. The percentage of Gen X super savers has climbed significantly from the 3 in 10 who had this status in 2019, a far bigger leap when compared to the tiny bump up in the number of Millennials and Boomers in that time period who hit this mark.

"The increase for Gen Xers is truly impressive," said Catherine Collinson, CEO and president of Transamerica Institute and Transamerica Center for Retirement Studies.

What's driving it? "Retirement is a light that is growing closer and brighter on the horizon for Gen X," she said. "Retirement is becoming more real—procrastination is not an option."

As we have noted, Collinson was quick to point out that in the early years of our careers, few Gen X workers were offered such plans. "And, if they were offered a plan, it's unlikely they were fully aware of how important it was to save in them," she told us. "Over their careers, Gen X has been required to navigate volatile financial markets in ways that were not expected of prior generations. Now that retirement is nearing, Gen Xers are increasingly engaged in finding ways to plan, save, and improve their retirement outlook, which is just what they need to do."

We all agree that being a super saver is a key ingredient for a comfortable retirement, but it's not all you need to do. Collinson adds: "It's also critical to safeguard your health and keep your job skills up to date, which, in turn, can help you work longer, save more, and grow your savings."

FOR ALL OF YOU DO-IT-YOURSELFERS

While we are delighted to see people ramping up their retirement savings, it's good to remember that this is just a slice of American workers. Nearly half of US private-sector workers—roughly 57 million people—don't have access to an employer-sponsored retirement plan, such as a 401(k), and so for them saving for retirement is all voluntary.[6]

Several relatively painless saving options are available, however, to help workers get traction on their own. If you have earned income, you can save for retirement in a tax-advantaged saving option, like an individual retirement account (IRA), even if you're starting with a small amount. These IRAs could be a traditional IRA, a Roth IRA, a simplified employee pension (SEP-IRA), a solo 401(k), and/or a health savings account (HSA).

Without employer-sponsored retirement benefits, it's easy to stop saving or trim back, especially if you feel like you can't afford to save right now.

Last year, Gen Xers accounted for 30 percent of independent workers, Millennials made up 33 percent, and Gen Zers were 19 percent.[7] In addition, women workers (74 percent of them) are less likely than men workers (77 percent) to be offered a 401(k) or similar plan by their employer, according to Transamerica data.[8] Twenty percent of women workers are not offered any retirement benefits, compared with only 15 percent of men. These findings are due, partly, to the fact that women are more likely to work part time, and many employers do not extend benefits to part-time employees. Only 46 percent of women who work part time are offered a 401(k) or similar plan compared with 81 percent of women who work full time.

So far, 20 states have enacted new programs for private sector workers, and in 17 of these states they are automatic IRA programs.[9] These 17 states require most private employers that don't sponsor a savings plan of their own to enroll workers in a state-facilitated individual retirement account (IRA) at a preset savings rate—usually 3 percent to 5 percent of earnings—which is automatically deducted from paychecks. The plans typically ramp up their employees' contributions by 1 percent each year until it reaches 10 percent unless an employee opts out.

"While these workers can set up any kind of IRA, there are a lot of choices to make in the private market," said John Scott, director of Pew Charitable Trusts' retirement savings project. "In contrast, the state programs provide a simple, easy option so they can start saving quickly."

OPTIONS FOR JOB CHANGERS

Retirement savings can be handled in several ways when leaving jobs. You can either keep your 401(k) balance with your old company or roll the money into a new employer's 401(k) plan or move it into an IRA. The downside to keeping retirement money at a former employer, of course, is that you can't add any more money to it. And you're stuck investing only in that specific menu of investments. An IRA will typically offer many more choices.

The upside: low fees. But it can have an advantage most people don't consider, Scott told us. "Employer sponsored plans typically get institutional pricing for the investments," he said. "So they're cheaper than the fees you might pay on the exact same mutual funds in your IRA, which are priced at retail." Another way to view it: Even though you may not be actively contributing to the account, it may grow more than an IRA with the same investments and higher fees.

When you roll your 401(k) account into an IRA, the company that administers the plan typically liquidates your holdings, then moves the cash into your IRA. However, you should be aware that it doesn't automatically invest it for you. "We often see people assume their IRA cash will be auto-invested, similar to a workplace plan such as a 401(k)," said Rita Assaf, vice president of retirement products at Fidelity Investments.

It's not that people intentionally want to make this money mistake. This is not deliberate or part of a master plan. It's just a case of out of sight, out of mind.

Until the laws are changed, your best move is to have a plan for how you want your savings invested before you initiate a rollover, said Lindsay Theodore, a senior manager in advisory services at T. Rowe Price. Call the firm where you're moving your money to and get an idea of what would be an appropriate investment, she added. "Having a good understanding up front as to what that process is going to look like can help you get your money invested right away, so it doesn't get stuck in a cash limbo."

Here's a scenario you hopefully didn't experience, and a cautionary one if you are tempted today. Kerry, for example, had access to her employer's 401(k) plan in her 20s, but no one really explained how it worked, or worse yet, the perils of cashing it out when she moved jobs. And so when she switched employers at 30, she took the money and ran. Just imagining what it might be worth today, after years of compounding, even if she had not added to that account, is stomach-churning. And yep, a regret.

She was cool with that move at the time. She needed the money right then—not in three decades. She used a portion of the money, after she paid taxes and the 10 percent penalty for early withdrawal, to pay down some credit card bills she had run up living in New York City on a modest reporter's salary. Another chunk was peeled off for traveling with friends.

Not one person told her that was a bad idea, and for gosh sakes who was thinking about retirement in those days? Her career was just launching. Retirement wasn't even on her radar.

It wasn't until much later that all of the great 401(k) features came onto the scene, things such as myriad investment selections, auto-enrollment and auto-contribution, and access to financial education about how these accounts worked.

ANNUITIES ARE GETTING MORE ATTENTION

At retirement planning conferences around the country, the topic du jour is about creating some organized way to help people pull money from their retirement accounts to, in essence, predictably pay themselves in retirement without all the angst of deciding which accounts to pull from and navigating the tax implications.

This topic is trending now for good reason. People freeze for fear of running out of money if they spend too much.

"Perhaps the hardest problem to solve is helping people to convert their savings into retirement income," AARP Public Policy Institute's senior strategic policy adviser, David John, told us. "Everyone's circumstances are at least slightly different, and all too often, people are just handed their money and told they have to make the decisions about how to use it." This leads some people to spend too quickly and others to hoard their savings so the money will be available when a future crisis appears, he added.

New ideas are coming on board all the time to solve this roadblock. A rising number of employers, for instance, are offering annuities in their 401(k) plans. And more people, for example, are building their own do-it-yourself income stream with a single-premium immediate annuity (or SPIA). SPIA sales are on track to meet or exceed the record sales this year, according to LIMRA, a trade association supporting the insurance and related financial services industry.

These annuities are the most basic plans: You pass along a chunk of your retirement savings to an insurer, and presto, you begin receiving a guaranteed paycheck until you die. The amount you get paid each month is calculated based on a variety of factors that include the amount you put into the annuity, your age, gender, and the current interest rate.

There are a few drawbacks. You cannot, typically, take refunds, so once you make that choice, you can't go back or change the amount you get each month. You can't have a beneficiary named to them, which means that when you die, the income screeches to a halt. Another niggle is that with SPIAs your payments will not be adjusted upward for inflation.

More widespread use of annuities could be a retirement life preserver, but for now, too many of them are baffling when it comes to comparing the terms, rules, and various fees, which can make them costly.

THE BEAUTY OF THE HSA

A health savings account (HSA) can be a shrewd way to stoke up saving for retirement. It should not be considered a replacement for traditional retirement plans, but it can offer a nice complement to them.

An HSA benefits from a triple tax advantage. It's the only account that lets you invest money on a tax-free basis, lets it build up tax-free, and lets it come out tax-free for qualified health care expenses. How much you can contribute to your account is set annually.

In order to put money into an HSA, you must be enrolled in a high-deductible health plan. With a high-deductible plan, you pay a lower premium per month than other types of plans, but a higher annual deductible—the amount you pay for covered medical costs before insurance kicks in.

You can also open an account as a self-employed freelancer or business owner if you have a qualified high-deductible health plan (HDHP).

Your HSA contribution with your employer can be made through an automatic payroll deduction where the funds are directed from your paycheck, tax-free, into the account. You can also add funds directly to your HSA at any time. While these contributions aren't tax-free, they are deductible on your tax return.

Some employers match contributions to HSAs similar to employer-provided retirement savings accounts. Your contributions roll over year after year and are yours to take along when you retire or change employers.

There's a hefty 20 percent penalty on any withdrawal amount that is not used toward a qualified medical expense, and you'll pay income tax on the disqualified sum. For anyone 65 or older, the penalty is gone, meaning you can withdraw funds for any purpose and only pay income tax on it, which is what makes these accounts so appealing.

The reality, though, is that most account holders use their HSAs to pay for current expenses and do not take advantage of the tax benefits HSAs offer. Many HSA account holders don't invest their HSA savings. Only about 3.2 million health savings accounts have at least a portion of their HSA dollars invested, per HSA advisory firm Devenir. Most just leave the money in cash, missing out on one of the account's key advantages.[10] A report from the nonpartisan Employee Benefit Research Institute (EBRI) that reviewed a database of over 13 million HSAs agrees. "On average, accountholders appear to be using HSAs as specialized checking accounts rather than investment accounts, though this behavior appears to change the longer an HSA owner holds an account," according to the researchers.[11]

We've heard that many financial advisers don't think HSAs are worth the trouble because people can't put enough money in them each year, but for these older couples who might be able to set aside, say, $10,000 a year for 10 years before they turn 65, that adds up to over $100,000 to help with health care expenses in retirement.

To put it mildly, that will come in handy. Medicare is not free, has lots of out-of-pocket expenses, doesn't cover most dental, vision, or hearing expenses, doesn't cover most long-term care, and most of us will likely need to use more and more health care the older we get.

"While an HSA is not explicitly a retirement savings vehicle, it's a smart move to use it in that way, if possible," Christine Benz, Morningstar's director of personal finance, told us. "The idea would be to contribute to the HSA, invest the money, and use non-HSA funds to cover health care expenses. It's pretty much a can't miss from a tax standpoint."

Why this matters: A 65-year-old retiring this year could easily spend more than $165,000 on health care and medical expenses throughout retirement. "Health care costs are among the most unpredictable expenses, especially when it comes to retirement planning," Robert Kennedy, senior vice president for Workplace Consulting at Fidelity, told us.

STUDENT LOANS AND RETIREMENT SAVINGS

Employers can consider student loan payments as qualifying contributions toward retirement-matching programs. That means if your employer provides a match to your 401(k) contributions, and you are paying down your student loan, you could count your monthly student loan payments as your "contribution" to your employer-provided retirement account, even though your dough isn't going in there.

Your employer's match does, however, go into a retirement savings account. Provisions from the retirement law makes it possible for employers to earn a tax break on that type of match. The precise matching formula and whether the employer offers this depends on the employer.

EARLY WITHDRAWALS FROM RETIREMENT SAVINGS

Early withdrawals from tax-deferred accounts, of course, are the most damaging for savers because it triggers some weighty taxes and penalties.

A withdrawal from your 401(k) account is typically taxed as ordinary income. Also, you'll pay a 10 percent early withdrawal penalty before age 59½, unless you meet one of the IRS exceptions. These include certain medical expenses, qualified tuition payments, and up to $10,000 for first-time homebuyers. Some employer plans, too, will allow a non-hardship withdrawal.

You may be able to pull up to $1,000 annually from a retirement account for specific emergency needs without owing the 10 percent early distribution penalty. And if you agree to pay it back within three years, you might not face a tax bill on the sum, either. That's provided the withdrawal can be tagged to a personal or family emergency.

Domestic abuse victims under age 59½ can now take up to $10,000 from their IRAs or 401(k)s without paying the 10 percent penalty tax.

With a loan, it's not a total loss. You pull money from your retirement savings and then pay it back to yourself, typically within five years, with interest—the loan payments and interest go back into your account. Depending on what your employer's plan allows, you can take out as much as 50 percent of your savings, up to a maximum of $50,000, within a 12-month period.

One caution: If you leave your current employer, you might have to repay your loan in full straightaway. When you can't repay the loan, it's considered defaulted, and you'll be on the hook for both taxes and a 10 percent penalty if you're under 59½.

Due to a new law, employers can now offer their employees the option of putting money into an emergency fund that is paired with their retirement plan. Although this provision is in effect, it may take some time for it to get going. "The very first of these emergency savings accounts is still in development, as a variety of quirks in the law raised administrative obstacles to implementation," Emerson Sprick, associate director of the Economic Policy Program at the Bipartisan Policy Center, told us.

And if you're sitting on unused funds in 529 education accounts, take heart. You can roll over those savings tax-free to a Roth IRA. There are restrictions, of course. For instance, there's a $35,000 lifetime cap, and rollover amounts cannot exceed the annual contribution limit for Roth IRAs. So, if you are under 50 and have $35,000 in unused 529 assets, you could roll over $7,000 per year (this contribution limit may change annually) over a five-year period. And the 529 account must have been open for more than 15 years.

MANAGING TAXES IN RETIREMENT

You might not be focusing on your future tax bill right this second, but once you start pulling money from your tax-deferred 401(k) plan and traditional IRA accounts, it will get your attention. Big time.

"These funds have not yet been taxed, so you need a plan to minimize these taxes [so you] can keep more of your hard-earned retirement money," Ed Slott, a certified public accountant in New York and an expert on IRAs, told us. "It's what you keep that counts."

People miss this critical point and often end up paying much more in taxes in retirement—when you'll need the money the most. Slott's advice is to convert those funds to a Roth IRA pronto.

People don't want to pay taxes before they have to. So the idea of converting to a Roth IRA bothers them, he said. "I look at retirement like a football game. The football game is easily divided into the first half and the second half. The first half is the accumulation phase.

"Everybody's familiar with that. That's when you do all your work. You're building, you're saving, you're investing, you're sacrificing to have more.

"The problem is, most people, when they get to halftime, think that's the end of the game. They'll come in and say, 'Ed, I'm retired. Look how much I saved for retirement.' They think the game's over. Meanwhile, the IRS comes out to play in the third and fourth quarter. They're playing nobody, so they win. Investing and saving is the first half, but protecting that money is the second half."

Slott wasn't done making his case to us. "For most people, their largest single asset, other than maybe their home, is their IRA and 401(k) account, and those are loaded with taxes. You could really blow it in the second half of the game through paying large amounts of taxes, excessive and unnecessary taxes, or lose it to unnecessary penalties, or not knowing simple rollover rules or early distribution rules. The minute you get those funds into tax-free vehicles, they grow and compound for you."

And you don't have to do this all at once. You can gradually transition to a Roth and pay taxes a chunk at a time. This is a move, however, that requires some expert help from your tax professional.

YOUR TO-DO LIST

- Take stock of which retirement accounts you currently hold.
- Consider if a conversion to a Roth IRA is a smart move for your situation.
- Review if it makes sense to add retirement accounts such as an HSA or an annuity.
- Do your research to see if your employer-provided retirement plan has a student loan feature, if that is a debt you are currently paying down.

In the next chapter, we'll investigate what to consider when you are dividing up and balancing the types of investments you hold in your retirement accounts, along with other assets you own in non-retirement accounts.

5

HOW TO DIVVY UP YOUR INVESTMENTS

In this building, it's either kill or be killed. You make no friends in the pits and you take no prisoners. One minute you're up half a million in soybeans and the next, boom, your kids don't go to college and they've repossessed your Bentley. Are you with me?

—Louis Winthorpe III
Trading Places, 1983

Simply saving more in your retirement accounts is not enough to get you over the finish line. Your money needs to grow, too, so you won't risk outliving your nest egg during your golden years. That's where savvy, but straightforward, investing comes in. You don't need to be Warren Buffett to get this right. And you don't need to pore over earnings statements of publicly traded companies to guess which one is going to be the next breakout star. In fact, you should avoid individual stocks altogether. That strategy is more like placing all your retirement chips on black 31 and spinning the roulette wheel in Vegas. Playing the market should only be for fun, with it's-okay-to-lose money. What gets you on the right track is diversifying your investments in a way that takes into account how long you have until your ideal retirement date and your appetite for risk.

To do that, let's go over what diversification actually is, how to diversify your investments in your retirement accounts, and how to maintain the strategy as time goes on.

WHAT IS DIVERSIFICATION?

Diversification is the strategy of putting your investments in an array of different assets to minimize your exposure to one asset type. Some assets, such as growth stocks (more on those soon), often increase in value and provide bigger returns for you when interest rates are low. When interest rates increase, these stocks may lose value. If you are invested only in growth stocks, you could lose a lot of money in a high interest rate environment. But if you put some of your investing dollars in growth stocks and some of your investing dollars in bonds, which typically have better returns when interest rates are higher, then you can smooth out those losses with wins from your bond investment.

Diversification also curbs your retirement portfolio's volatility over time. Remember in Chapter 3 when we mentioned how the S&P 500 stock market index yo-yoed quite a bit from 2021 to 2023? Up 27 percent, then down 19 percent, and then back up 24 percent, all within three years. You want to avoid that kind of seesawing, that volatility.

Instead, you want your investments to grow by an average rate over your time horizon. One way to do that is by smoothing out volatile years by spreading out your investments so that if one asset has a really down year, your investment in another asset that's having an up year can offset that dip and average out your return. The flip side of that means that if one of your investments really takes off, you stay disciplined and don't funnel everything into that asset, even if you're getting not-so-great returns on the other pieces of your investment portfolio.

Diversification is also good for your blood pressure and will help prevent you from making rash moves when, say, the stock market tanks. Of course, while diversification is a time-tested strategy that has historically worked, there is no guarantee against losses. Sometimes assets you expect to increase in value just don't, due to unforeseen economic circumstances. The point is that diversification is your best way to insulate yourself from big, unwanted swings even if it means you may miss some upside.

DIFFERENT ASSETS

The main way to diversify your portfolio is by investing in different asset classes. Some may be familiar to you such as stocks, bonds, and certain cash investments. Others may be a little more obscure, such as commodities. And there are alternative asset classes that seem sexy. Take art or cryptocurrency, for example. Let's go over each.

Cash and cash equivalents: These assets are actual dollar bills you have on hand or in deposit accounts (like your savings or checking account) or securities that are easy to turn into cash, such as US Treasury bills, also called T-bills; guaranteed investment certificates (GICs), money market funds, and shorter-term certificates of deposit (CDs) that mature within 90 days and can be redeemed without penalty. Longer-term CDs are considered fixed income assets.

These investments are considered very low risk because there's very little chance or no chance at all that you could lose your money. But you also receive lower returns versus other, riskier asset classes. Because of this, cash and cash equivalents are best used to park your emergency savings, rather than your retirement savings, which needs to grow as much as it can over time.

Equities or stock: Stocks are ownership shares in a company typically listed on a stock exchange like the New York Stock Exchange or the Nasdaq stock exchange. Stock investments are considered riskier because they are typically more volatile and you could lose money on your investment. But because they offer the greatest growth opportunity for your money over the long term they should represent the largest share of your total investments, though that share will shrink over time. (More on that later.)

Generally, you will want to invest mostly in US stocks, which can be broken down into smaller subcategories. We'll hit the big ones. For instance, large-cap, mid-cap, and small-cap describe stocks based on the size of the company, determined by their market capitalization value. That value equals the number of outstanding shares—or the total number of shares issued and held by investors—multiplied by the price of the stock. Typically, large-cap stocks are from big, established companies and are less risky investments than small- or mid-cap stocks.

Then there are growth stocks and value stocks. Growth stocks are from companies that typically expand a lot when the economy is chugging along and interest rates are low, such as tech companies. These stocks tend to outperform the greater stock market during periods of economic growth and are more expensive. On the other end are value stocks that come with a more attractive price and provide reliable income streams. Some examples are financial and energy stocks, which often outperform the broader market as the economy recovers from a setback. Health care can be a good value stock as the economy appears to slow and enter a recession. Of course, these are generalities and no type of stock is 100 percent predictable.

Last, there are international stocks that are issued by non-US companies. Their performance can differ from US stocks because they reflect the economic performance of other countries rather than the US. Often, foreign stocks offer higher potential returns than US stocks, but also come with more risk.

Fixed income investments or bonds: Bonds are issued by governments and companies when they want to raise money. When you buy a bond, you're lending money to the issuer, which agrees to pay back the loan on a specific date and pay you interest before then, usually twice a year. These investments offer regular income from interest and are considered safer than stocks. Because they are less volatile, bonds are used to blunt those swings in the stock market.

The safest bond investments are US Treasury bonds or other high-quality bonds, but they generally provide lower long-term returns than stocks. To get better returns, investors can turn to high-yield bonds and international bonds, which are also riskier. Longer-term CDs are also considered fixed income investments.

Commodities: These are generally considered the raw materials used to make goods and services. Some are so-called hard commodities like metals, natural gas, and crude oil, the latter of which plays a role in the price of gasoline at the pump. And then there are soft commodities, or agricultural products, such as wheat, sugar, coffee, soybeans, and frozen concentrated orange juice. Commodities are often traded through futures contracts, so investors don't have to exchange the actual commodity itself. A fun example of this is the climax of the 1983 comedy *Trading Places*, which centers on commodity trading, specifically with Eddie Murphy's and Dan Aykroyd's characters tricking the villains of the movie to corner the frozen OJ futures market.

The best way for more novice investors to add commodities to their portfolios is through mutual funds that invest in commodity-related companies. More sophisticated investors may turn to more complex investments like futures contracts, which is a legal agreement to buy or sell a commodity at a set price at a certain point in the future, or exchange-traded products (ETPs) that track a commodity index.

Alternative assets: These types of assets include an array of investments that can range from real estate—such as rental property (not your personal home that you own) and funds directly invested in commercial real estate—to valuable personal property like artwork and other collectibles. Alternative assets can also include investments in hedge funds or venture capital, cryptocurrencies, and even peer-to-peer lending. Often, these assets are harder to convert to cash quickly because it takes more time to find a buyer. But they can still offer big returns despite this difficulty. Overall, though, alternative assets should comprise only a small portion of your portfolio, if included at all.

HOW TO DIVERSIFY YOUR RETIREMENT INVESTMENTS

Now that you have a handle on different assets, let's talk about how to use them to create a diversified retirement portfolio that reduces volatility and also provides high-enough returns to hit your retirement goals.

The key to diversification is balancing how much risk you're comfortable taking with how much time you have until you plan to retire. If you're too risk-averse and invest too conservatively, you risk inflation outpacing the growth of your investments and your savings not growing enough for your goals. On the other hand, if you're too aggressive, especially as you get older, your assets could get hit hard by a market downturn and you have less time left to recover from those losses.

Risk appetite: To understand your risk appetite, try taking an investment risk quiz. One of our favorites is the University of Missouri's "Investment Risk Tolerance Assessment."[1] It takes about 10 minutes and gives you a tolerance assessment based on five risk levels: low tolerance, below-average tolerance, average/moderate tolerance, above-average tolerance, and high tolerance.

Typically, people with a higher risk tolerance are more likely to feel comfortable investing in riskier assets like stocks, even picking individual ones, and also investing in alternative assets such as cryptocurrency, because they focus on the growth opportunity. Those with low risk tolerances would likely prefer investments that won't lose their value, such as bonds or even cash in savings accounts, even if that sacrifices higher returns. They are more focused on potential losses. Many of us may fall somewhere in the middle. That said, your tolerance can fluctuate based on your life circumstances or the economic environment. For instance, you may feel more willing to invest in riskier assets after securing a promotion at your job. Conversely, you may want to put more of your investments into safer assets when the economy is in a recession and layoffs are high.

While it's good to understand how much risk you're comfortable with, you may find that you need to be more or less aggressive than what you're naturally inclined to be. This may be a good reason to bring in a professional to help you navigate any investment anxiety or temper your riskier impulses. Chapter 12 provides advice on how to find one.

Time horizon: In addition to risk tolerance, the number of years until you want to meet your goal is a huge factor in how to invest those savings. The general guideline is the shorter that time frame is, the more conservative you want to be in your investing. And the reverse: The longer your time frame until your goal, the more aggressive you can be because you have time to recoup losses along the way.

Think of it this way. If you're saving to buy a car in two years, you would want to put that money into a high-yield savings account or even a two-year CD. The goal isn't to make as much money as you can on the savings, it's to safeguard it until you have enough to buy that car. Imagine if you had invested that money in the stock market and in year two, the market swooned into a bear market, falling 20 percent, taking your car money along with it. You might not have enough to buy that car when you wanted to.

Now, retirement is a goal that's well down the road, even if it's not as far away as it was in your 20s. You still have time to recover from short-term losses if needed, so you can take on additional risk—such as a bigger exposure to US and international stocks—to pursue long-term growth.

Of course, the time you have until retirement continues to shrink and so the makeup of your retirement portfolio should reflect that shortening time horizon. Recall what we mentioned earlier: the shorter the time horizon, the more conservative the investments. So as time goes by and you get closer to your retirement date, you will want to reduce the share of high-risk investments in your retirement portfolio and increase the percentage of more conservative ones. You don't want to be two years from retirement and overexposed to stocks during a major market downturn.

ASSET ALLOCATION

So what is the ideal asset allocation for your portfolio based on your risk tolerance and time horizon? We've got you covered. If you're in your 40s and have about 20 years left until retirement, you want to invest 80–100 percent of your portfolio in stocks and 0–20 percent in bonds. You should have three to six months of your basic expenses saved in cash. Alternative investments, especially riskier ones like cryptocurrency, should make up a small portion of your portfolio (if at all)—up to 5 percent—with money that you can afford to lose. The ranges allow for your risk tolerance. If you can swallow more risk, you may feel comfortable with a higher percentage of stocks in your portfolio. If you're in your 50s and have about a decade left until retirement, you may want to be slightly more conservative. Kerry likes to use a handy, easy formula to roughly determine what share of your portfolio should be in stocks: Subtract your age from 110. So a 50-year-old would have 60 percent in stocks and the rest in bonds and cash. Again, adjust higher for stocks if you are riskier or need to catch up more.

The other thing to consider is your actual number of years until retirement. This helps couples who may have an age gap. If you both plan to retire in 20 years—even if one of you is in your 50s—then plan based on that. Similarly, if you're in your 40s and plan to retire early, you may want to have a portfolio that looks more like the portfolio of a 50-year-old, if you're on track with your savings goals. If you are behind on your savings goals, you may want to invest on the more aggressive side and increase your share of stocks to the higher end of the ranges. You may also need to extend the number of years until retirement.

"I think that for specifically Gen X who are trying to catch up, I don't think there's anything wrong with still holding a 100 percent stock portfolio," Judson Meinhart, a certified financial planner in Winston-Salem, North Carolina, told us. (By the way, Meinhart's favorite movie as a teen was 1993's *Dazed and Confused*, and his first car was a Saturn SL2.) "And as long as your time horizon is at least 10 years out, it makes the most sense to invest aggressively and ride out that market volatility."

Still, and this is key, "Within that 100 percent equity allocation, it's super important that you're diversified," he added.

That means having varied types of stocks within your stock portion of your retirement portfolio. You'll probably want to have more exposure to larger companies balanced between growth and value stocks, and then gradually less exposure as companies get smaller. You'll also want a healthy share of international stocks to balance out the portfolio. For instance, Janna's stock portfolio with her husband, who is in his 50s, is about 30 percent large-cap growth, 16 percent large-cap value, 13 percent mid-cap growth, 5 percent mid-cap value, 5 percent small-cap growth, 2 percent small-cap value, and 29 percent international. Overall, Janna's portfolio is 86 percent stocks, 12 percent fixed income, and 2 percent cash.

In the next section we examine some products out there that can help you with diversification.

CHOOSING YOUR INVESTMENTS

Okay, so you know what your asset allocation should be. Now we bet you're wondering which stocks and bonds to pick to create that retirement portfolio. Fortunately, your employer-sponsored 401(k) and 403(b) likely comes with products to help you make these investment decisions. For IRAs and other retirement vehicles, a plan provider such as Vanguard or Fidelity offers investment options and often can provide customized advice for you.

There are several ways to go about making this choice. Some investments require a more hands-on approach, while others provide what Kerry likes to call the set-it-and-forget-it option. Let's go through your options.

The first investment choice to consider is **index funds**. These come in two types. **Index mutual funds**: These funds combine money from investors to buy a stock or bond portfolio that reflects a broader index like the S&P 500, which tracks the 500 largest publicly traded US companies. A mutual fund company sells shares in these index funds to investors. The second type is an **index ETF**. This type of fund also pools money and tracks a market index, but is traded on exchanges like stocks.

So, for simplicity's sake, if you want your retirement portfolio to be 80 percent stocks and 20 percent bonds, you would choose index funds that your retirement plan offers to reflect that. If, for example,

Vanguard was your provider, you could choose the Vanguard Total Stock Market Index Fund ETF (VTI) for 80 percent of your money and the Vanguard Total Bond Market Index Fund (BND) for that 20 percent. The VTI stock fund represents all investable US companies and blends large-, mid-, small-, and micro-cap stocks. The BND bond fund measures an array of fixed-income assets including US government, corporate, and international dollar-denominated bonds, and other securities backed by mortgages and other assets. You could get a little more granular and choose index mutual funds or ETFs that track more specific indexes, so that the stock portion of your portfolio is made up of an S&P 500 index fund as well as one that tracks the Russell 2000, an index that includes just small-cap US stocks.

The advantages of index funds is that these are not actively managed funds, meaning there are no managers deciding which stock investments should be in the fund. The funds passively follow the index they are benchmarked to. This means the fees associated with index funds are much lower than funds that are actively managed. (More on that later.) Fees are expressed as an expense ratio, which is a percentage. So, if you invested $10,000 in an index fund with an expense ratio of 0.04 percent, you'll pay the fund $4 each year.

The potential drawback to these funds is that you'll need to do the math to make sure your asset allocation reflects your time frame and risk appetite, and you'll need to rebalance your portfolio if the asset allocation gets out of whack. (You're making a trade-off here—because you're not paying much in fees, you have to do more of the management work yourself.) Allocations can get unbalanced when the stock portion of your portfolio goes gangbusters, while the returns on the bond portion are lame, or vice versa. Here's an illustration. Let's say Bill and Ted invested $100,000 on the last trading day of December 2020, with $80,000 in VTI and $20,000 in BND. A year later, the VTI is up 24.4 percent and the BND is down 3.9 percent. Now they have an excellent $99,520 in VTI, but $19,220 in BND. Their stock portion makes up 84 percent of their total portfolio and bonds comprise 16 percent. They might want to adjust their investments to get closer to that 80/20.

The general rule of thumb is rebalance when your allocation is off target by 7 to 10 percentage points. A good book on index fund investing is John C. Bogle's *The Little Book of Common Sense Investing: The Only Way to Guarantee Your Fair Share of Stock Market Returns.*

A second investment method is **asset allocation funds**. These also come in the mutual fund or ETF varieties. These funds invest in a mix of asset classes that align with your risk tolerance. There are typically three risk types: balanced funds, growth or aggressive funds, and income or conservative funds. A manager actively manages the investments in each of these funds to align with the risk profile, and rebalances to maintain the risk allocation. But you may need to rebalance your investments in asset allocation funds if your risk tolerance changes as you get closer to your retirement date. Because these are actively managed, your expense ratio will likely be higher than those on index funds. Look for anything lower than 0.75 percent for actively managed funds.

A similar investment are **target-date funds**, which are actively managed with a specific retirement year in mind. This is the set-it-and-forget-it option. So, if you're 45 and plan to retire at age 67 when your full Social Security benefits kick in, then you would choose a target-date fund that's dated 22 years into the future, or the one closest to that. If you would rather a slightly lower risk, choose a target-date fund that's 20 years into the future. If you need to take on more risk—say to catch up—choose one further away, say 25 years in the future. The fund will invest in a mix of assets that is appropriate for that targeted date. As the target date nears, that mix of investments changes to become less risky, typically by reducing your exposure to stocks and increasing the level of bonds you carry. Because target-date funds are actively managed, you also don't have to worry about rebalancing.

Speaking of which, it's also good to revisit your investments when you change jobs and get a new 401(k). The options in your new employer's 401(k) may be better and you may want to roll over your old 401(k) into the new one, if it's allowed. Janna and her husband like to check back on their progress once a quarter.

If you're interested in a more hands-on, personalized approach, you can also work with a financial planner or wealth adviser firm on managing your portfolio. Again, watch out for the fees, which can eat into your investments. An adviser can be helpful if you have a complex financial situation, such as a huge age gap between spouses, a dependent child with special needs who will require lifelong care, financial stakes in businesses, or a large amount of real estate that requires a customized approach.

YOUR TO-DO LIST

- Figure out how many years you have until retirement.
- Take a risk tolerance assessment test to determine your risk appetite. If you're planning with a partner, he or she should take it, too.
- Check out the investment options provided in your retirement savings plans and find the one that best fits your risk profile and time horizon.

We've covered the very basics of investing for retirement. Next we'll go into the many ways you can increase your income during those golden years so that you don't outlive those savings. We'll start with examining ways to maybe work a little bit longer, but differently, as you get older.

PART THREE

Increasing Your Cash Flow

6

PLANNING FOR A LONGER WORK LIFE

Just when I thought I was out, they pull me back in.

—Michael Corleone

The Godfather Part III, 1990

You may have heard that old metaphor of the three-legged stool to describe the sources of our retirement income: Social Security benefits, retirement savings from your 401(k) or other retirement funds, plus your non-retirement account investments and assets.

That model has shifted. Today, especially for those of us who may lag behind in our retirement savings, working longer is a viable fourth leg. What that means for you will depend on your individual situation.

This stage of your working life is *not* typically a linear path. You might do something for a few years and transition to something entirely different, or do several things at the same time. For some, working longer could mean retiring from your role at one employer and moving over to a full-time opportunity elsewhere to keep your momentum going for a few more years. It might be launching a microbusiness and pursuing your entrepreneurial spirit—an effort that can be richly rewarding, particularly if you're pursuing a passion.

Working longer could simply mean staying at the job you have, but downshifting—working fewer days per week, or reducing the number of projects you work on.

For many of you, we suspect, it will play out in stages as you add paid part-time projects and jobs into your retirement-life mix of spending time with family, traveling, volunteering, and creating a balanced life. Think of it as a patchwork quilt. Some examples: A freelance financial adviser who sells pies on the side at the local farmers market. A contract writer who adds speaking and teaching to the mix. A retired corporate lawyer who teaches business law and business ethics as an adjunct professor at a university, but also serves on a corporate board in a paid capacity and volunteers on a nonprofit board.

You might circle back to an earlier interest of yours from childhood. Don Covington, for example, retired from the military and ran away with the circus, a passion of his since his childhood after he attended the circus with his dad in Baltimore, Maryland. He became the manager of a traveling nonprofit troupe of performers, the Big Apple Circus, for a few months each year.

In this chapter, we lay out what you can do now to prepare for the new reality of working longer. This scenario includes up-to-date advice on the financials of working in retirement, how to find your what's-next, networking, working with a career coach, and more. We also review which jobs will likely be in demand in the future. Many of you are years away from putting all of this information into practice, but these are the issues that you should think about, and things you should remember to do when you're there.

COSTS AND BENEFITS OF WORKING IN RETIREMENT

The idea of continuing to work in some fashion after you retire from your primary career is not a far-out concept for most workers, even if it's not on your personal radar *yet.* A Transamerica Center for Retirement Studies report found that three in 10 retirees they surveyed retired after age 65 or older and did not expect to stop working due to financial reasons and for healthy aging-related considerations such as staying active, enjoying their work, and keeping their brain sharp.[1]

Most Gen X workers (54 percent), in fact, do plan to work after they retire, including 40 percent who plan to work part-time, per the Transamerica data.[2] A global survey by WTW, a leading global advisory firm, found that half of workers age 50 and older now expect to work past age 70, nearly double those who did prior to the pandemic.[3]

We see this as a positive trend for several reasons. A report from the Pew Research Center on how Americans view their jobs discovered that it's the older workers who are the happiest.[4] Two-thirds of those 65 and older say they are highly satisfied with their jobs, compared with 4 in 10 of those 18 to 29, just under half of those 30 to 49, and about half of workers between 50 and 64.

"Older workers have expressed higher job satisfaction levels overall, and they are more likely to feel respected at their job," Luona Lin, a coauthor of the report, told us. "Plus, they don't feel left behind—the vast majority of older workers say they have the education and training they need to get ahead."

The majority of workers 65 and older say they work because they need the money and because they want to work. A little over one-quarter of this age cohort say they work mostly because they want to, while 17 percent say it's mainly because they need the money, according to the data.

A contributing factor to the high satisfaction levels is autonomy. Workers ages 65 and older are the most likely to express high levels of satisfaction with flexibility about when and how much to work, and with the amount of feedback they receive from their manager, according to the report. And when you're happy at work, you're engaged.

You can't ignore the purely psychological benefits of being needed, of feeling relevant, of participating in a network of people, a community, of contributing to the world in a meaningful way that maybe you couldn't have done in earlier parts of your career. "Work provides routine, structure, connection, mental stimulus, purpose, and relevance," Robert Laura, the retirement coach you previously met, told us. "These are all things that many people don't realize they are losing when they leave work and that aren't easily replaced with golf, grandkids, and crossword puzzles."

As we mentioned earlier, Becca Levy, a researcher at the Yale School of Public Heath, refers to a study that shows people who have purpose—and you can find your purpose in your work—tend to live seven years longer than those who don't have that reason to get up in the morning for a purpose. There's also a sense of "use it or lose it" in terms of your mental acuity.[5]

The truth is, many Americans are not financially ready to retire, and they do enjoy what they do. A twofer. These older workers are reenvisioning the workplace and work-life balance through flexible opportunities, and that's key to their ability to enjoy healthier, longer lives, and may very well be key to your life, as well.

If you're not feeling that you've saved appropriately for retirement, it's really important to continue in the workplace to earn some kind of salary for as long as you can. That income will help you stave off the need to dip into your retirement accounts so you can let them continue to grow. If you continue working full-time, you can even keep adding to those accounts.

"I'm a big fan of adding income in retirement," Stephanie McCullough, the founder and chief executive of Sofia Financial, said, "and I'm always encouraging people who are still employed to think about planting this seed now for how they might be able to work part-time or consult or start their own gig."

It can be a game changer. "The one thing that jumps out at me every time I run the 'do you have enough to retire' projections for a client using my financial planning software is that any kind of income after 'retirement' makes a huge difference," she said.

Stephanie added that if it's $25,000 coming in as income, for example, that's $25,000 of your retirement savings you don't have to spend yet, and it can stay invested and keep growing for you.

Continuing to work for longer means you can push back tapping into Social Security benefits from age 62, the earliest you can claim, until your full retirement age 67. Or you may be able to wait until age 70 when you get the biggest bang for your monthly check by taking advantage of the roughly 8 percent annual increases in your check after reaching your full retirement age.

"Additional income can give you more time to contribute to your savings and it can also help you pay down debt and increase your cash reserves ahead of full retirement," Judith Ward, a certified finance planner at T. Rowe Price, told us.

While this applies to both men and women, for women, in particular, working into their 60s and 70s can deliver financial security from the very real threat of poverty in their 80s. "Financial problems in retirement and senior debt arise with insufficient income as a result of lower lifetime earnings and less in savings, costs of family caregiving, and divorce," said Cindy Hounsell, the founder and president of the Women's Institute for a Secure Retirement, or WISER (wiserwomen.org), a nonprofit organization dedicated to women's financial education and advocacy.

A review to determine how much additional income you actually need for a successful retirement will set your guardrails here. Our magic number exercise in Chapter 3 is a good place to start. It can give you a ballpark estimate of what that means in terms of how long you might need to keep working. If you have a gap, for example, you can do a calculation to see how that translates to five years' take-home pay.

We totally get it if the thought of working for five more years fills you with dread. But what about switching to something more enjoyable? It might not get you to your goal as fast as possible, but it can make your life right now much more satisfying.

"Not saved enough is one reason for working longer, but many people still really do want to do some work and use their knowledge and wisdom," said Sharon Emek, founder, president, and CEO of Work at Home Vintage Experts (WAHVE), a contract staffing service that matches older professionals with clients. "They just don't want to be a 40-to-60-hour employee with all the stress."

In recent years, contract work opportunities that offer flexibility have soared as the gig economy and new technology have wiped out many of the barriers of self-employment. For many white-collar workers, all you need is fast Wi-Fi and a laptop and you're good to go. The range of services for the self-employed span the scope of finance, law, marketing, tech, and many more. There is more opportunity than ever before.

The shift to contract or short-term projects can help you stay on the job or keep the work experience on your resume current while you look for a full-time position. It can also get you in the door at a potential employer that in time might roll into a full-time position. Employers are more likely to hire you at this age for a contract position. (More on this later.) Contract positions can also benefit you if you simply want to keep earning a paycheck but don't want the "pedal to the metal" full-time duty.

The downside, however, is if you rely on benefits that come from a full-time job that you wouldn't get with contract positions, such as an employer-provided retirement account and access to an employer-provided health care plan. To forego these benefits can be an issue. Be sure to consider the full value of the benefits package you receive from work as you think about downshifting, or shifting roles entirely. How will you replace those benefits? For example, will you tap into Medicare for your health insurance needs, or increase contributions to your own IRA?

Moving in and out of the job market before permanently retiring can also have implications for your Social Security benefit. As we discuss in Chapter 7, if you continue to work after claiming Social Security benefits after age 62 and before your full retirement at the age of 67, the Social Security Administration (SSA) will *temporarily* withhold a portion of your benefits for earnings over a certain threshold (roughly $23,000). In the year you hit full retirement age, that limit increases threefold; and in the month you hit full retirement age, the annual earnings test ends. From that point on you can earn without limitations, and while you don't get the amount you forfeited previously in a lump sum, your monthly benefit amount is adjusted upward so you will *recoup* all the benefits withheld. There is a calculator on the SSA website to walk you through the calculation.

MAKE WORKING FOR YOURSELF WORK FOR YOU

Maybe your vision of working after retirement means giving up the nine-to-five and starting a new business where you can be your own boss. If that's you, keep in mind that launching a full-blown business demands a level of financial fitness to weather those initial years when your business is getting up to speed. One way many retirees make this second act work is to launch the business in baby steps as a side gig while they are still on a payroll.

If you do end up running a business from your home, there are some additional issues that you must address.

Get your paperwork in order: Find out if you need any special permits—tax registrations, business and occupational licenses, and state and local government permits. If you belong to a homeowners association, find out if there are any restrictions to running a business out of your house. It's a good idea to add an insurance rider to your homeowners or renters policy to cover any expense should someone get injured on your property who is there for business purposes. Each state has its own rules about insurance. The Insurance Information Institute (iii.org), an industry trade group and information clearinghouse, is a place to begin your research.

Taxes: Set up automatic quarterly estimated federal taxes on business income each quarter with the IRS. Depending on where you are situated, it may be necessary to pay state and local income and business taxes, too. The IRS's Small Business and Self-Employed Tax Center is a great resource to learn more. And, of course, make sure you have a trusted accountant on board.

As for paying taxes, consider taking a tax deduction for 100 percent of expenditures directly related to your home office, such as the purchase of a work computer. Direct expenses are deducted in full.

Taxpayers who qualify may choose one of two methods to calculate their home office expense deduction. The simplified option has a rate of $5 a square foot for business use of the home. The maximum size for this option is 300 square feet. The maximum deduction under this method is $1,500. When using the regular method, deductions for a home office are based on the percentage of the home devoted to business use. Taxpayers who use a whole room or part of a room for conducting their business need to figure out the percentage of the home used for business activities to deduct indirect expenses. These are things like your mortgage or rent, insurance, and utility bills. To get the deduction, you must file Form 8829, Expenses for Business Use of Your Home. For full details, go to IRS Publication 587.[6]

Retirement savings: If you have earned income, you can continue to save for retirement in a tax-advantaged saving option, like an individual retirement account (IRA), even if you're starting with a small amount. Without an employer and employer-sponsored retirement benefits, it's easy to procrastinate or skip it, but even if you can slide some money into a Roth IRA, you'll be doing yourself a favor.

Health insurance: If you are not 65 and enrolled in Medicare, or are not covered by a spouse's plan, you will need to shop around for health insurance.

Getting paid: One stressful thing about running your own business as a freelancer or contract worker is getting paid in a timely fashion. Particularly if you are starting a business to increase your income in retirement, this is a real concern. Most self-employed freelancers have problems getting paid at some point, according to research by the Freelancers Union (freelancersunion.org), the nonprofit group that promotes the interests of independent workers through advocacy, education, and services.

Our advice here is to pause before you accept a project from a new client and do some sleuthing. Do you know anyone who has worked for them? What has their experience been with timely payment? Consider asking privately in a members-only online LinkedIn or Facebook freelance group (or an independent workers group associated with your field) about what others have experienced with that client.

If you're responsible for your own billing and are not part of a platform such as Upwork (upwork.com) or WAHVE (wahve.com) that will do the paperwork for you and collect the money, along with their cut, you need to pay attention to billing and know what's outstanding.

A 30-day grace period is reasonable. For some assignments you might bill for half up front when you sign the contract and bill the remainder when it's completed and accepted by your clients. A written contract that both you and the client sign and date is critical. It outlines the project, what you will be paid, and the due date. If the client doesn't offer to send one, then create your own. The Freelancers Union has a link on its website to walk you through the process of setting up a customized freelance contract. If it is a substantial project, it's a good practice to hire a lawyer to vet it for you.

When you take on a new client, you should be sure to obtain, up front, the contact information of the person in accounting who will manage your contract and payment.

Finally, set up a regular billing system that works for you. You might invoice when a project has been completed and accepted, or bill periodically if it's a longer time period. But longer-term projects may require a different approach with periodic payments that have been agreed upon in the contract.

Don't cut your client too much slack if they drag their feet on paying you. Email and call, and be sure to save all your documentation of your collection attempts. Hiring a lawyer to collect for you is expensive, so it's better to be aggressive before it comes to that.

A REMOTE JOB CAN BE YOUR TICKET

The rise of virtual job opportunities has changed the workplace for workers over age 50. Remote work can resolve many issues for those who have mobility issues, or experience the stress of a commute.

Remote work helps push back on ageism, too, because older workers won't be judged by their book cover so to speak, in the same way they might be while working alongside colleagues decades younger. Instead, it is a worker's performance and productivity that matter.

"Typically, someone might want to work 25 to 30 hours a week, but some think 35 or 40 hours is fine if they can work from home," Emek said.

For those of you who might have caregiving duties, the ability to find remote work is huge. "We have some of our retirees who are 60 or older taking care of a 90-year old parent and some taking care of grandkids, even some taking care of their children who are ill," she said. "One of my managers is taking care of a grandchild. She works from home and she babysits him in her home office. If she needs to do something with him, she makes up the time and gets her work done. In fact, she works more than I ask because she appreciates how I respect her needs and what she brings to the company."

The number of remote jobs has expanded exponentially in recent years, allowing workers access to a trove of potential jobs across the globe. You can find work as a bookkeeper, consultant, a graphic designer, a web designer, a social-media expert, and much more. You might helicopter in for project-based contract jobs, too. Remember these contract posts usually don't come with health care and retirement benefits, so you're on your own there.

If you'd like to find a job where you can work remotely, you might check out:

- FlexJobs (flexjobs.com) and WAHVE (wahve.com), which lets professionals aged 50+ work from home in insurance, accounting, and human resource positions.
- Rat Race Rebellion (ratracerebellion.com), SideHusl.com (sidehusl.com), and Working Nomads (workingnomads .com) all offer remote job listings.
- Some of the bigger freelance platforms include Upwork (upwork.com), Freelancer (freelancer.com), and Fiverr

(fiverr.com), which has over 700 different job categories. FlexProfessionals (flexprofessionalsllc.com) has a catalog of part-time jobs.

- GLG (glginsights.com) is a global network of fee-based executive-level experts. Accepted members of GLG are connected to paying clients for problem-solving tasks and more. The GLG network currently has roughly a million top professionals and subject matter experts on board. GLG network members consult with clients over the phone or in person, through small group meetings, longer-term projects, or board opportunities.

GETTING STARTED ON YOUR NEXT ACT

To get a jump-start on extending your working life, we recommend that when you're 55, you start thinking about what you want to be doing at 60. If you want to get rolling on this process sooner, have at it. Our interviews with hundreds of workers have shown that landing on what work you want to do in retirement is often a process that takes time.

It's probably best not to make rash moves in terms of making a quick shift or expecting you can do it overnight. Leapers can succeed, but it's the planners who have better odds. It starts with your research. What sorts of things might you want to do that really would turn you on and bring joy to your life that maybe you haven't been able to do?

What do you do best? Take one minute. Look across the span of your career so far. What do you feel like you are best at? What have others told you you're good at? When do you feel most in control and on top of things? Select one skill, talent, or personality trait you'd call your superpower—something you're confident puts you in the top 1 percent of the world. Have some swagger here. No one but you is looking at what you pick.

Transferable skills. What was your first job? What's your favorite hobby? What are some activities in your daily life right now? Maybe they are caretaking, chores, organizing your home, family time, or friend time. What skills do you use now? What skills have you used in the past? How does doing those things make you feel? Connecting the dots between your first jobs, your hobbies, and even the sports you participate in can help you build your secret superpower. The key is looking for patterns about the kind of work (and play) you value and that enriches you, and the skills that are connected to them. Is there a skill you still use today? Is there a lesson you learned that's stayed with you? You might surprise yourself here.

Now take some quiet time to write in your journal to connect the dots. Begin to brainstorm five to 10 sectors or fields that interest you, and then create a document with two columns—right and left. In the left column, enter the fields or sectors, and in the right column write the positions or roles you can imagine doing. These roles and positions can be a combination of things you have done previously or are doing now, or they can be new ones you'd like to move toward. (Bonus points if you name some specific employers/companies/organizations you'd like to work for.)

David Conn, now in his late 50s, started the second act dance by working as a consultant for private equity firms, earning pay as a board director, and teaching and mentoring students at New York University, which was perhaps his favorite activity.

In 2022, he stepped out of his full-time position as a chief executive officer at Sequential Brands Group, Inc., a company that owns, promotes, and licenses a variety of consumer brands. He was in charge of some biggies, such as Jessica Simpson, Joe's Jeans, Ellen Tracy, The Franklin Mint, FAO Schwarz, and Sharper Image.

The COVID-19 pandemic made him pause and consider what it was he really was looking for to build a second act into his next decade and beyond. "Even when I was much younger, I always envisioned myself having a kind of second career like athletes do," Conn told us. "I looked at professional athletes who go on to be media personalities, or are successful in the business world, and at some point, I knew there would be a pivot where I was going to keep earning, but do something very different, a second career for me."

The Role of Experiments in an Encore Transition

Marci Alboher is a leading authority on career issues and workplace trends, the chief engagement officer at CoGenerate, and author of *The Encore Career Handbook: How to Make a Living and a Difference in the Second Half of Life*. She suggests thinking about making a job transition as a set of experiments.

1. Test out hunches. (This sounds really good!)
2. Narrow down options. (Can I take something off the table?)
3. Answer specific questions. (Will I like this environment?)

"Think of some experiments you've done," Alboher says. "Maybe you have taken a class, joined a board, volunteered. You might even have had a failure." Alboher tested out being a substitute teacher for a day and realized that particular avenue wasn't quite right for her. Take 10 minutes and write down a hypothesis about your encore that you'd want to try out, Alboher advises. Is it one more big-responsibility job? Going to part-time from full-time? Joining a board—nonprofit or for-profit? How might you craft an experiment to test your hypothesis? What obstacles do you see to doing that?

Similar to Alboher, John Tarnoff, a midlife career coach, suggests picking a time, say 10 or 15 minutes a day, and writing down your thoughts about what it is you might want to do next. You want to write down what it is that you're thinking about, because a hard thing to do, particularly if you're busy, is introspection. This exercise is cumulative and it builds over time, and no one sees it but you.

Conn admits he was fortunate to have financial flexibility to be able to start anew with plenty of runway still ahead to keep earning on his own terms and have enough time to let it play out. "It felt like the right time to do something different with my life," Conn said, "and at my age, it was the perfect time to start. I still have a lot of energy and passion."

And he has another dream he's unpacking. Conn wants to be a writer. "Throughout my career, I felt like I was always a very good writer," he said. "I wrote my speeches and other communications and have already started writing a novel. Blogs and podcasts interest me, too, and building out a speaking business."

He didn't make this shift alone. As the idea spawned from his pandemic days percolated, Conn began working with a career coach to focus his efforts. "I've had executive coaches throughout my career," he said, "so when I made this decision to look at what kind of work would keep me going for the next 15 years, I reached out to Nancy Ancowitz, a New York City–based career advancement coach, whose sweet spot is personal development."

Ancowitz helped Conn focus on what could come next, and how he might go about getting there, paired with a dollop of encouragement to think about what was going to make him happy and how that would match up with what he was good at before it was too late.

"She pushed me to lean into something that I enjoy very much and that I have a passion for doing," he said. "I enjoyed being a CEO of different businesses tremendously, but these other pursuits are giving me joy."

ADVICE FROM A CAREER COACH

We reached out to Ancowitz for her insights on how Gen Xers like Conn can make working into their 60s and beyond a reality for financial, social, and mental health reasons.

"Staying relevant in the work world as you move into your 50s and beyond doesn't mean mimicking 20-somethings," Ancowitz told us. "It's less about sounding trendy and more about speaking the language of your industry. Mastering just enough tech jargon to stay sharp and credible can make all the difference—without trying to sound like someone you're not."

Finding a Coach

A career coach can give you a fresh look at what you have in your wheelhouse right now, help you find ways that you might be able to change your current work, and set you up for a longer shelf life. But they can also help you look for a new beginning, weaving the threads of your background together for you in a way only an outsider might be able to do without the emotion attached.

To find a coach that's right for you, you might sign up for a virtual workshop taught by a coach, take a class from one at a community college, or connect with one via the career center at your alma mater. If you have been laid off or taken an early retirement package, your employer might also provide you a coach for a few weeks of counseling. The most common way, though, is to ask friends and family for recommendations.

Coaching is a self-regulated industry and there are all sorts of specialists running about. They include career coaches, executive career coaches, retirement coaches, life coaches, and so on. Many coaches have been doing it for years without adding professional designations. The International Coach Federation (coachingfederation.org), however, awards a global credential. These coaches have met educational requirements, received specific coach training, and achieved a certain number of experience hours. Other groups that provide access to coaches are the Life Planning Network (lifeplanningnetwork.org) and the Retirement Coaches Association (retirementcoachesassociation.org).

In today's world, there's no need to hire a coach who lives close enough to meet in person. Most coaches offer online get-togethers via Zoom or Google Meet, or phone sessions. Hourly session fees can run anywhere from $85 to $300. We advise interviewing three or four potential coaches before selecting one. Most will provide one free session so that you can get a feel for whether the two of you will be a good pairing.

To get the most from your sessions, consider in advance what you expect to gain from their professional guidance. Is it plain advice about job searching, or someone to provide writing suggestions for your resume? Do you need a coach to show you ways to pare down your decades of work experience onto two pages, or to spiff up your LinkedIn profile? (For many white-collar jobs, a profile on LinkedIn is a prerequisite.) Perhaps you're seeking someone who can kick-start your approach to networking or a partner to explore a more psychological approach to your next work stage.

One caveat: Coaches will want you to be honest about your finances and what your income needs are for a new role. "I always say, no matter how much or how little money you have, it's important to figure out where the financial piece fits in and how much money at this stage you need to earn," Dorian Mintzer, a retirement coach and speaker, told us.

Many of her clients have successfully pivoted mid-career by refreshing their skills, adopting the latest tools, and confidently using terminology that resonates in their fields, all while leaning on their experience, perspective, and insight to stand out, she said.

The way to do this is to focus on what matters for the roles you want, per Ancowitz. "This phase of life doesn't have to be about climbing the corporate ladder—instead, it can entail pursuing work that energizes and inspires you," she said. "Several clients transitioned from corporate roles to teaching part-time, rediscovering satisfaction through mentoring the next generation, as Conn has."

That's the charm. "Whether you're launching a business, freelancing, joining boards, or contributing to your community, design your next chapter around what excites you and makes an impact," Ancowitz said. "Retirement doesn't have to mean hitting the greens or swimming with sharks. It's about crafting a balance that sustains your finances, passions, and energy," she said.

"Whether you're managing eldercare, taking on part-time work, or exploring passion projects, build a plan that honors your wallet and your well-being. You're steering toward a future that's energizing, fulfilling, and entirely yours."

PEOPLE POWER

Once you have a sense of the kind of work you might like to do in retirement, you have to find that work. And one of the most valuable assets when looking for a job in your 50s and 60s are your friends, your colleagues, and your network, said Chris Farrell, a retirement expert and author of *Purpose and a Paycheck: Finding Meaning, Money, and Happiness in the Second Half of Life*. "The thing about your network is they know you, and you know them. And so if you're thinking about what you want to do next, one of the first things you do is you tap into your network, and you start asking them, 'What do you think I should do next?' 'What do you think I would be good at?' They can really help you hone in on what your skill set is, and also come up with some ideas."

Some might be really unrealistic, but that's okay, he added. "It's about getting you thinking about what you might want to do."

Your network is also who you are going to need for references for jobs and for connections you might reach out to for informational interviews. "A lot of times those contacts are going to come through your network—the second-degree or the third-degree separation," Farrell said.

BACK TO SCHOOL

Another way to help your retirement job search is to up your learning game. As they say, if you aren't learning you aren't earning.

You might check out training available online from your local library, LinkedIn Learning, Coursera, Udemy, and YouTube. Microsoft provides on-demand training videos for its apps. Google provides workshops for its office apps suite, including Docs, Sheets, and Slides. GetSetUp (getsetup.io) offers live online classes for adults on everything from Excel basics to Zoom protocol. AARP Skills Builder for Work (jobskills.aarp.org) is a suite of free courses including Microsoft Office fundamentals and other options.

A growing number of midlife and later-life transition programs are gaining traction across the country. Driving the trend are Baby Boomers and Gen X eyeing retirement from their primary careers and looking for new directions. The programs, commonly based at large universities such as the University of Colorado Denver, Notre Dame, Harvard, Stanford, and Yale, generally have about two dozen students per class and involve anywhere from four months to one year of on-campus and hybrid sessions.

"The concept is to create a blueprint of what you've done and dig into that, along with your values and strengths, to discern what you want to do next," Anne Button, the founding director of the CU Denver Change Makers program, told us. "Most of our fellows are recently retired or on the edge of doing so and are looking to make a social impact."

Now, tuition runs from under \$4,000 to more than \$70,000 for these programs, so you should consider if the cost of tuition at the higher end of the spectrum will pay off, especially if you are planning on working for only another 5 to 10 years, or in a part-time capacity. Explore scholarships and financial aid possibilities, which are a standard offering for most programs, or consider lower-cost alternatives.

Take the example of Destiny Burns, who, at 52, launched CLE Urban Winery (cleurbanwinery.com), a boutique winery and tasting room in her hometown of Cleveland. She earned a certification in food service while still employed. (Burns, by the way, is a huge fan of the Foo Fighters, Green Day, and The B-52s.)

Community colleges, business schools, and other postsecondary institutions offer classes on the basics of starting a business, and there are also online tutorials. For instance, you might want to sharpen your marketing or finance chops, or get an understanding of employment law.

Many state colleges offer tuition-free classes for people 60 and older. Keep in mind that paying students get first dibs. Programs don't open up for the older crew until registration for classes has closed and the add-drop period has ended.

Osher Lifelong Learning Institute (OLLI), offers 125 programs on university and college campuses across the country to provide education to people who are 50 years of age or older. By paying an inexpensive membership fee, which varies between colleges, seniors can attend non-credit courses solely for the sake of learning—there are no tests or grades.

And we can't emphasize enough the importance of looking for opportunities to work with younger people. Teaming up with someone two decades younger, whether they're your coworker or manager, can revitalize your work in a way you never imagined. You can see what may have become old hat to you, or you're a tad jaded about, through a new lens. It's exciting. And you may begin to learn new ways of doing things, new technology, new ways of communication. It's a reset. Finding ways to work with younger people will keep you sharper about what's going on in your industry and may even push you to do your best work yet.

CHALLENGES ASSOCIATED WITH WORKING LONGER

People will say they're going to work until 65 or older, and they're out the door by 62. The reason for stepping away is often due to a physical health issue, a layoff, or because they need to care for a family member. Ageism, embedded in the workplace culture, can also make it hard for older workers to get back into the workplace again. According to many employers, 62 is the cutoff for working, and 58 for hiring, per Transamerica.[7] What planet are they on?

Even today, workers over 60 are clocking in more hours, on average, than in previous decades. Today, 62 percent of older workers are working full-time, compared with 47 percent in 1987, according to the Pew Research Center. And they're more likely to have a four-year college degree than in the past.[8]

"Older workers want and need to work beyond traditional retirement age," Transamerica Institute's Catherine Collinson said. "They're not financially ready to retire, and they may enjoy what they do. However, they can only succeed if employers are welcoming and supportive."

More than half of employers say that their company culture "emphasizes professional growth and development among employees of all ages, including those age 50 and older," according to the Transamerica data, yet a fraction—two in 10—emphasize it a "great deal."

"Without thought to this part of the labor force, I fear that these older workers won't have the opportunity to advance in their jobs and will be relegated to lower-wage, lower-skill work," Ramona Schindelheim, editor in chief at WorkingNation (workingnation.com), an online media site focused on work and jobs, said.

Historically, employers' recruiting practices have overlooked older workers, but among those with job openings recently, more than half said they gave "a great deal" or "quite a bit" of consideration to job applicants ages 50 and older, according to the Transamerica Institute's Workplace Transformations report. That's encouraging, but the word "consideration" doesn't necessarily translate to getting hired.

Nearly seven in 10 workers (69 percent) consider their employers to be "age friendly" by offering opportunities, flexible work arrangements, and training and tools needed for employees of all ages to stay on top of the changes in their field and rapidly changing technology.

That's swell, but almost 9 in 10 employers consider themselves to be age-friendly. Can you say *disconnect*? The most frequently cited programs they offer include traditional and/or reverse mentorships (50 percent), job training (44 percent), internships for individuals starting their careers or individuals reentering the workforce (40 percent), and professional development programs (35 percent). Where they lag behind is providing work arrangements that can keep older employees working and earning longer. These include a phased retirement option, flexible work schedules, letting employees dial back hours and shift from full-time to part-time, or allowing them to take on jobs that are less stressful or demanding.

The majority, roughly six in 10 employers, don't offer a formal phased retirement program for workers who want to transition into retirement. Only half of employers are willing to adjust to flexible work schedules to help employees transition into retirement. And a fraction, three in 10, are up for shifting older workers who want to stay on the job to work that's less stressful or demanding physically.

That adaptability matters because the bulk of the Baby Boom generation is now rolling into retirement with Generation Xers on their heels, and many are expecting a gradual transition into retirement as opposed to a cold stop.

Some employers, to be fair, are getting gold stars. "Retaining and hiring older workers has become critical to our organization because it is more difficult in the rural environment to find qualified workers," Suzanne Cooner, CEO of Audubon County Memorial Hospital and Clinics in Audubon, Iowa, told us.

To make the workplace age-friendly, the hospital reduced the biweekly number of working hours to qualify for full-time benefits from 72 hours to 60 hours and now offers job sharing, phased retirement, and retire-to-rehire opportunities and retraining.

Al Comito, the hospital's chief information officer, was hired in 2023 when he was in his early 60s. For Comito, it's not about the income. "I've been planning for retirement for a long time, and I am to the point where I feel financially secure," he told us. "If I wasn't enjoying what I do, I would not be doing it. It gives me a sense of accomplishment and satisfaction . . . and purpose."

At Drake University in Des Moines, Iowa, finding qualified workers to fill open positions hit a bad patch. "We had to start thinking about looking for candidates in places we previously had not explored," Maureen De Armond, executive director of human resources, told us.

"In the hiring process, for example, we are now much more thoughtful about really whittling down our list of required qualifications. We may not need new employees to arrive with every skill set, so long as they are eager to learn," she said.

In the end, the aging population may be the impetus for change when we are ready to extend our working lives. "A steep drop in fertility rates has already eviscerated working-age populations in leading economies around the world, causing employers to seek out new sources of labor, including older workers," Bradley Schurman, the demographic strategist and the author of *The Super Age*, told us. "And that's pushing some leading employers to devise new retention and recruitment strategies."

Whether you are looking for part-time or full-time work, it's smart to review employers who have signed on the AARP's Employer Pledge Program (aarp.org/work/employer-pledge-companies) or the Age-Friendly Institute's nonprofit-generating Certified Age Friendly Employer (CAFE) program (institute.agefriendly.com/initiatives/certified-age-friendly-employer-program) that identifies organizations committed to being the best places to work for employees aged 50+.

WHERE THE JOBS ARE

One of the best places to get an inkling of what's happening in the job market is the analysis produced by the economists and researchers in the "Occupational Outlook Handbook" by the US Bureau of Labor Statistics (BLS) (bls.gov/ooh). It provides a detailed look into industries, jobs, educational requirements, and pay, predicting the overall growth potential over the next decade.

Another terrific source to get a sense of jobs and industries on the rise is the "Career Exploration Tools" developed by the Occupational Information Network (O*NET OnLine) under the sponsorship of the US Department of Labor's Employment and Training Administration. It includes career assessment tools to help you consider job options, complete job applications, create resumes, and prepare for interviews and to shift fields. Then they can link you to nearly 1,000 occupations described by the O*NET database, as well as to occupational information in the Department of Labor's CareerOneStop (careeronestop.org) resource center. The information spans the entire US economy. And the good news is that it's free and regularly updated. You can tap into it at the O*NET Resource Center (onetcenter.org /tools.html).

There are also hot jobs debuting that you might not have thought about. Six in 10 of LinkedIn's 2025 "Jobs on the Rise" showcase "the evolving world of work and emerging opportunities that job seekers may not have considered before." The list tracks the fastest-growing positions.

The positions include artificial intelligence engineer, artificial intelligence consultant, and physical therapist. Workforce development managers who design and implement training programs to upskill employees are in demand. Travel advisers are on the rise. Event coordinators, directors of development who run fundraising strategies, and sustainability specialists who analyze a company's environmental and social impacts and create strategies for resource efficiency also made the cut.

Several engineering roles showed up for the first time on the list, including bridge engineer, nuclear engineer, and instrumentation and control engineer.

As a self-proclaimed bookworm and research nerd, Kerry was pleased to discover that research librarians are back in vogue.

"Only about 30 percent of job seekers say they want to switch industries, but more than 50 percent of recently hired workers got their jobs in a new industry," Julia Pollak, chief economist at the US Department of Labor, told us. "That suggests that workers who keep an open mind, expand their search, invest in new skills, and follow opportunity are disproportionately successful."

SKILLS IN DEMAND

Some of the most in-demand skills, according to LinkedIn's research, are customer service, project management, communication, leadership, teamwork, sales, and strategic planning.

For AI enthusiasts, the tide is moving in your direction. "We've started to see a growing number of employers asking for integrative artificial intelligence skills," Cory Stahle, a labor economist at Indeed Hiring Lab, told us.

Transferable skills, of course, can open doors to new roles, too, Amy Glaser, senior vice president at staffing agency Adecco, told us. "Part-time roles also offer a valuable way to gain experience, build connections, and transition to full-time opportunities.

"Overall, adaptability and a willingness to learn are critical for workers looking to thrive in today's multigenerational workforce," she added.

With folks like our parents, and ultimately us because we're living longer lives, there's a burgeoning demand for home health and personal care aides, technicians, senior massage therapists, and other wellness health professionals. And new jobs are coming online all the time. For now, here are a few on the rise: patient advocate, home modification professional for aging in place, senior fitness trainer, retirement coach, financial planner specializing in seniors, senior move manager, personal driver or assistant.

These jobs are often for those in their 50s and 60s who provide services to those in their 70s, 80s, and 90s. The COVID-19 pandemic also ramped up the awareness of mental health as people of all ages struggled with all manner of issues, including the loss of family and friends to COVID-19, burnout, disruptions in work, loss of jobs, and fear about the future. Employment of substance abuse, behavioral disorder, and mental health counselors is on the rise, and that momentum is likely to continue for years. Jobs like behavioral health care manager, risk reduction manager, social worker, and case manager fall under this category. Titles include therapist, psychologist, counselor, and mental health clinician.

The Labor Department also anticipates an uptick in demand for people with information technology (IT) and computer-related skills, especially in cybersecurity, in the next 10 years. It expects job increases in IT support and telehealth.

Keep in mind though, all of these jobs can offer flexibility as far as your time, but you should expect to spend some up-front dough to get the necessary certifications and training. That said, if you are in your 50s and potentially have two decades to keep working in some manner, it can certainly make sense to spend up front. Ideally, you will start adding some of these courses and training on the side before you retire from your primary career. If you're fortunate, your employer may even pick up some of the cost of education. Under federal law, employers can offer up to $5,250 a year in tax-free education-assistance benefits for undergraduate or graduate courses. You don't need to be working toward a degree.

A PARTING THOUGHT FROM A RETIREMENT EXPERT

"It's not too early to start thinking about working longer," Richard Eisenberg, a retirement expert and retirement columnist for *MarketWatch* and other national publications, told us. "In fact, it's really beneficial to start thinking about it when you're in your 50s, rather than waiting until you're just on the precipice of retirement and/or in your mid-60s or later."

He knows the drill personally. Eisenberg retired in 2022. At 65, he stepped away from his job as managing editor for *Next Avenue*, the PBS website for people over 50, where he had worked for a decade. "I had a rough idea of what my retirement would be," Eisenberg told us. "I knew I would be 'unretiring' since I still wanted to be doing some writing, some editing, and some teaching, but not all the time."

So far, he has. Eisenberg, who lives in Westfield, New Jersey, explores "unretirement" in his expert columns, podcast, and teaching posts, including an online NYU master class.

His big-picture advice: Start thinking about how you want to keep working longer, where you want to keep working longer, and how much time you want to spend working each week when you leave your full-time job.

"Those are big questions that most people don't think about," Eisenberg said. "And think about what skills you could learn or skills you could bolster to make you a more impressive candidate to keep working longer. Because the older you get, the more age discrimination you may encounter when you're trying to find work."

Eisenberg is spot on. The more you can do to show an employer that you are going to be a talented and capable worker for them, the greater the chances that you'll be able to continue working. If you can show that you've got current skills, you're curious, and that you've been learning the latest technology, you will be able to combat their thinking that you won't be able to do the work.

"A lot of us want to work part-time in retirement," Eisenberg said. "We want to stay active, have social connections, bring in some income, and stay mentally engaged, but we also want to have time to do other things."

Plus, there's the freedom to do what you want to do this time around, Eisenberg said. That means choosing a working routine that isn't stuffed with meetings and administrative duties—all "the parts of our former job that we didn't like so much."

We know that right now you don't know precisely what your next work chapter is going to be, but you can have a good idea of what you want it to be by early planning. For some of us, we want to continue doing the same kind of work we were doing before, like Eisenberg has, or something similar to that because we enjoy it, and because that's who we are, and working longer allows us to retain some of that identity, just slightly differently.

In the end, it's your dance. Improvise and see where it takes you. There's a certain freedom in having the time to do just that and get paid for it at the same time.

YOUR TO-DO LIST

- Run your numbers to see what kind of paycheck will meet your retirement needs.
- Meet with your financial adviser to get an idea of how working longer fits into your financial plan.
- Figure out if there will be any associated expenses related to a shift in your work that you will need to cover.

- Journal about what kind of work you might want to do.
- Deep dive into what your skills are and which ones you might add, and research courses while at your current employer. See if they offer an educational assistance program.
- Consider working with a career coach.

In the next chapter, we'll parse out how Social Security benefits fit into the mix of sources for your future retirement income.

7

OPTIMIZING SOCIAL SECURITY

Well, I've been with the best, and I've beat the best. I've retired more men than Social Security.

—Apollo Creed
Rocky IV, 1985

For almost 100 years, Social Security has been a major pillar of our retirement preparedness. It has been providing a guaranteed source of monthly lifetime income to participating individuals since 1940, five years after President Franklin D. Roosevelt signed the Social Security Act into law. Just as important, since 1975, the benefit is adjusted for inflation annually to help recipients stay apace with rising prices. No other investment does that for you.

The program is critical for women, who typically outlive men, still earn less than their male counterparts, and are more apt to take time out of the paid workforce to meet family caregiving responsibilities, resulting in far lower levels of retirement assets than what men accumulate.[1] The program is also vital for people of color and others who have faced headwinds in the workplace—such as having jobs that don't offer retirement benefits and provide lower earnings—that make it tougher for them to save.

So optimizing your Social Security strategy is paramount for a successful retirement. It's important you understand the ins and outs of Social Security and what it can offer, and how to make this critical entitlement program work the hardest for you. Let's start with the basics.

NUTS AND BOLTS

Throughout your working years, you and your employers contribute to the Social Security system. You may have seen these contributions—called Federal Insurance Contributions Act, or FICA—taken out of your paycheck. Your eventual Social Security benefit amount is established by how much you earn, and thereby contribute to the program.

Using a formula known as the average indexed monthly earnings (AIME), Social Security takes 35 years of your highest earnings, adjusts them to factor in wage growth, and averages them to generate a monthly figure, which is the amount you are eligible to receive. Social Security benefits are determined by your history of wage income—you earn credits toward benefits automatically during your working years. After you claim your benefits, they start flowing on a monthly basis and they continue as long as you live.

To qualify to receive a retirement benefit, you must work long enough to become insured. You need to earn 40 Social Security credits to be eligible for benefits and Medicare. One credit equals a certain amount in earned wages or self-employment income. The threshold amount changes from year to year. You can earn a maximum of four credits per year, and so you need 10 years of work to get the 40 total credits needed to qualify for benefits.[2] In 2025, for example, you earned one credit for every $1,810 in wages or self-employment income, meaning you needed to earn $7,240 during the year to obtain the yearly maximum of four credits. You can also claim Social Security benefits while still working, but there is a limit to how much you can earn, depending on your age.

While some pension plans, long-term insurance policies, and a handful of annuities provide inflation protection, Social Security is the only component of our retirement income system built to provide risk-free, automatic inflation protection.

The Social Security Administration (SSA), the federal government agency that oversees the benefits, reviews the amount it pays out and adjusts it for inflation every year. This is called the cost-of-living adjustment, or COLA, which began in 1975 under a formula made into law by Congress. Before then, special acts of Congress increased benefits on an irregular basis.

The COLA is calculated by averaging together the Consumer Price Index for Urban Wage Earners and Clerical Workers (CPI-W) for July, August, and September and then comparing that figure with the same data from the previous year. The CPI is one measure of consumer price growth released by the federal government.

In general, the SSA announces in October how much benefits will increase the following year. People who receive Social Security benefits are notified by mail in early December about their new benefit amount. Most beneficiaries can also view their COLA notice online through their personal Social Security account at My Social Security (socialsecurity .gov/myaccount).

It's important to point out that about 28 percent of state and local government workers do not pay Social Security payroll taxes and therefore aren't eligible for Social Security benefits when they retire. California, Texas, Ohio, Massachusetts, Illinois, Colorado, Louisiana, and Georgia comprise 73 percent of noncovered state and local government employees.[3] Instead, these workers are part of public sector retirement systems that are required to provide a comparable level of benefits. That's why the public pension benefits for these government employees are typically higher than pensions of other government employees who also receive Social Security coverage.

DOING THE MATH

While the average monthly benefit is around $2,000, that amount changes depending on when you start taking Social Security. There are three key ages for Gen Xers to know—62, 67, and 70.

Age 62 is the earliest age you can claim Social Security benefits, but it comes with the smallest payout. You get only about 70 percent of what you would have if you had waited until you reach full retirement age, or FRA. The FRA for folks born in 1960 and after is age 67, and that's when beneficiaries receive 100 percent of their Social Security benefits.[4] For many years, the FRA was age 65, but Congress passed a law in 1983 that gradually increased the FRA to account for people living longer and healthier. Then there's age 70. If you wait until then before claiming, you get the largest monthly amount. How much more? If you were born in 1960 or later, you'll receive 124 percent of your FRA payout if you claim at age 70.[5] That payment is for the rest of your life, and over 15 or 20 years that difference becomes very significant indeed.

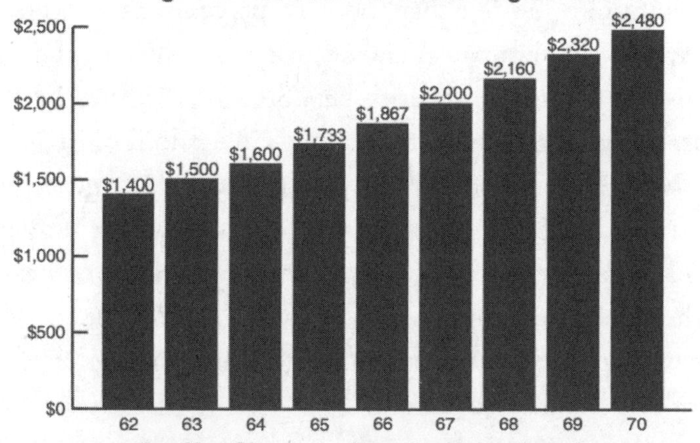

Source: Social Security Administration

Of course, you must live long enough for the cumulative benefits of claiming later to catch up with the total amount of reduced payments you would receive by claiming earlier. That catch-up point is called the break-even age, when the total amount of claiming later exceeds the total value of claiming early. To get an idea of your personal break-even age, use the Social Security "break-even calculator" provided by Carroll Advisory Group in Texas (www.carrolladvisory.com/free-break-even-calculator-for-social-security).

The Social Security Administration provides another good calculator. To find this calculator, visit the Social Security website (ssa.gov) and search for "early or late retirement" and click the appropriate link. To get a more personalized calculation and see how different retirement ages change your estimated benefit, create and sign into your own personal My Social Security account.

WHY DON'T WE WAIT TO CLAIM?

Waiting to claim Social Security until you reach or pass your full retirement age is "like finding gold on the street," Laurence Kotlikoff, a Boston University economist and Social Security expert, told us. "We Americans under-save, under-insure, under-diversify, pay for bad investment advice, rely on dying early, retire too soon, take Social Security at the first chance."

For instance, in 2023, 55 percent of retirees claimed benefits before their full retirement age, about 24 percent claimed when they hit their full retirement age, and about one in five (21 percent) delayed until after their full retirement age.[6]

To Kotlikoff, one of the biggest stumbling blocks that pushes retirees to turn on their Social Security benefit as soon as they're eligible is that they're reluctant to spend down other savings accounts first, particularly by tapping money invested in their retirement accounts such as 401(k) plans.

"They think they're going to make a killing in the market one day," he said. "That's largely Wall Street convincing them that they need to leave it in there and the reward will come. It might. But you certainly can't count on the kind of return you get in Social Security checks for the rest of your life if you have the planning and patience to wait."

A recent working paper published by the National Bureau of Economic Research mapped out other reasons people claim their Social Security benefits early. Perhaps the biggest factor in the grab-the-money-ASAP decision is the psychological ownership of one's Social Security benefits, according to the research. The second psychological factor is a feeling that if you don't live long enough, the government gets to keep some of your money, the paper found.

"The more you feel like it's your money that the government has been sitting on, the sooner you want it back," said Suzanne Shu, the paper's other coauthor and a professor at Cornell University's Dyson School of Applied Economics and Management. "That is not how our Social Security system works in the US, which uses the money contributed by current workers to pay current beneficiaries. And yet people are looking at the money that they've contributed into Social Security as being held almost like a 401(k) account that they're going to cash out once they retire."

RESIST THE URGE TO CLAIM EARLY

Understanding what's behind your urge to claim early could help you delay making this costly mistake. Think of it this way: What advice would you give someone? Hopefully, you would advise them to wait until they reach or even pass their full retirement age before claiming benefits. Now think about your own strategy in terms of your own advice. Chances are that you can reframe your own mindset to one of patience.

If you can delay retirement for a little while longer, you give yourself an opportunity to delay Social Security and meanwhile allow the money in your employer-provided retirement account to continue to grow, because you will be contributing to it. You can also opt to tap into other investments or retirement accounts to tide you over. Or you can look for ways to generate cash by downsizing your home. You might move to a location where the cost of living is less, freeing up your budget some.

As insurance, Social Security provides protection against what is called longevity risk. "Most people don't think of living a long time as a risk—but it is in financial terms," Mark Miller, a retirement expert and author of *Retirement Reboot: Commonsense Financial Strategies for Getting Back on Track*, told us. "Even relatively affluent retirees can exhaust their savings if they live to very advanced ages—especially women, who tend to outlive men."

Bottom line: It is prudent to delay claiming Social Security if you are in an economic position to do so, Miller added. "Delaying protects you against insufficient income in very old age, when other assets are likely spent."

IF YOU HAVE TO CLAIM EARLY

Still, not everyone can wait to claim Social Security later. This may be due to health issues, or because they need the money now to make ends meet.

"For some, the choice is made for them, due to financial stresses or health care needs," Shai Akabas, director of economic policy at the Bipartisan Policy Center, told us. "Notably, these challenges are faced more often by people of color and those with less education."

Most people claim benefits when they need them, Linda Benesch, communications director at the social advocacy group Social Security Works, told us. "The most common age to claim benefits is 62 because many people—especially if they've been pushed out of the workforce, or forced to take lower paying jobs due to factors like age discrimination and inability to do physically demanding jobs—can't afford to wait."

UNDOING EARLY CLAIMING

If you claimed early because you found yourself laid off, but have since landed a job and no longer need the monthly check, you have an option. You can suspend your payments up to age 70.

You can call Social Security directly at 1-800-772-1213 or write and make the request. Your benefits will be suspended beginning the month after you make the request. If your benefit payments are suspended, they will automatically start up again the month you reach age 70. You can restart earlier than that, of course.

To put the brakes on your checks, you'll have to file what's known as a withdrawal of benefits using Form SSA-521. You can only do this for up to 12 months after you became eligible for retirement benefits. At that time, and this is the whopper, you'll have to repay everything that you've received from Social Security to date. You'll then have up to 60 days to reconsider and withdraw your application.

"That's a complete undo, and you can only do this one time," Justin Smith, a certified financial planner with Savant Wealth Management in Phoenix, Arizona, told us. "That means you have to pay back the benefits you received. I don't see it all that often because people don't typically like to pay back those benefits."

Take a breath, though. If you miss that window, there's another strategy.

Once you reach full retirement age at 67, you can elect to suspend your retirement benefits. You won't be on the hook for paying back any benefits you've already earned. And the good news is that you'll start earning those delayed retirement credits. This means that when you do turn your benefits back on—no later than age 70—your monthly Social Security payouts will be around 8 percent higher for each year that you defer them.

Getting the most out of Social Security also depends on your life circumstances. The most important factors include your life expectancy, marriage, whether you can claim benefits based on someone else's record, and whether you plan to keep working. Taxes are also a factor to keep in mind. Let's work through each one by one.

HOW LONG WILL YOU LIVE?

Your life expectancy is a big piece of the equation as to when to tap your benefit. We went over longevity in Chapter 3 so that you can better understand that key metric in terms of adequately planning for retirement. Remember: Today's 65-year-old man will live on average to 84 and today's 65-year-old woman to 87.

But that's just an average. It's important to make an educated guess for yourself. That guess is a good way to inform your Social Security strategy. If your life expectancy is longer, then you might consider delaying those benefits to get the maximum amount for what could be decades of retirement. If it's shorter, you may decide to get your benefits sooner. One way to get a bead on this is to utilize a life expectancy calculator. You can find one on the Social Security website by searching for "life expectancy calculator."

You should also review your family's longevity record. If your relatives tend to live long lives without a history of disease such as diabetes and cancer, then you may want to delay receiving Social Security benefits because those bigger checks will make a difference when you're rolling into your 80s and 90s. But if your relatives lived shorter lives than average, or if you have a history of chronic illness, claiming Social Security before 70 may be more beneficial to your financial security. This is especially true if you're single and don't have to worry about how claiming early can affect a surviving spouse's benefits, which brings us to...

SOCIAL SECURITY FOR TWO, PLEASE

The complicated rules that are used to calculate the size of a person's Social Security benefits can get even more confusing for married couples. The reason: When each partner might want to start claiming Social Security will depend on the amount of employment income each has earned annually, as well as their age.

While delayed claiming often optimizes Social Security benefits, some people have compelling reasons to claim early. A couple can often optimize benefits if the lower earner claims early while the higher earner delays.

If you're a married couple, one strategy is for the spouse with the higher benefit to wait until 70 and thereby earn those delayed credits. The one with the lower earnings from their working life would then start earlier, if the extra cash flow is needed to make ends meet. If the spouse who delayed dies, the surviving spouse would then step up to the higher benefit. A coordinated delay strategy increases the odds that lifetime benefits will be greater, because one of the two are very likely to beat their break-even age.

BENEFITS ON SOMEONE ELSE'S RECORD

If you are divorced, you can claim on your ex's record, provided he or she is 62 or older and you were married for 10 years or more. They don't have to be collecting yet, as long as you divorced at least two years before applying. If you have since remarried, though, you can't collect benefits on your former spouse's record unless your later marriage ended by annulment, divorce, or death. If your current marriage ends in divorce or the death of your spouse, you can claim on the higher of the two benefits—your first ex's or your second ex, or deceased, spouse's. You can't claim on the records of multiple people.

The amount of benefits you get has no effect on the benefits of your ex-spouse and his or her current spouse. The SSA won't notify your ex that you've claimed on his or her record.

Your benefit will be capped at 50 percent of your spouse's benefit. If the benefits you'd receive by collecting on your own earnings record are more than what you'd collect on your ex's record, consider collecting on your own record instead. The SSA will pay the higher of the two benefits for which you're eligible, but not both.

Keep this in mind, however: If you collect Social Security before you reach your full retirement age (67 for Gen X), your benefits will be permanently reduced whether you're collecting on your own earnings record or your ex's record.

If your ex dies, you can claim benefits the same as a surviving spouse, provided that your marriage lasted 10 years or more. Benefits paid to you as a surviving divorced spouse won't affect the benefit amount for other survivors getting benefits on the worker's record. If you remarry before age 60 (age 50 if you have a disability), you cannot receive benefits as a surviving spouse while you are married. If you remarry after age 60 (age 50 if you have a disability), you will continue to be eligible for benefits on your deceased spouse's Social Security record.

If you qualify for benefits as a widow, widower, or surviving divorced spouse on another individual's Social Security record, you can opt to apply for survivors benefits immediately and delay your own retirement benefit until your full retirement age or later, when your monthly benefit will be higher.

If you receive widow's or widower's benefits and will qualify for a retirement benefit that's more than your survivor's benefit, you can switch to your own retirement benefit as early as age 62 or as late as age 70, with the usual rules on payout sizes by age applying.

If you are getting benefits on your spouse's record already, you generally will not need to file an application for survivors benefits. The SSA will automatically change any monthly benefits you receive to survivors benefits after it receives the report of death.

If you are getting retirement or disability benefits on your own record and your spouse dies, you will need to apply for the survivors benefits. The SSA will check to see whether you can get a higher benefit as a widow or widower, and you'll receive the higher of the two benefits.

STILL GETTING A PAYCHECK?

If you plan to work in retirement, it's important to know how that might affect your Social Security benefits once you claim. Your paychecks could trigger the Social Security retirement earnings test, a formula that withholds a portion of benefits if your wage income exceeds a set level.

The earnings test applies only to people who are collecting Social Security between age 62, the earliest age of eligibility, and their full retirement age—again, for Gen Xers, that's age 67.

In general, the way the earnings test works is if you're between age 62 and your full retirement age and earn more than the annual limit (which changes each year) and you're collecting Social Security, the administration will withhold $1 for every $2 over that limit. The good news is that the earnings test goes away at full retirement age. And the withheld benefits are not lost—Social Security recalculates monthly benefits when you reach full retirement age to credit back the withheld benefits.

But retirees caught in this situation are often baffled.

For instance, sometimes months can go by from when wage income is reported to the SSA and when Social Security starts withholding from your check. If you're a contract worker, that sum might not be revealed until you file your taxes. As a result, you're overpaid by their calculations and so you have to pay back the benefits.

DON'T FORGET ABOUT THE TAX MAN

As we write this in early 2025, roughly 40 percent of people who get Social Security must pay federal income taxes on their benefits.[7] This is typically because they earned income in addition to Social Security from wages, earnings from self-employment, interest, dividends, investment income, and other taxable income that must be reported on their tax returns. That additional income is subject to federal taxes, too. Only a handful of states tax Social Security benefits in addition to the federal income tax, so check with your state's tax department to determine if it's one of them.

If you file a federal tax return as an individual and your combined income is between $25,000 and $34,000, you may have to pay income tax on up to 50 percent of your benefits no matter when you claimed them. Same thing for spouses filing jointly that have a combined income between $32,000 and $44,000. If, as an individual, your combined income is more than $34,000 (or more than $44,000 for couples), up to 85 percent of your benefits may be taxable. Combined income is calculated as your adjusted gross income plus nontaxable interest plus half of your Social Security benefits.

"For retirees with significant savings, it makes sense to develop a tax-efficient strategy for timing their benefit claim with drawdowns from portfolios," Miller told us.

Eliminating federal taxes on Social Security benefits is part of President Trump's economic plan for his second term, so we encourage you to keep up-to-date on new policymaking on this front so that you can plan your future accordingly.

SEEKING SOCIAL SECURITY ADVICE

Whew. A lot goes into optimizing your Social Security strategy to get the most for your retirement years. For many of you, a little outside help may be desired. It's important to know where you should—and should not—turn.

It may seem obvious that the Social Security Administration is the first place to call, but significant staffing cutbacks and an increase in the number of beneficiaries over the last decade has left the agency scrambling. The waiting time on SSA's phone line averages 36 minutes. In 2013, the average wait time was only 10 minutes. The quality of advice also may make you pause. Research conducted by Kotlikoff discovered that people who made claiming decisions based on guidance from Social Security employees lost out on thousands of dollars in benefits they could have received. A 2018 government report found that the Social Security Administration collectively cost 13,000 widows $130 million in lost benefits.[8] Even worse, there's no redo option.

"The basic rule of Social Security is that if they make a mistake, it's your mistake," Kotlikoff told us.

So, who should you get advice from?

Start online to get a foundation. The Social Security Administration's calculator compares retirement benefit estimates based on your selected date or age to begin receiving benefits with retirement estimates for age 62, full retirement age (age 67 for Gen X), and age 70.

You can also get ballpark figures for your Social Security benefits at different ages by using free online calculators from places like financial services firms, the federal Consumer Financial Protection Bureau, and AARP, or by paying for Social Security claiming strategy software. Kotlikoff's Maximize My Social Security calculator, for instance, costs $40 a year; Social Security Solutions' SSAnalyzer software runs $300 a year.

If you have a financial adviser, he or she may be able to lay it all out for you in a way that makes sense, and that dovetails with your current retirement plan and overall income plan for your golden years. To choose an adviser, you might seek out a financial pro who has taken special courses and certification in Social Security.

Where to look? You may want to hire an independent Social Security adviser (such as a member of the National Association of Registered Social Security Analysts or someone who earned a certificate from the National Social Security Advisor) to help make the right decisions. Consultations with independent experts cost roughly $400 to $1,500, depending on the complexity of your case.

"The closest thing to my heart is being able to help others make this decision," Martha Shedden, president of the National Association of Registered Social Security Analysts (NARSSA), told us. "Because I've seen the huge amount of difference it makes financially."

FUTURE OF SOCIAL SECURITY

Before we tie things up, let's address the anxiety among Gen Xers about the future of Social Security. First, the anxiety is not totally misplaced. The entitlement program's reserves are projected to run out in the early to mid-2030s—the estimates change from year to year—at which point the program will be able to pay out just 75–80 percent of benefits to seniors.[9] That has repercussions for many workers who plan to rely on Social Security for a major portion of their retirement income, and it's created "a crisis of confidence in the Social Security system," Deb Boyden, the head of US defined contribution at Schroders, an asset management company, told us.

Just ask Laura Heller, a 59-year-old Indiana resident who retired from her day-to-day job in 2024, but is looking for different ways to increase her income beyond a take-home salary.

"I am very skeptical about Social Security. We were always told it's not going to be there when we need it, and I believe that," said Heller, whose husband owns his own business and is still working. (Heller's first car was a Ford Mustang and her first job was at McDonald's.) "So I have to continue to operate on that. If it's there, great, that's gravy. But if it's not, I need to be prepared."

That's why Heller has spent her life socking away money for retirement. She had side hustles before those became trendy. Waiting tables. Bartending. On top of her career in journalism and then communications. She was "too scared to ever not have a net." An older Gen Xer, she's seen more than her share of recessions that created a lifetime of instability and a great amount of fear.

"It's just like we came of age during a time when we were transitioning out of pensions into private retirement funds, we are now going to come into retirement age at a time when Social Security is more precarious," she said. "So to be caught short on that would be just devastating."

This is also not the first time Social Security's reserves have faced a funding problem. In fact, in 1983 the Social Security system was literally months away from being unable to pay full benefits on time. Congress acted with several major reforms, including:

- Delaying the cost-of-living adjustment for six months.
- Accelerating the enacted payroll tax increase from 10.8 percent to the current 12.4 percent.
- Extending Social Security coverage to new federal and nonprofit workers, which added to the number of workers paying into Social Security.

- Taxing Social Security benefits of high-income seniors.
- Phasing in the increase of full retirement age from age 65 to age 67.

The reforms were supposed to keep Social Security solvent until 2060, but the economic and demographic expectations at the time were too optimistic. And so here we are facing a looming solvency crisis again—and unfortunately it's bigger than the last one.

Still, if you're worried your benefits won't be there when you retire, let's dispel that concern right now, said Kotlikoff. As the insolvency date nears, lawmakers will be pressured to provide a solution, which like last time, will probably include some mix of tax increases and a phased-in increase in retirement age.

"It's absolutely right to assume that current retirees and near-term retirees are going to get what they've been promised. Politicians are not going to touch that third rail," he said. "Assume that the benefits are there for sure."

But as a concerned citizen hoping for a sunny retirement, it's an issue that should be at the forefront of your mind when you walk into any voting booth for federal elections. That is, until our elected officials finally fix Social Security.

YOUR TO-DO LIST

- Sign up for a My Social Security account (ssa.gov/myaccount) if you haven't already, and review your most recent Social Security statement and benefits estimates.
- Run a Social Security benefit calculator to get a ballpark figure of your benefits at different claiming ages.
- Write down reasons why you might need to take your benefit before age 70 and consider ways you could mitigate them. If you can't, plan a future with a smaller lifetime payout.

- Seek out a financial expert with expertise in Social Security.
- Make Social Security a voting issue.

Now that you have figured out this major source of your retirement income, it's time to discover how you can augment that income.

8

OTHER INCOME SOURCES

You see that building? I bought that building ten years ago. My first real estate deal. Sold it two years later, made an $800,000 profit. It was better than sex. At the time I thought that was all the money in the world. Now it's a day's pay.

—Gordon Gekko
Wall Street, 1987

The biggest worry when it comes to retirement is the potential to outlive your savings. With people living longer and savings not keeping up, this has become a real possibility. For most Gen Xers, Social Security is the only guaranteed income stream we have. The savings in our retirement accounts are finite, and a really bad year in the stock market at an inopportune time could deplete those savings when we need them the most.

It's important to consider other ways to fund your retirement, especially if you feel you're behind on saving. In this chapter, we'll consider how you can use your housing wealth to increase your retirement savings. We'll also go over annuities, which, on top of Social Security, can offer you a monthly check for the rest of your life. We'll also touch on what's dubbed the Great Wealth Transfer, the money flowing from your parents to you, and whether that's enough to fill in your retirement preparation gaps. But first, let's look at your house.

REAL ESTATE

More than seven in 10 Gen Xers owned their homes in 2023. And home values have largely marched upward—with a few months of dips here and there—since crashing during the fallout of the Great Recession.[1] This is a huge well of wealth that could serve Gen Xers in many ways for their retirement. The question is how to unlock that wealth? This is an especially tricky question because, on average, Gen Xers have a very low 4 percent interest rate on their mortgages.[2] For those Gen Xers with a higher mortgage rate, one option may be in trading in that higher interest rate for a lower one, if the math works out. There are other options, too. Let's see the various ways you can use your home to help fund your retirement.

One way to release home equity is by selling your current home and buying a more affordable one, a process known as downsizing. That could mean moving to a smaller property like a townhouse or condominium that requires less maintenance as you age or by moving to a more affordable city or state. This option is especially attractive for homeowners who have paid off their mortgage. You literally get to pocket the difference between the sales prices of your old home and the purchase price of your new one. If you still have to pay off a mortgage, the equity you're able to cash out will be less. You may also end up with a higher interest rate, but on a smaller mortgage amount. How that affects the difference between your new and old payment depends on how large the new mortgage amount is and the gap between your old and new interest rate. If the new mortgage and interest rate are large, you may find the new payment doesn't save you as much money as you'd like.

You could also cash out some of your home equity by refinancing, but again the preferred way to do that is if prevailing interest rates are close to or lower than your current one. Perhaps you want to put that extra money in the stock market to earn more or buy an annuity (more on that later) to get a guaranteed income stream. If you do this after you retire and are no longer working, it may be harder to qualify for a refinance if your income is much lower than when you were working. You also have to figure in that your new monthly mortgage payment may be larger than before. Talk with a mortgage professional who may be able to sort out your best options.

The last way to use home equity to help fund your retirement is through a reverse mortgage. A reverse mortgage allows you to withdraw a portion of your home equity to use for maintenance, repairs, or general living expenses. Your home is collateral for the loan, but the title stays in your name. You also don't make monthly payments. Instead, the reverse mortgage is paid off when you no longer live in the home and you or your heirs pay back the loan, usually by selling the property. Now the amount you owe on the reverse mortgage increases as time passes because interest and fees are added to the balance every month. As the loan balance grows, your home equity goes down. You can live in your home indefinitely as long as you pay the property taxes and homeowner's insurance on time and keep up the property's maintenance. How much equity you can withdraw depends on several factors, including:

- Age of the youngest borrower or qualified nonborrowing spouse.
- Current interest rate.
- The appraised value, mortgage limit, or the sales price, whichever is less.

The most common type of reverse mortgage is a home equity conversion mortgage, or HECM, which is available through a Federal Housing Administration–approved lender only. These loans are also only available to homeowners who are 62 and older, who own their house outright or have paid down a substantial amount, and live in the house as their principal residence.

Before the FHA's HECM, reverse mortgages were the Wild West of home loans. Now you're required to attend a consumer information session by a federally approved counselor before finalizing a reverse mortgage. There are still scams to watch out for, according to the Consumer Financial Protection Bureau. Look out for contractor scams, where contractors approach you about getting a reverse mortgage to fund upgrades to your home. Some ads also falsely promise veterans special deals on reverse mortgages. Steer clear! The best place to find out information about reverse mortgages is the US Department of Housing and Urban Development (HUD). Its website on reverse mortgages provides a search tool to help you find a trusted reverse mortgage counselor and/or a HUD lender.

If you own a second home, you may consider renting out that property for a steady income while you're retired. You could go the Airbnb or Vrbo route, or you could rent full-time on a yearly or two-year lease basis. For short-term rentals, you need to make sure your HOA, if you have one, allows these kinds of deals. You should also consider other costs, such as cleaning services and an on-call handyperson. Similarly, for long-term rentals, check into the costs of using a real estate agent to find renters and expenses related to landlord responsibilities.

Laura Heller, a 59-year-old, lives in a house she owns along Lake Michigan. She also owns two other homes that she rents out. One is her husband's old house and the other is her husband's late parents' home that they bought out from his siblings. Heller retired from her full-time job in communications last year and is looking for ways to generate income beyond a traditional salary. Real estate has been one solution so far.

"I am considering future real estate investments," she told us. (Heller loved *M*A*S*H* and *Seinfeld* when she was younger and "anything John Hughes, but *The Breakfast Club* above all else.") "It's something I'm talking about with my adviser and a couple of like-minded friends in the area who have been investing in real estate at a higher level than what I have. So that's an interest of mine in terms of a different way to build wealth."

ANNUITIES

One of the ways to use the equity that you unlocked from your home through downsizing or refinancing is to consider purchasing an annuity to help guarantee a lifelong stream of income on top of Social Security. You can also use the cash you saved up in your retirement accounts to pay for an annuity. But don't use it all. The rule of thumb is to take a third of your retirement savings for an annuity, according to Benny Goodman, vice president at the TIAA Institute. Of course, the exact percentage will vary by individual.

So what is an annuity anyway? At the most basic, you give an insurance company a lump sum and they provide a monthly check for a certain amount of time. Sometimes that stream of income starts immediately, and at other times it starts at some later date. Those monthly payments could last a lifetime or they could come for a specific period of time, say 10 or 15 years. The key here is that an annuity provides a guaranteed income check in addition to Social Security benefits.

In many ways, annuities are a way to substitute for traditional pensions, which also provide a guaranteed income stream. The way to calculate how much you would need from an annuity is to add up your expenses you will need to pay—consult that Chapter 3 cash flow exercise for help here—and subtract your estimated monthly Social Security benefit payment from that. (We went over how to find that estimate in Chapter 7.) Whatever that gap is can be covered by an annuity. Any money left over in retirement and brokerage accounts could go to more discretionary spending like eating out or traveling.

"The real value of an annuity is to make sure that you've topped up your Social Security income so that your [guaranteed lifetime income] at least covers your basic [expenses]," said David John, a senior strategic policy adviser at the AARP Public Policy Institute.

There are two main types of annuities: a fixed annuity and a variable annuity. A typical fixed annuity works like this. You give an insurance company a chunk of money, say $100,000, and the company will send you $7,500 a year, or $625 per month, for every month for the rest of your life. It's very straightforward.

"There's no bells, no whistles, nothing," Goodman said. "That's an easy product to understand."

Fixed annuities get slightly more complicated when it comes to couples. When one spouse passes away, you want the surviving spouse to still receive income during their retirement. In that case, you want to include both spouses in a joint annuity, which lasts until the second spouse passes away. That adds more risk for the insurer, so maybe that $100,000 annuity pays out $7,000 a year rather than $7,500 a year to accommodate both people.

Another variation of this is a joint annuity with a 20-year guarantee, which says that if both spouses die within 15 years, a beneficiary designated by the owners of the annuity receives a check for the next five years. But to get that perk, you may only get $6,800 in monthly income for the same $100,000 annuity. Folks like this plan, Goodman said, because they feel like they're not losing their money, since the minimum guaranteed 20 years of payments will be more than the amount they gave the insurance company.

Then there are "pure" variable annuities, where the income is variable. You provide a lump sum to the insurance company, which invests that money and in turn provides you a lifetime check every month, but the size of the check can go up or down, depending on how those investments perform. So if the company's annuity is invested in, say, the S&P 500 stock market index, your monthly check increases when the index is up and the check shrinks when the market goes down.

"The beauty of that is, historically over long periods of time, the market has done well," Goodman said. "So those annuities have done well, but you have to watch out for when the market crashes."

For instance, in 2008 and 2009, the pure variable annuity income dropped by 50 percent, so a senior who was getting $1,000 per month one year was getting $500 per month the next year. That sort of scenario creates a difficult cash flow situation for seniors who are on fixed incomes.

"On the other hand, in 2022 retirees got a 62 percent raise when the market went crazy," Goodman said.

Variable annuities also come with a lot of extras, which may make it harder to know if you're getting a good deal. Some insurers will throw in a death benefit, which provides a lump sum to your estate after you die. But the annuity doesn't offer this for free. The insurer may charge something like 1 percent for this particular benefit. That means if the S&P 500 index, which your annuity is tied to, goes up 10 percent, your monthly annuity payment will only increase 9 percent because you have to pay that 1 percent for that death benefit.

Other variable annuities may provide an income floor, meaning that even if the index your annuity is tied to tanks, your monthly benefit can decrease by only so much, or perhaps not at all! But to get this perk, the insurer charges you another 1 percent. That's where you need to be careful. The fees for these extras can add up, and that 2 to 3 percent, "eats away a lot of the potential increased value," Goodman said. There are other snags. If you bought an annuity at age 65 and you suddenly receive a terminal diagnosis, unwinding that contract could cost you as much as 30 percent of the principal, depending on the terms of the policy.

"You may be locked into an annuity contract that is not suitable for your needs and they're hard to get out of," John said.

As if that wasn't difficult enough, now some employer-sponsored 401(k)s have the option to purchase an annuity if the retirement plan provider offers one. This can work in two ways. In one scenario, starting around age 45, you would automatically start to buy slices of an annuity over the next 20 years in your 401(k). By the time you reach retirement, a certain proportion of your retirement savings pool is an annuity.

This is all well and good if you stay with one employer for much of your working life. But these slices can't be ported over to another employer. So if you change jobs frequently, you could have five years of annuity purchases in one provider and 10 years with another provider and five years from a third provider.

"You're getting a bunch of tiny little checks," John said, "and you're probably paying much more for it than you would if you had just had one annuity."

To solve this dilemma, several 401(k) providers offer contributors the ability to buy an annuity, rather than buying slices of annuity. Some are adding this feature to their target-date funds. Starting around age 55, depending on the provider, part of the money you invest each month is earmarked for annuity contracts. Once you hit age 65, say, about 30 percent of your portfolio is in this annuity fund, while the rest is allocated to stocks and bonds. If you don't want to buy the annuity, those funds are yours and act like a bond allocation in the target-date fund.

"It is a rapidly developing field," Goodman said.

Because of this, we believe you should proceed with extreme caution, especially with newfangled annuity features and the more complex annuities that increase the fees. Be aware of the other drawbacks, like no refunds and the inability to name a beneficiary. If you do end up considering an annuity, keep to the simple, straightforward ones and always, always buy from a triple-A rated insurance company, rather than a smaller outfit that may not be there 20 years down the line.

THE GREAT WEALTH TRANSFER

Another source of income could be your parents. Over the next two decades, $84 trillion in assets is set to transfer down to younger generations. Of that total, Generation X is expected to get the largest amount and share. They will inherit $30 trillion, or 36 percent of the total. Millennials are expected to get $27 trillion; Gen Z and younger will inherit $11 trillion; and the youngest Boomers are set to get $4 trillion.[3]

Many of us may be banking on this transfer of wealth from our parents to fill in those holes in our retirement savings. Maybe our parents have already been gifting this inheritance to us by helping with down payments on a house or funding our children's education. If that's the case, when you get something, it might not be as much as you expected.

"I have not seen my clients inherit life-changing money," said Bridget Grimes, a certified financial planner in Coronado, California. Inheriting $100,000 is helpful, but it generally won't be enough so that you can retire immediately.

And if that inherited money is in an individual retirement account (IRA) or 401(k), accessing that money gets a little thorny. Let's say Alex Keaton is inheriting money in an IRA from his dad. Typically for an IRA, Alex would need to liquidate the account by the end of the 10th year after the year of his dad's death. If Alex's dad had begun taking required minimum distributions (RMDs), or yearly withdrawals required by the IRS, then Alex may be required to take these from the account in each of the nine years after his dad's death. If Alex doesn't, the IRS may levy a penalty. His withdrawals would be taxed as well, so Alex may want to consult with a tax pro to figure out how to best empty out the account with the softest tax hit possible. After the money is withdrawn and taxed, it's Alex's to do with however he wants.

If Alex inherited a 401(k) instead, he could take his portion of the inherited 401(k) balance as a lump sum penalty-free, but taxed as ordinary income. Or he could transfer the funds of an inherited 401(k) into an inherited IRA, but Alex must follow similar rules as if he inherited the IRA. Two quick notes: Once a lump sum is taken, the remaining balance can't be rolled over. And Alex as a child beneficiary can't roll over the inherited assets in his own retirement account. Only spouse beneficiaries—in this case, Elyse Keaton—can do that.

Also, don't discount the emotional aspect of inheritances, said Adam Wojtkowski, a certified financial planner in Mansfield, Massachusetts. He's worked with clients who inherited stock from the company their dad worked for. The child has an attachment to that stock because that was the employer that helped Dad put food on the table and funded the holidays. They may have a hard time cashing in that stock to use for other purposes, such as funding a grandchild's college education, even though Mom and Dad would want that.

"I'm pretty sure 99 times out of 100, your parents would say, 'Yes, do that for my grandchild, that's a great legacy that I'm going to have,'" Wojtkowski said.

Finally, the financial planners we spoke to said an inheritance shouldn't be considered a given, especially as you plan for your retirement. Don't count it in your plans; instead, it's an unexpected bonus that you get. Why? Because bad luck and bad timing can shrink an inheritance in no time.

"I've had a few clients that are in their 70s and 80s who have had strokes and health care problems and that million-dollar portfolio is quickly disappearing," said Jon Ulin, a certified financial planner in Boca Raton, Florida. (A Gen Xer himself, Ulin had stand-in parts in the *Rocky* and *Mannequin* movies during college.) "So maybe some of us might inherit a half-million to a million dollars, but I would work on your savings as if you were not getting that money."

YOUR TO-DO LIST

- Discuss if downsizing seems like a good fit for your retirement vision. If you want to stay in your current home, but need more retirement income, research more about reverse mortgages.
- Check to see if your 401(k) offers an annuity option and research the pros and cons of it.
- Talk with your parents about what to expect from them in terms of an inheritance. But don't mark that down as a 100 percent guarantee.

Now that you have a grasp on what money sources can fund your retirement—from your savings and Social Security to working longer and tapping home equity—it's time to turn to other parts of your financial life that need upkeep. The next chapters explore how to juggle the many financial responsibilities you might have aside from retirement saving and provide strategies to protect your wealth and accommodate health care expenses as you stare down retirement. We'll also give you advice on moving to a new crib in a new state in retirement, and on how to find a trusted professional to be in your corner. In the meantime, take a breather. You're doing great so far. You deserve a break.

PART FOUR

More Than Money

9

MANAGING COMPETING FINANCIAL PRIORITIES

ANDREW: My God, are we gonna be like our parents?
CLAIRE: Not me... ever.
ALLISON: It's unavoidable, it just happens.

THE BREAKFAST CLUB, 1985

If only saving for retirement was the sole financial goal you had to think about. But so many of us have other obligations that require attention and, quite frankly, our money. You need to save for that proverbial rainy day. There may be debts that you need to repay. Your kid's higher education is just around the corner. Or you're worried your parents will need more help as they age. Is there enough money to go around?

"Financial planning is about the trade-off of the different options or different opportunities and how they align most closely with your goals," Judson Meinhart, a certified financial planner in Winston-Salem, North Carolina (Janna's hometown!), told us. "If you pay for your son or daughter's college tuition, that is money that's not going to be there for you when you want to retire."

As you weigh each financial priority it's important to understand what sacrifices or adjustments you may need to make as a result. In this chapter, we hit on the competing priorities you may encounter on your way to your retirement goals. Let's start with your emergency fund.

BUILD YOUR EMERGENCY FUND

Your emergency fund should be your first financial priority, before retirement or anything else you might be saving for. An emergency fund is a cash reserve for unplanned expenses, such as medical bills, home repairs, or car repairs. "Lack of savings are hurting everyone–whether you're Gen Z entering the workforce saddled with student loans or Gen X supporting both kids and parents," Sid Pailla, chief executive of the Sunny Day Fund, a financial technology company that helps workers establish emergency funds, told us.

Nearly a quarter of consumers have no savings set aside for emergencies, according to the Consumer Financial Protection Bureau.[1] "So when a financial emergency inevitably hits, our research shows that one in five people are sacrificing their retirement security by taking 401(k) early withdrawals or loans," Pailla said.

Most financial advisers suggest you set aside six months of living expenses for an emergency. But if you can gradually ramp up to a year's worth, do. And you want to stay liquid. A money market mutual fund or a high-yield savings account is a smart, safe place to stash this money since they don't fluctuate in value and are easily accessible when you need them.

Before socking away money in an account that bills itself as high-yield, check to see if there are any restrictions. There may be fees for withdrawing money more than a certain number of times each month or a monthly balance requirement.

A growing number of employers are now helping workers ramp up their emergency savings while also providing ways for them to save for retirement. Workers who qualify and have a defined contribution retirement plan, such as a 401(k), are able to add an emergency savings account that's a designated Roth account.

Participants are able to take out funds at least once a month, and the first four withdrawals in a year are tax- and penalty-free. Moreover, participants don't have to provide proof of a qualifying emergency cause. Depending on plan rules, employee contributions may be eligible for an employer match.

"All it takes is one financial shock—like a major car repair or an unexpected illness—to destabilize a household," Craig Copeland, director of Wealth Benefits Research at the Employee Benefit Research Institute (EBRI) in Washington, DC, told us.

One way to pump up your emergency savings is to earmark your tax refund into that account, or if you get a bonus at work, set some of that aside for this purpose, too.

You can also set up automatic transfers each month from your checking account into a money market account or another savings account that's earmarked for emergencies. You can start by transferring small amounts and then ratchet up the contributions until you reach the amount you feel comfortable with having as your cushion.

Now that you have the big unexpected expenses covered, it's time to check in on other financial obligations you might have.

CREDIT CARD DEBT

As we mentioned in the Introduction, Gen X has the largest average credit card balance of all generations at over $9,200. Their balances have grown by a whopping 44 percent since 2012.[2] This is not necessarily because the generation that once spurned the consumerism of Baby Boomers is now a bunch of spendthrifts. Generally, spending peaks between ages 45 and 54 when folks hit those prime-earning years. Spending typically declines after that, until those last years when health care spending usually accelerates.

But, of course, that doesn't mean there aren't individuals who are relying too heavily on credit cards now and may be in a bit of trouble. Often this can happen if you don't have an emergency fund. If that sounds like you, it's high time to slay that dragon. (To determine the extent that credit card debt makes up your liabilities, take some time to go through the exercises in Chapter 3, if you haven't already.)

"Given how high interest rates are, getting rid of credit card debt is super critical," Jennifer Grant, a certified financial planner in Dallas, Texas, told us.

Eliminating credit card debt also takes precedence over maximizing your retirement savings. It's simple math. Putting money toward a debt that's accruing 25 to 30 percent in interest is better than placing that cash in an account that returns 7 to 9 percent.

Before embarking on a quest to vanquish credit card debt, it's also important to know exactly how you got into this type of debt in the first place. There's a difference between leaning on a credit card during an emergency and spending more than you're taking in by using your credit card to fill in the gaps. (The cash flow exercise in Chapter 3 is there to help you figure that out.) The latter explanation describes your spending habits, requiring you to make some major day-to-day changes or else you risk finding yourself back where you started.

Digging out of debt may sound daunting, but it's surmountable. Just ask K. Sommer from Texas, who had been on track for an early retirement at age 55, but the Great Recession disrupted those plans. The 17-month bear market, a yearlong bout of unemployment—common during the time—and a divorce erased his retirement savings and put him tens of thousands of dollars in credit card debt. Once he regained his footing in the job market, Sommer spent years whittling down his debt.

"I was basically starting from scratch," Sommer told us. (Sommer's Gen X bona fides: His first concert was Run-DMC with LL Cool J as an opening act.)

He canceled his cable and subscriptions, limited eating out, and forewent any trips. He played the balance transfer credit card game and got a debt consolidation loan. He even froze his credit cards in Tupperware to prevent any spontaneous decisions. In 2021, he sold his house and finished off the debt completely. Now, at 56 years old, he is maxing out contributions to his employer-sponsored retirement plan, adding catch-up contributions on top of that.

"Obviously retiring at 55 is no longer an option... [but] I'm in a much better place than I was five years ago," said Sommer, who hopes for a partial retirement in nine years when he hits Medicare eligibility at age 65, with part-time work on the side. "I also am cautious because all of a sudden life could happen and then it derails these great plans for retirement."

Here are some of the strategies Sommer used to get out of debt. Like Sommer, you may want to combine some of these methods to tackle all of your debt.

Balance transfer card: First, use a credit card to get out of credit card debt. We know that sounds counterintuitive, but it can work as long as you remain disciplined. The key here is to look for a 0 percent balance transfer credit card. These cards come with a 0 percent interest rate for an introductory period—often six to 18 months—on a certain balance amount transferred from another credit card. The no-interest period provides folks time to pay down their debt without interest charges piling up. There's an up-front fee to do this, typically 3 to 5 percent of your overall rolled-over balance. And you need to have a decent credit score to qualify.

There are two pitfalls to watch for. First, if your outstanding balance is large, the new card may not have a big enough credit limit to transfer the entire debt. In that case, you will need a payoff plan for the remaining balance. Second, if you don't pay off your balance before the 0 percent intro period ends, the remaining balance will start accruing interest and the rate could be higher than the one on your original credit card. The best way to avoid this, obviously, is to stick to your payoff plan.

To find a balance transfer card, check out Yahoo Finance's "best balance transfer credit cards" list that is reviewed monthly.

Debt consolidation or personal loan: Transferring your outstanding credit card balance to a debt consolidation or personal loan also offers a set timeline for getting out of debt. It requires that you make monthly installment payments for an established term, often two to seven years, helping you avoid the temptation to pay just the minimum. The loan is unsecured, so it doesn't require that you put up collateral—like a home, car, or personal property—to qualify. But unlike a balance transfer card, a personal loan comes with a nonzero interest rate, but the rate will be far lower than what you're charged on your credit card. Yahoo Finance also puts out a "best personal loan rates" list that's updated regularly.

Again, you may have some outstanding balance left over even if you employ a balance transfer card and/or a personal loan. In that case, it's savviest to pay as much as you can on the balance that carries the highest interest rate and the minimum on the rest of your balances. After the balance with the highest interest rate is paid off, attack the balance with the next highest rate, and so on. This is the snowball strategy. In the meantime, call up your credit card issuers and ask if they would lower your interest rate to make it easier for you to pay off those balances.

"It works more often than people imagine," Matt Schulz, chief credit analyst at LendingTree and author of *Ask Questions, Save Money, Make More: How to Take Control of Your Financial Life*, previously told us. (Schulz still owns all 107 issues of the original *Star Wars* comic book series from Marvel.)

While there are two other ways to pay off credit card debt, approach these methods with some caution.

Tapping home equity: As we learned in Chapter 8, Gen X homeowners are largely flush with home equity—thanks to a long run-up in home prices after the housing crash that preceded the Great Recession. You can unlock some of this housing wealth to pay off your higher interest debts by borrowing at a lower rate against your home. There are two ways to do this: a cash-out refinance or a home equity line of credit, otherwise known as a HELOC.

A cash-out refinance is simply replacing the mortgage on your home with a new one, but with a bigger outstanding balance. Let's say you still have to pay off $100,000 on your home that is worth $400,000. That means you have $300,000 worth of equity. Say you cash out $50,000 of that equity, then you now owe $150,000 on your mortgage. But that $50,000 is accruing interest at a much smaller rate than when it was on your credit card, which was accruing interest at something like 20 percent. In this scenario, it's likely your monthly mortgage payment will go up. By how much depends on the difference between your old interest rate on your mortgage and the new one. If the new rate is a lot larger than the old one, you may want to consider a HELOC. This is likely the case for most Gen Xers who refinanced when rates were at historic lows. Almost two-thirds have a mortgage rate that's 4 percent or lower.[3]

A HELOC is "like a giant credit card tied to your house," Scott Sheldon, a senior loan officer at Sonoma County Mortgages in California, said. (A young Gen Xer, Sheldon said he was "a sucker for anything with Chuck Norris, Jean-Claude Van Damme, or Sylvester Stallone" growing up.) Except the interest rate on these lines of credit are a lot more favorable than what credit cards offer. Like a mortgage, HELOC rates can be fixed, where the rate doesn't change, or variable, so it goes up and down based on where the Federal Reserve sets its benchmark rate. Just like a credit card, you have to pay at least a monthly minimum payment, though to get out of debt, you should pay more than that. Of course, the biggest downside is that your home is collateral. If you can't pay back what you borrowed on the HELOC, the lender can move to take your home. A mortgage professional can help you decide if these options fit your budget.

Borrowing against your 401(k): Last and probably the least favorable option is taking a loan from your 401(k). This is not a withdrawal, which would deplete your balance and cause you to incur taxes and penalties, as we discussed in Chapter 4. A 401(k) loan is not great, especially because it does not help you save up for retirement. But at least with a 401(k) loan you pay yourself back with interest, typically 1 to 2 percentage points above the prime rate, which is the rate banks charge creditworthy customers. One big potential stumbling block: You may be required to pay the entire remaining balance back in one go if you switch jobs.

"If you're paying 25 percent to 30 percent interest on a credit card, taking a loan from your 401(k) is certainly an option," Grant said. "Sometimes it's the best of several crummy options."

STUDENT LOANS

While the generation that succeeds Gen Xers are the ones moaning loudest about student loans, it's the MTV generation that has the biggest problem with them. Of the 21.2 million Gen Xers carrying student debt, one in nine of them owe $40,000 to $60,000![4] That's rough. And it's an obvious drag on their ability to save for retirement.

Tackling student loan debt head-on is a great strategy. Using your results from the cash flow exercise from Chapter 3, determine how much money you have left over after paying for your basic needs. Is there enough to set aside for your 401(k) to get your employer match, and also to pay your student debt bill every month? If so, do both. If there's even more left over, split it between your retirement savings and your student loans. This way you build up your nest egg further while chipping away faster at the debt. Because the interest rates on student loans are close to returns you can get from investing long term, the aim is to balance these two priorities as much as you can. This strategy contrasts with dealing with outsized interest rates on credit card debt, as we mentioned before.

If you don't have enough money to make your student loan payment and invest for retirement, talk to your human resources department to see if your employer can base their matching contributions to your 401(k) on your payments to your student loans, a provision in the SECURE 2.0 Act that went into effect in 2024. If so, that, at least, will allow you to build up retirement savings until you earn more and can put more toward retirement, in addition to paying your student loan obligations.

You can also look into consolidating your loans, but do this with eyes wide open. Consolidating typically means replacing your federal loans with private ones. Once you do that, you lose many of the benefits of federal loans, such as enrolling in income-driven repayment programs and applying for forgiveness programs. As of this writing, there are several ways to obtain loan forgiveness for federal debt. If you work for the government or a nonprofit, you may be eligible for the Public Service Loan Forgiveness program that eliminates any remaining debt after 10 years of payments. There's a similar program for teachers called Teacher Loan Forgiveness. Check these out at Federal Student Aid (studentaid .gov) before consolidating.

Just like with Social Security, political forces affect your options for student loans. How easy it is to qualify for forgiveness programs can depend on which administration is running the Department of Education. New repayment programs also come and go depending on who is in charge, so it's important to keep tabs on what lawmakers are promising and delivering.

PAYING FOR YOUR CHILD'S EDUCATION

Speaking of student loans, you're probably wondering about how your own kids are going to pay for their higher education. Adjusted for inflation, the average sticker price of attending college—which includes tuition and fees, living expenses, and other related costs—has almost tripled in the last four decades.[5] While students often pay less than the sticker price, the costs are still incredibly high, especially for students from lower- and middle-income families. And if you're behind on your retirement savings, the question of helping your kids pay for college is even more consequential. There's a saying in personal finance: "You can borrow to go to school, but you can't borrow for retirement." And the financial planners we spoke to take this saying to heart.

"I always tell people if you're going to pull money out of a retirement account, which I see people doing to pay for college, is your child going to come back and fund you in retirement?" said Paul Caylor, a certified financial planner in Huntsville, Alabama, and an older Gen Xer himself who paid his way through school while taking on some loans. "Are they going to pay your monthly mortgage payment, because that's equivalent to what you want to do right now? My guess is no."

In fact, we're not huge fans of taking on debt yourself to pay for your kid's education. Federal loans that you can take out on behalf of your child's college education are called Direct PLUS loans for parents, also referred to as Parent PLUS loans. You, not your child, are responsible for repaying these obligations, with repayment starting as soon as you take out the loans. With PLUS loans, you can't qualify for all the income-driven repayment plans available to other federal student loans. These loans also come with large borrowing limits, which increases the possibility of taking on too much debt. The other problem is these loans are very hard to discharge even in bankruptcy.

Bottom line, and this is hard because we often want to give our children the world: Do not sacrifice your retirement savings to pay for your children's higher education. And the sooner you let them know about this, the more time you and they have to plan how to take that next step. Having this frank conversation now will prevent a situation down the road where you are unsustainably in debt. It may also help your child understand what she's signing up for and what's manageable and what's not.

"I think a lot of kids apply to school and [families] don't realize the [financial] impact it will have. They think, 'That looks expensive, but we'll figure it out' and then later realize all of the unintended consequences of making these decisions," Judith Brown, a certified financial planner in Finksburg, Maryland, said. (A Gen Xer herself, Brown remembers growing up without cable and air conditioning, and exploring the outdoors.)

Families should explore all sorts of other options when it comes to addressing the cost of higher education. (A fantastic book on this is Ron Lieber's *The Price You Pay for College: An Entirely New Road Map for the Biggest Financial Decision Your Family Will Ever Make.*) This can be considering two years of community college and then going to college. It can mean hunting down scholarships, both small and large, to help foot the bill. Janna's niece became a residential adviser, or RA, in a dorm at her school to cover her room and board, a move Chuck Hansberry, Janna's brother-in-law and a fellow Gen Xer, said was "a game changer to be honest with you because the cost of living is a huge part of the college thing."

It's also about making the financial aid packages that schools offer a big deciding factor. That's what Christine Condry and her daughter did.

"It did come down to looking at different offers and different amounts. And there was one choice that did seem like the best one as a matter of, 'can we make that happen?'" the 58-year-old from New Jersey told us. (Condry was a big Kate Bush fan when she was younger, and her first job was operating a Six Flags toll plaza.) Condry and her husband decided against utilizing a 529 college savings plan for their daughter's education, because "What if she wanted to be a potter?" Condry said. (Fortunately, there may be a workaround for that now. A new law that went into effect in 2024 allows the beneficiary of a 529 plan—such as your child—to use any leftover funds in the plan for retirement savings, but the kinks of it are still being worked out.)

Instead, Condry timed paying off her mortgage with when her daughter went to college. Without the mortgage payment, Condry was able to make up the difference for her daughter's tuition payments "without having this put aside for exactly that purpose." Condry and her husband, in the meantime, stayed the course with their own retirement savings. And now that their daughter has graduated, they can use some of that extra money toward home projects they had delayed. (Condry first got serious about her finances in her 20s after reading the quintessential book *Your Money or Your Life*, by Vicki Robin and Joe Dominguez, first published in 1992. The book is largely considered the precursor to the Financial Independence, Retire Early [FIRE] movement, which encourages living frugally and investing aggressively with the goal of retiring well before age 65.)

Other options for parents can mean looking at alternatives like the military or trade or vocational schools. You can also budget into your retirement savings some money you plan to give your kids each month to help them pay back student loans or launch into adulthood. So maybe you're not there on the front end, but you can be there on the back end. But it all starts with this hard conversation.

"It's so much more helpful to say, 'Here's what we've saved, here's what we budgeted. We don't want you to graduate with a ton of debt, so let's figure out a way to do this in the most economical way,'" said Grant, a Gen Xer with twin teenage daughters who are also on the cusp of this next big step. "And so we're helping our kids do that, but we're also not taking on school debt."

AGING PARENTS

That may not be the only tough conversation that you need to have with your family. The others involve one with your aging parents and a related one with your siblings, if you have any. Let's start with that conversation with your parents about how they envision their lives as they get older and more dependent.

"Have these conversations early before Mom and Dad get into trouble," said Carolyn McClanahan, a physician, certified financial planner, and founder of Life Planning Partners Inc. "Having that when everybody's alive, well, and happy makes it easier when the poop hits the fan."

McClanahan offers four questions that your parents need to think about so you have an idea of how to proceed when their aging starts to take a toll. Financial ramifications are also related to the questions. Let's go through each one by one.

- Where are you financially and when are you going to get help with financial decision-making?
- Where are you going to live as you age?
- When are you going to quit driving?
- What are your health care wishes when you need help with these decisions?

Where are you financially and when are you going to get help with financial decision-making? This one has the biggest potential impact on your finances. In many cases, parents don't disclose to their adult children how much money they have or how they're faring financially. Then all of a sudden, parents start asking for help and the adult children realize that their parents haven't financially prepared for aging.

Christine Condry got a read on her mother's finances only after her father, who had managed the financial affairs, declined cognitively from Parkinson's disease. Condry ended up being a joint power of attorney with her mother and sat in on meetings with their financial planner. What she learned provided relief.

"I know she's in good shape," Condry said. "I don't know if she would have shared as much, except for the circumstances with my dad."

That's why you want to have these conversations as early as you can. It's good to find out if they have a pension that pays out until the end of their life and if it continues for the surviving spouse, what kind of supplemental health coverage they have, if the house is paid off, and if they have long-term care insurance. You don't need to get the answers to these questions all at once. The key is to start this conversation and continue it until you and your siblings have a good understanding of where your parents stand financially, and if part of their plan is relying on you.

Some advanced preparation is required when it comes to financial decision-making. If your parents want you or your sibling to step in eventually to take over their finances, they need to have the proper documentation in place—primarily a financial power of attorney, which often needs to be drawn up by an estate planning attorney. Chapter 13 goes over this in more detail. You will also need them to create a list of their financial accounts (banking, pension, Social Security, other retirement savings, and insurance) and creditor/payment accounts (mortgage, credit card, utilities, phone, and so forth) and the passwords to those accounts. This needs to be updated every time they change passwords. Ask them to provide answers to common security questions and make sure you can access their cell phone for multiple-factor authentication. Janna and her husband faced some of these hurdles when her father-in-law was in decline. Trust us, having this information makes it so much easier during what can be a very emotional time.

If your parents would prefer a professional take over their finances as they age, make sure they have engaged someone already. This is especially critical for older couples where one spouse does all the finances.

If something happens to that spouse, then the other one has a professional already in place to turn to.

Where are you going to live as you age? The answer to this question comes with a lot of costs and potential accommodations. If Mom and Dad would like to age in their home—as so many parents desire—is their home suitable for that? If not, can they afford to pay for needed modifications? Would they be willing to move? (The AARP *HomeFit Guide* can help with this.) Maybe their plan was to move in with one of their adult children—whether or not you and your siblings were aware of that. Regardless, caring for them probably requires getting professional help to come in for a certain time each week, with the level of engagement increasing over time. Who pays for that? Bridget Grimes, a certified financial planner in Coronado, California, sometimes helps her clients figure out how their budget can include paying for a long-term insurance policy on their parents.

"Others will save money in anticipation of their parents needing the money later for their health care," she said.

Last, you need to know if your parents are willing to move to a nursing facility if they need a significant amount of care. This is also a substantial expense that savings or insurance needs to cover. Your parents may also qualify for Medicaid if they spend down their assets. An estate planning attorney can help with this. To understand the costs related to these decisions and help you plan, check out the tool "Cost of Long Term Care by State" (www.carescout.com/cost-of-care) by Genworth, an insurance company.

When are you going to quit driving? "This is when people stick their head in the sand and then all of a sudden it's like, 'Oh my God, we have to take Dad's keys away,'" McClanahan said. "And it's not pleasant."

What you need is a transportation plan. Find out if your parents will agree to take driving tests to make sure they're still safe to drive when the time comes. If they no longer can drive safely, have a plan in place so they can get to their appointments and the grocery store. Maybe that means hiring someone part-time to drive them around, or perhaps it means sharing those responsibilities among family members.

What are your health care wishes when you need help with these decisions? Another key piece of information is who will make health care decisions for your parents when they are not able to do so. Whoever they choose to take on this responsibility will need a document called a health care proxy or a medical power of attorney, depending on the state, and these will be drawn up by the same attorney who deals with the financial documents.

Additionally, your parents need to fill out a living will that outlines what medical interventions the health care proxy should undertake, depending on differing scenarios. These include whether or not to use a feeding tube or a ventilator. An estate planning attorney can help create these documents for you. You can also check AARP's "Find Advance Directives Forms By State" directory online to download forms from your state.

THE TALK WITH YOUR SIBLINGS

Once you and your siblings understand your parents' wishes as they age, you need a second talk, just among yourselves, especially if it's apparent that Mom and Dad are going to need your help, financially and physically. The discussion among your siblings should center on who can provide what kind of help when the time comes.

This can become complicated because one sibling may live closer to your parents than the others, so that sibling, almost by default, becomes the one who drives Mom and Dad around to run errands or takes care of household chores. But there are ways for those other siblings who are farther away to stay involved; it just might not look the same. Maybe they can pitch in financially for a house cleaner, a landscaping service, or a part-time aide to give the caregiving sibling a break. Perhaps they can FaceTime in on doctor's appointments.

"It just is so much easier to have that conversation when it's not an imminent need," Grant said. "Because once Mom gets sick, then everybody's worried and everybody's scared and it's hard to deal with it because you're also hurting."

These conversations will be ongoing, but chances are they'll get easier as time goes on. In fact, we'd wager that everyone involved will feel a lot more comfortable knowing they won't be entering uncharted waters without a map when things turn south.

YOUR TO-DO LIST

- Set aside six months or more of living expenses for an emergency.
- Come up with a credit card payoff plan and follow through. Use a combo of the methods noted in this chapter, if needed.
- Chart a course to pay off your student loans by looking at all avenues available to you: 401(k) matching, forgiveness programs, and consolidation.
- Consider what financial help you can provide your child or children without sacrificing your retirement, and initiate a discussion with them as they near high school graduation.
- Start conversations with your parents and siblings about your parents' plans for the future.

Life in our 40s and 50s is a lot more complicated. We're carrying more debt and many of us are worried about the generations before and after us. It's stressful, but smart trade-offs now give you the best financial footing for the future. Another way to plan for the years ahead is by preparing for one of the biggest costs you'll face as you age: health care. That's the subject of the next chapter.

10

PLANNING FOR FUTURE HEALTH CARE COSTS

It's not the years, honey, it's the mileage.

—INDIANA JONES

RAIDERS OF THE LOST ARK, 1981

Your health is your wealth. Overall health care costs have consistently been climbing every year, especially for older Americans. For instance, the average after-tax, out-of-pocket costs for medical expenses throughout retirement for a single, 65-year-old who retired in 2024 is $165,000, more than doubling since 2002 when Fidelity first released its estimates.[1] Another reliable estimate from the Employee Benefit Research Institute (EBRI) finds that some couples could need as much as $413,000 in savings to cover health care costs in retirement.[2] That's not chump change, and many Gen Xers may find themselves on the higher end of any average because, generally speaking, we're unhealthier than previous generations.

A 2021 study found that the physical health for both Gen X and Millennials has deteriorated from Baby Boomers at the same age.[3] The two younger generations also have higher levels of unhealthy practices, such as drinking and smoking, and more anxiety and depression.

If that wasn't bad enough, the MTV generation is also more likely to be diagnosed with cancer than Boomers, a 2024 study found.[4] These statistics drive home why Gen Xers must plan now for what's likely to be one of their biggest living expenses when they step out of the workforce.

Fortunately, things can be done now to address those future costs later in life. First you need to understand how much of those big estimates apply to you as an individual. To do that, you need to take an honest accounting of your current health, what kind of health care consumer you are, and how you can reduce your health costs by increasing your wellness before you retire. We'll show you ways to save for future health expenses, including a health savings account (HSA), which allows investors the trifecta of contributing, investing, and withdrawing money tax-free when used for qualified medical expenses. This chapter also discusses the ins and outs of Medicare coverage, the pros and cons of long-term care insurance, its viability as a program (a common worry for Gen X), and the long-term care insurer of last resort—Medicaid. We'll also touch briefly on the worries Gen X have over the challenges facing Medicare and long-term care. Here we go.

WHAT IS YOUR HEALTH CARE MINDSET?

Understanding your own health care mindset is the most important factor you need for estimating your costs for health care in retirement. And how much you spend boils down to how you utilize the health care system. Some people visit the doctor only when they have a very big medical issue going on. Others visit the doctor more often to manage chronic conditions or to stay on top of preventative care. A good way to figure this out is to check out your cash flow exercise from Chapter 3 and see how much out-of-pocket spending goes to doctor visits, medications, and other health care services. That should provide a snapshot of whether you're a high or low health care user.

"So, if you're a low health care user, then you're probably on the lower end of spending on health care in retirement," said Carolyn McClanahan, a physician, certified financial planner, and founder of

Life Planning Partners Inc. "If you know you're going to go to the doctor [often], you're going to pay a heck of a lot more for health care."

It helps to put yourself, and your partner or spouse if you're planning for retirement together, in one of four buckets, McClanahan said. These are:

- **Healthy high health care user:** This is you if you're an athlete or health nut who wants to maximize your health. You may often visit sports medicine doctors and chiropractors to stay in tip-top shape, thus generating higher-than-normal health care spending, but you're healthy as can be.
- **Healthy low health care user:** This is you if you're healthy with few to no drug prescription needs who gets the recommended 150 minutes of exercise per week and eats a balanced, healthy diet. You visit the doctor only when you really need to, keeping a lid on your spending.
- **Unhealthy high health care user:** This may be you if you have a lot of medical conditions such as diabetes or heart health issues, or need to manage health concerns such as high cholesterol and high blood pressure. You go to the doctor often and rely on several medications to maintain your body's working order, increasing your health care spending.
- **Unhealthy low health care user:** This may be you if you have similar health issues as the unhealthy high health care user, but you don't visit the doctor very much to manage those conditions. As a result, your health care expenses are low and the savings you'll need for these expenses are lower because your life expectancy may not be that long.

WHAT IS YOUR HEALTH NOW?

You're not stuck in these buckets. You actually have time to change which bucket you belong in based on your health behavior now,

McClanahan said. What does that look like? It means that around age 45, minor health conditions begin to crop up—such as hypertension, obesity, or diabetes—that require more attention and maintenance. Exercise and eating right also become much more crucial. Your youth can no longer help you outrun these health issues.

"I actually call the ages of 40 to 50 'the point of no return,'" McClanahan said. "If you start taking good care of yourself, even if you have minor problems in your 40s and 50s, you're just as likely to live a good, long, healthy life as anybody else."

That also translates to lower health care spending. But if you don't take the time to course correct, those chronic diseases of aging are going to get worse. Hypertension will turn into heart disease. Diabetes will turn into renal issues such as diabetic nephropathy and retinopathy.

"Your 60s is when you start seeing all those things happen, just when you're getting ready to retire," McClanahan said. And that means spending more time in the doctor's office and more money going to health care expenses if you ignore or don't manage your earlier issues.

BE AN ENGAGED PATIENT

Another way to limit your health care spending is by being an engaged patient. Instead of just doing everything your doctor tells you to do, make sure you understand why you're doing those things. Doctors are busy, so be proactive and help your doctor understand where you are with your health. At every visit, provide a narrative that goes over your health history, the medications you're on and why, your exercise regimen, and your diet.

"What doctors do more often now instead of taking a good history is they just order tests reflexively because it's become more protocol-driven instead of truly based on your history and needs," McClanahan said.

So if a doctor wants to order tests, ask if that test is really necessary and how the results will possibly change what the doctor will recommend. Inquire if there is a cheaper way to get the needed tests. It's okay to tell your doctor that you are trying to minimize out-of-pocket spending or that your insurance plan has limited coverage, if you need an excuse to lean on.

You should be just as vigilant about your medications. Often, at follow-up appointments a provider won't necessarily question if you still need to be on your medications, especially if they are not the person who originally prescribed the medication. Or you may see several specialists regularly who each prescribe drugs for certain conditions, but they may not look at your medication regimen holistically. A good practice that McClanahan recommends is bagging up your medication bottles and bringing them to any doctor's checkup. This will help your doctor help you understand why you're taking each. What you discover may surprise you. "Sometimes you'll find that they're on two different types of the same class of medication they shouldn't even be doing," McClanahan said.

And if you're prescribed a new medication, check whether it's on your health insurance's formulary or preferred drug list. If it's not, then you will have to pay out of pocket for it. To avoid that situation, ask for a similar medicine that is on your insurance's list. Do the same thing with brand name drugs, which can cost hundreds of dollars, versus generic versions that are much cheaper. A good pharmacist can also recommend a more affordable substitute if you forget to ask your doctor.

Last, really understand your health care coverage. Employers often provide more than one option. As a guide, if you're a high user of health care, you want to choose the more premium plan, which may cost a bit more on a monthly basis but will likely limit how much out-of-pocket spending you have to put forth. A high-deductible plan means more out-of-pocket costs for you now, but does provide a health savings account, or HSA, which can help with retirement costs down the road. (More on that later.) You need to weigh the pros and cons of these options.

If you're shopping in the private market for health insurance, make sure to compare plans annually, especially if your health needs change. Make sure you can afford the deductible yourself and that your preferred doctors are in the insurance plan's network. Going out of the network adds up real quick.

"This is your health care cost hygiene," McClanahan said. "Adopting these practices when you're in that 45 to 60 age range will make it easier to control your health care costs when you actually retire, when it's even more important."

HEALTH SAVINGS ACCOUNTS

One way to save for your expected health care costs in retirement is through a health savings account, or HSA. We covered these briefly in Chapter 4. As a reminder, to get one you enroll in a high-deductible health plan, or HDHP. These plans come with a lower monthly premium than other plans, but a higher annual deductible—the amount you pay for covered health care costs before your insurance kicks in. You contribute to your HSA through automatic payroll deductions where money is directed from your paycheck, tax-free, into the account. You can also add more directly to your HSA at any time. These additional contributions aren't tax-free, but they are tax-deductible. Some employers may also match the contributions you make to your HSA. You can withdraw anytime from your HSA tax-free to pay for qualified medical expenses. Unqualified withdrawals are subject to a hefty 20 percent penalty and you will have to pay income tax on the disqualified sum.

Any unused balance of your HSA rolls over from one year to the next. These funds can also be invested and grow tax-free. Once you hit 65, your HSA is practically another retirement account. Withdrawals can be made for any purpose, not just approved medical expenses, and you only pay income tax on nonmedical withdrawals. It's the only account that allows you to fund it on a tax-free basis and grow tax-free. Qualified health care expenses come out tax-free at all times.

"The triple tax advantages that HSAs offer are more tax-efficient than retirement plans," HSA specialist Roy Ramthun, who led the US Treasury Department's implementation of HSAs after they were enacted into law in 2003, told us. "They should not be considered a replacement for traditional retirement plans," Ramthun cautions, because what you can put in is relatively small and withdrawals only avoid taxes on qualified medical expenses, "but can offer a nice complement to them."

That's if you take advantage of them correctly. Most people don't. They use HSAs as a specialized savings account rather than an investment account. But the opportunity is "most significant" for older married couples. They can contribute the annual limit for a family, plus each individual can make a catch-up contribution reserved for those 55 and over. That can add up to over $10,000 per year.

"For these older couples, $10,000 a year for 10 years before they turn 65 adds up to over $100,000 to help with health care expenses in retirement," Ramthun said.

HEALTH INSURANCE IN RETIREMENT

If you have substantially amped up your retirement savings because you want to cut and run from the workplace as soon as you can, that's going to up your health care spending in retirement. That's because you can't go on Medicare before 65. Your employer's human resources folks can tell you if you will have health insurance benefits after you retire, which is unlikely these days, or if you are eligible for temporary continuation of health coverage called COBRA. If your spouse is employed, you may be able to switch to their health insurance. Perhaps you can take on a part-time job that offers employer-based insurance. Otherwise, you will need to pay for a private plan yourself. This can be pretty pricey. Private health care coverage is the biggest expense for Janna's semiretired sister and brother-in-law, Dawn and Chuck Hansberry. In general, private health care coverage for two relatively healthy people can cost around $1,100 a month.

"It's just obnoxiously expensive across the board," Chuck told us. (Hootie & the Blowfish played in the restaurant where Dawn, Chuck's wife and Janna's sister, worked in her 20s, but she prefers the hair bands, such as Def Leppard and AC/DC.)

It pays to shop around for health care plans, and consider how much you use health care services as part of the equation. You might also quality for tax subsidies to help make the overall cost a little bit more palatable. Working with a tax accountant or financial planner can help you figure out what you're eligible for.

MEDICARE

At 65, folks can enroll in traditional (or original) Medicare, which is the government-run health care coverage for seniors. Original Medicare is made up of two main parts: Part A and Part B. There are also two supplemental options called Part D and Medigap that you can choose to sign up for. We'll also touch on Medicare Advantage (Part C) in the next section. Here's what to know about Part A, Part B, Part D, and Medigap.

Part A, also called hospital coverage, pays for the inpatient care you get while in the hospital and in skilled nursing facilities. Part A also covers hospice care and short-term home health care when you're recovering from an injury or disease. Most people pay $0 for Part A because they or a spouse paid Medicare taxes for at least 10 years while working. But this coverage does come with a deductible.

Part B, or Medicare's medical insurance, covers medically necessary services, such as cancer treatments, as well as preventive services. You typically pay nothing for most preventive services if you get the services from a medical provider who accepts Medicare. Otherwise, you must cover 20 percent of the cost for each Medicare-covered service after you've paid your deductible. Part B also charges a monthly premium, which right now is less than $200 a month.

Part D is drug prescription coverage, and the amount you pay per month varies by income. Part D is optional coverage, and it is provided by private insurance companies that follow rules established by Medicare. You must be enrolled in Part A and/or Part B to get a separate Medicare drug plan.

Medigap is also called Medicare Supplement Insurance. It's extra insurance you choose to purchase from a private health insurer to cover your share of out-of-pocket costs from Original Medicare. Medigap policies often pay for that 20 percent that you're on the hook for in Part B coverage, plus your deductible and copayments. You generally must be enrolled in Part A and Part B to buy a Medigap policy. There are a range of Medigap policies designated by the letters A–D, F, G, and K–N, and they are standardized across insurance companies. Plans with the same letter may, however, offer different pricing depending on the insurer.

A crucial note on Medigap: If you sign up during the six-month Medigap open enrollment period that starts after the first month you have Part B, an insurer can't deny you a Medigap policy for preexisting conditions. After that period, though, an insurer can deny you or charge you more for a Medigap policy.

MEDICARE ADVANTAGE (PART C)

Medicare Advantage is also part of Medicare; the government oversees the funding of the plans. But the actual health insurance plans are administered by private insurers. These Medicare Advantage plans have grown in popularity over the last decade or so, largely because of their attractive perks and low costs.

Medicare Advantage plans offer benefits traditional Medicare doesn't provide, such as dental, vision, and hearing coverage, in addition to perks like a grocery or transportation allowance, depending on the plan. Many also come with a low or $0 monthly premium. However, those enrolled in Medicare Advantage plans still have to pay the Medicare Part B premium. But Medicare Advantage plans often come with drug prescription coverage, or Part D, that you must purchase separately under Original Medicare. Another benefit is that there's usually a yearly limit on out-of-pocket costs for Medicare Advantage plans. That doesn't exist for Medicare, unless you have purchased a Medigap plan.

There's a trade-off, of course. You have to go to a network of providers who have contract agreements with the insurer. If you go out of that network, you either must pay more for the care or you may not be allowed to see that doctor at all. Unlike Original Medicare, you also have to jump through pre-authorization hoops to get approved for treatment, and you will likely have to deal with changing in-network and out-of-network medical providers.

"That is a danger each and every year," David Lipschutz, the associate director for the Center for Medicare Advocacy, previously told us. "People don't have much recourse if their doctor leaves the network."

The benefit of enrolling in traditional Medicare is that almost every doctor and hospital system in the country accepts Medicare. You can choose the doctors you want to visit and find the very best specialists to treat you. Also, no prior authorizations are required before getting treatment. Your health care experience should be easier than what you're used to dealing with now: unexpected denied claims, out-of-network costs, and a changing network of providers from year to year.

"Traditional Medicare is a little bit more expensive. But, man, if you're ever sick, you're going to be grateful you're on traditional Medicare," McClanahan said.

One last word on Medicare: If you opt to push back your Medicare benefit because you are covered elsewhere, you still have to take some action. It's a bit convoluted, but the way the system works is that you need to go online to Medicare.gov and file for traditional Medicare (Part A and Part B) three months before you turn 65, even if you don't plan to use it until later. If you don't sign up for Medicare Part B when you're first eligible at age 65 (by declining Part B coverage during the sign-up process), you may have to pay a late enrollment penalty for Part B for as long as you have Medicare coverage.

ORIGINAL MEDICARE VS. MEDICARE ADVANTAGE

Which type of health care insurance coverage you choose also plays an important role in how much you will need to save for health-related costs. How much exactly? Well, the EBRI provides more precise estimates based on whether you are a high, average, or low user of health care services, as well as if you have median or high drug prescription needs and if you choose Original Medicare or Medicare Advantage.[5] (You need to create an account with EBRI to download the institute's full report.) These estimates are updated annually, but they should give you a rough estimate to aim for in the future.

The following charts derived from EBRI's data show the total health care savings needed for a 65-year-old man, woman, and heterosexual couple with median drug prescription needs. Chart A shows the savings needed to cover premiums related to Original Medicare, including Part D and Medigap, their deductibles, and out-of-pocket expenses through their lifetime. Chart B shows the savings needed for those enrolled in Medicare Advantage to cover Part B premiums, Part D premiums, and out-of-pocket expenses through their retirement.

Chart A: Savings Needed for Original Medicare

	If you want a low Medigap premium	If you want an average Medigap premium	If you want a high Medigap premium
Men	$134,000	$184,000	$247,000
Women	$158,000	$217,000	$292,000
Couple	$256,000	$351,000	$473,000

Chart B: Savings Needed for Medicare Advantage

	If you are a low health care user	If you are an average health care user	If you are a high health care user
Men	$61,000	$99,000	$137,000
Women	$71,000	$116,000	$161,000
Couple	$117,000	$189,000	$261,000

LONG-TERM CARE COSTS

Another looming cost for Gen X is long-term care. Medicare doesn't cover these costs and neither do Medicare Advantage plans. But these expenses are considerable, especially if you are healthier and expect to live longer. About 70 percent of folks end up needing some sort of care as they age, with their needs progressing from meal prep and housework at the start to more intensive care like bathing and feeding as they advance.

The median cost of in-home care now is about $30 per hour in the United States, which works out to more than $20,000 a year for just one two-hour visit every day.[6] You'll eventually need more than that. McClanahan's rule of thumb is to have enough money to cover two years of long-term care. Healthier older people tend to be at greater risk of dementia because they live longer, according to McClanahan, so they may want to plan for up to five years. Starting around 69, the risk for dementia roughly doubles every five years.[7]

"Nursing homes always like to make sure you have money to pay them and if they see that you can afford at least two years of long-term care, it makes it much easier to get into a good nursing home," McClanahan said. To get a bead on how much that adds up to, you can use Genworth's "Cost of Long Term Care by State" tool (www.carescout.com/cost-of-care) to help you plan.

One way to prepare to finance this care is by purchasing long-term care insurance. Unfortunately, it's pricey. How pricey? As of this writing, the average annual premium for a $165,000 policy with no inflation protection is $950 for a 55-year-old single male and $1,500 for a 55-year-old female.[8] Together at that age, the average combined annual premium is $2,080. If they wait until they're 60 to purchase, the combined cost rises to $2,600. A 60-year-old single man would pay $1,200 and a single 60-year-old woman would pay $1,900.

No wonder only a fraction of people have bought this insurance. Just 11 percent of adults and 14 percent of those 65 and older reported having a private long-term care insurance policy.[9] There's also an issue of longevity for the insurance company itself. "You don't know if these insurance companies are going to be around 20 to 30 years down the road when you actually need to utilize that long-term care," McClanahan said.

Other ways to plan for long-term care is by saving for it and earmarking, say, your HSA savings for these expenses. Or perhaps you can use the equity in your house for your long-term care costs. Of course, that would mean your house and its equity can't be passed down to your heirs. But that's better than saddling them with the burden of finding care for you in your old age.

Medicaid is the only federal aid that covers long-term care costs, but you must spend down most of your assets before you can qualify. You can also structure your estate's assets, often utilizing trusts or joint owners—something we'll go into further in Chapter 13—to help you qualify for Medicaid without spending down all of your wealth. This restructuring typically needs to happen at least five years before you need Medicaid to cover your long-term care. Otherwise, some states, which administer Medicaid's funding, will try to claw back assets that you may have tried to shield by transferring ownership to your children or spouse. Talk with an estate planning attorney or a financial planner experienced with Medicaid to help plan out your long-term needs.

MEDICARE'S SHAKY FUTURE

These are all imperfect solutions for growing issues of long-term care. Americans are generally living longer, but require more costly care in the last years of their life. How we pay for that makes long-term care, health care, and health insurance in this country a political issue. Already, funding for Medicare Part A is on shaky ground. The reserves for that are expected to run out in the mid-2030s, right when a lot of Gen Xers will be signing up for the coverage. If the reserves are exhausted, payroll taxes earmarked for Medicare only cover a portion of the program's costs, which could mean that seniors' "access to health care services could rapidly be curtailed," the Boards of Trustees for Medicare said.[10] Our generation and those younger than us are concerned about this. A 2024 survey found that almost two-thirds (65 percent) of Gen Xers and Millennials who were familiar with Medicare worry that it won't be there for them.[11] How Medicare is funded for the future, whether it's expanded, or if a new government program is created to provide long-term care coverage, depends on what federal lawmakers do. The future of health insurance before and during retirement could also change depending on the political winds. It's smart to stay abreast of what proposals are out there, how they may impact your golden years, and vote accordingly.

YOUR TO-DO LIST

- Determine how much money you will need in retirement for health care costs based on your health and if you're a high or low user of health care.
- Make changes now to your health care practices to help lower costs by staving off worse health conditions in the future.
- Get familiar with your health insurance options in retirement, especially if you plan to retire early.
- Use the Genworth calculator to determine your long-term care costs, and make a plan for how to cover those costs in the future.
- Make Medicare a voting issue.

We've gone over a host of ways to buttress your retirement savings by prioritizing the many responsibilities you have now and making sure your health and health care are in the best place possible. The next chapter addresses whether you are physically in the best place possible for your retirement and what factors you might consider if relocating is part of your retirement plan.

11

RELOCATING IN RETIREMENT

You think you can keep us out of Florida? We're moving in lock, stock, and barrel. We're gonna be in the pool, we're gonna be in the clubhouse, we're gonna be all over that shuffleboard court. And I dare you to keep me out!

—FRANK COSTANZA
SEINFELD, "THE SHOWER HEAD," SEASON 7, EPISODE 15, 1996

Where do you want to wake up most days in the next decade or so ahead? What friends or family do you want to share this next leg with? Is there a new chapter out there for you?

You may have no intention of retiring *yet*, but as the decades click by, you might pause and ask yourself: Is this where I want to spend the rest of my days? We're not trying to be morbid, just realistic. For Kerry, who lives in Washington, DC, the idea that she will spend the rest of her life waking up looking at an alley is a hard no.

What about a major move to another part of the country where you've never lived and have always dreamed of? What about a return to your childhood roots and the comfort of roads once traveled and the company of your family and hometown friends?

Of the four-million-plus Americans who retire each year, many opt to stay put, or perhaps downsize to smaller digs nearby.[1] Others toss the dice and move a thousand miles away to be closer to family or to pare back costs. Then too, there are those who let it rip and relocate abroad or to a place in the United States that's more aligned with what they love to do for a hobby or fun.

"If you had asked me when I was in my 20s or 30s where I wanted to retire, I'd have told you I'd like to own a ranch in Wyoming or Colorado," Sallie Cosgrove, a former clinical veterinarian at Virbac, a pharmaceutical company, now living in North Carolina, told us. "As I got older, the idea of 'riding the range' and 'mending fences' became less attractive."

Cosgrove has always been outdoorsy. She enjoys trail riding on her two horses, so finding a small farm in a horse-friendly area that offered unlimited land where she could ride (protected space that would never fall prey to development) was key. Having a climate that would allow her to pursue her passion year-round was also very important.

"Friends that had already retired suggested that I identify what I thought would be my top five retirement locations and then vacation in those locations," Cosgrove said. "This was the best suggestion that I could have received. I did exactly that and settled on Southern Pines, North Carolina."

The housing market in Michigan where she had lived for 17 years was wobbly, and she didn't feel comfortable buying a new home without first selling her existing home. Another prerequisite was to have at least one acquaintance in the town in which she was planning to move. Her parents had both passed and she had no siblings, and so her new circle of friends was (and still is) very important to her.

Cosgrove continued to work remotely in North Carolina for her employer for three years after she purchased a home in Southern Pines. "This was tremendously beneficial in that I had an income to buffer the moving costs and an income that allowed me to perform some home improvements without dipping into my retirement savings," she said.

"While I'd like to take credit for a well-thought-out move, there were many things that I never thought about, which I now realize were actually very important. By some miracle, I just lucked out. Specifically, moving to a location where at least a subset of the population has a similar educational background and work history," she said. "You have access to a state-of-the-art health care network. There's at least one 'big box' store and a grocery that are easy to reach. The community supports the arts and music. Your friends want to come and visit, and there's an airport within an hour's drive."

For Jeb and Dianne Sanford, who were living in a rural area outside of Sperryville, Virginia, their quest was to find a retirement home while they were still working. And it was the lure of a new lifestyle in a small town within commuting distance to the cultural life in Boston and the joy of watching the boats going up and down the Essex River out into Ipswich Bay, among other factors, that made their move to Hamilton, Massachusetts, appealing. Plus, it was a place where they could continue to work remotely.

They both have roots in the region. He was born in Boston. She went to Harvard Law School. And they're committed Red Sox fans. It's a return to roots in a way, but also a launch into a new adventure.

As Gen Xers gradually move toward retirement, the question of where to live may begin to percolate. In addition to some of the criteria we've mentioned, many Gen Xers are layering on finding a new home with a design that will allow them to age in place as they step into their seventh, eighth, and ninth decades of living.

The financial consideration of where to live should be a key consideration for all of us, since housing costs beyond the actual purchase price include utility bills, homeowners insurance and other natural disaster coverage, taxes, health care costs, gasoline, groceries, and more. If you have a few locations to choose among, making strategic money decisions can streamline your future retirement budget. Deciding where to move isn't something to decide on a "let's give it a whirl" basis, and if you're moving with a partner, there will be all kinds of decisions to make about where you'll land. Compromise, anyone?

The best advice we can give here is to be deliberate and do the legwork. There are myriad community, cultural, financial, and health factors to consider when planning to relocate.

WHERE YOU LIVE AND WELL-BEING

"Where you live and how you choose to engage with your surroundings is one of the most important decisions in life," says Ryan Frederick, the Gen X founder and CEO of Here (www.here.life), a platform dedicated to "place planning." (*Star Wars* and sitcoms *Silver Spoons*, when he was younger, and *Cheers*, as a teenager, made his must-watch list.)

Frederick's book, *Right Place, Right Time: The Ultimate Guide to Choosing a Home for the Second Half of Life*, explores why our living situation needs to complement our life stage and health. According to Frederick, this alignment can mean the difference between a vibrant, fulfilling life and one burdened by loneliness and health challenges.

Generation Xers are already taking stock of their homes now that their kids have launched, or a parent has moved in. "If you are concerned about living a long, healthy, and financially secure life, start with finding the right place, and good things will follow," Frederick advised. "Ultimately, successful place planning involves individuals being more informed about what's best for them and taking action. People don't necessarily understand how significant a place is in the context of living longer and healthy aging. Where you live not only influences your current life, it shapes your future self."

When people think about "place," it's generally their physical environment, their single-family home, their apartment, their cottage, their RV. "I see place as being much broader than that," Frederick told us. "You have a physical dwelling, but then you have a neighborhood, a street, a metropolitan area."

So, when we choose a place, we must look at the bigger picture, he said. "Am I living in, or do I want to live in, an urban, suburban, rural area? What region of the country? What country? What's the economic trajectory of the region, the city, even the neighborhood, because all of those things matter in your well-being."

In other words, you might totally love your house, but you should step outside and assess your neighborhood. Is it getting better or worse? Consider your metropolitan area. Does it face challenges, such as aging infrastructure, onerous taxes, or climate change risks? Are you in a region that is set up to be successful over time and growing economically? Is this a region you will want to stay in for the rest of your life?

CONSIDER THESE BIG PICTURE QUESTIONS

As you begin to think about where you might like to live, start with self-evaluation:

- What do I want my life to look like?
- Do I have a purpose? Am I socially connected?
- Am I physically active?
- Is my current place physically appropriate for me?
- Do I have this sense of connectedness to it?

There might be a way to redesign your current home, or you might move into an apartment or a condo, or age-restricted housing, or senior living, or accessible dwelling units—a smaller, independent living space located on the same lot as a stand-alone single-family home, Frederick said. Granny pod, anyone?

You should consider the design of your living space, he said. Does it have universal design elements incorporated in the physical space? Universal design focuses on making a house safe and accessible for any age or physical ability—from wider doors and hallways to accommodate walkers and wheelchairs to a range of countertop heights in the kitchen, or slip-resistant tiles and grab bars in the bathroom and shower. Many elements of universal design can be incorporated into the design of a home in a way that does not require a trade-off with attractive aesthetics.

"Sometimes people fall in love with a house on Zillow—oh my gosh, my dream house," Frederick said. "Then they make this big financial decision, and they're there, and maybe they love the Zillow version of the house, but they find out it isn't helping them with purpose. They're not socially connected and so on."

Does the neighborhood create a sense of hospitality and connectedness? Not that you need to be best friends with all your neighbors, and they need to know everything about your life, but is there social capital? "That's part of really thriving at any age," Frederick said. "But particularly as we get older, that social fabric where people help each other, and you can be a part of the community together, matters."

You might find a cohousing arrangement with family or your friends that can help your financial well-being and at the same time add some social connection or a multigenerational one. "The pandemic put a spotlight on this issue of social disconnection and loneliness, and how important social connection is at any stage in life," he said.

TAKING A TRIAL RUN

Once you have a good idea of where you'd like to live and what kind of home you're interested in, then what? Test it before fully committing to it. Is it really what you want? If you're moving from a single-family home, and you're curious about having a downtown condo, take a few weekends, maybe even a couple of weeks, and just rent an apartment through a service like Airbnb. This will give you a sense of the community and how much space you are comfortable living in. Maybe you thought 1,500 square feet would be right for you, but after spending some time in a space that size, you find that it's too small. Moving can be costly, and if you pick the wrong location, jeepers, it's not so easy to unwind. "Place is a direct element in your well-being," Frederick added. "Are you picking the right place to thrive as you age?"

Before they retired, Don and Reina Weiner bought an acre of land in a mixed-age community in Chapel Hill, North Carolina. At the time of the purchase, the couple was living in Leesburg, Virginia. Chapel Hill met three of their prerequisites: warm weather, top medical care nearby, and a robust cultural life spawned by several universities in the area.

They hired an architect to design their new digs, sold their townhouse in Virginia, and rented an apartment near their future home. And that's when their dream retirement home imploded. "I had a significant allergic reaction to the environment with severe headaches and throat issues," Reina said. "The question was: Could I live here?" she said.

She decided to jettison the plan and they ultimately decided on Asheville, North Carolina. The Blue Ridge Mountains surround this town, which is an artists' conclave as well as a swell place to hike. And its elevation of 2,100 feet makes summers a tad cooler than other southern locales. The state income tax rate is a flat 4.5 percent, with Social Security income exempt, and there's no state estate tax or inheritance tax.

As Mark Cappone and his wife, Molly, inch toward their mid-50s, they're in the midst of defining their next chapter and figuring out how, when, and where to relocate from their home in Columbus, Ohio. At age 45, Cappone was diagnosed with kidney cancer. "That very much changed my outlook on retirement," Cappone said. "As a Gen Xer having a potentially life-ending experience in middle age gives one pause, to say the least. I think it's fair to say that part of our approach to relocating in retirement *now* is that stark reminder that we're all only here for a while and we don't really know how long that is. We have dreams and there's no better time than the present to get out there and live them, within reason, of course."

Wherever they choose to live in retirement, Cappone needs to have purpose and connection, and he probably wants to keep working. "And so when it comes to location, part of Molly's and my equation has been, 'Is this a place that we feel we can find both of us purpose and connection in whatever way that that looks like?'"

Cappone retired as a colonel in the US Army in 2016, a hair short of 23 years of service, and he pivoted to a second act as a teacher at the Fisher College of Business at The Ohio State University, as well as an executive and leadership coach. For the couple, memories of living in the south when he was stationed in Augusta, Georgia, keep popping up as they consider where they might relocate for their retirement years. Both of their children are in their 20s and launched, so empty-nester reality has settled in.

(Cappone adds that their long roster of go-to flicks from back in the day include *The Breakfast Club*, *Back to the Future*, *Ferris Bueller's*

Day Off, *Top Gun* ["probably why I joined the military, lol," he said with a wink], *Ghostbusters*, *E.T.* and, of course, *Star Wars*.)

"Molly, to this day, says she always felt like she was on vacation even when she was driving to work there," he said. Now that their hunt for a new place to live is on in earnest, that glow of the sunny warm south lingers. As they narrowed their choices of places, the one that has risen to the top is Charleston, South Carolina. "Some visits down to South Carolina in the recent past have reminded us how much we really love being in that climate, so we spent a month renting a townhome there."

With enough days with boots on the ground there, they have moved past the shiny vacation-town feel of the place to really allow them to pull the emotion out of it and think longer term.

"Living there has allowed that luster to kind of move to the side and let us really talk and think about: 'What if we have a home here, what kind of life would we be leading versus this idealized life?'" Cappone said.

The couple has meanwhile seriously "put some weight to the criteria such as living costs, location, type of home, distance from family, traffic, how much home can we afford and where that is," he said. Importantly, they began working with a real estate agent recommended by a friend who's a retired military person. "She has been very helpful in just educating us and explaining the realities of living in a coastal area with flooding or hurricanes," Cappone said.

"We're being deliberate and we're taking our time. And I'm glad we are, because I'm seeing our priorities shifting," he added. "So, film at 11—we still haven't decided on exactly what, but we will definitely move in the next year or two. If I were to crystal ball it—maybe sooner."

One last smart move worth noting for the Cappones is that they are working with a financial planner. "I lean on him to get a perspective on the financials," Cappone said. "I have a military pension and portable health care that goes with us. We're not overly wealthy, and yet we have a lot of choices, and I feel gratitude for that. We're blessed and we're taking money into consideration."

YOUR RELOCATING CHECKLIST

Home prices. One big payoff of relocating is cashing in the equity you've built up in your home and moving to a more affordable area where you can buy a place for a fraction of what it costs where you live now. You might even be able to step up to a bigger home or larger property if that's what you fancy. If your projected income from Social Security, pensions, and other retirement account sources isn't going to be enough to meet your living costs, you may need that cash generated from selling your house for living expenses down the road. It could also be helpful if you're looking to pay down or wipe out credit card and other consumer debts. If you choose to buy your new digs with cash, you can eliminate your monthly mortgage payment.

Married couples can exclude up to $500,000 in capital gains from the sale of a primary residence (single homeowners can exclude $250,000). This rule can be a windfall for retirees who own highly appreciated residential property, as long as they have owned and used the house as a primary residence for two of the past five years. You can find median home price data from the National Association of Realtors, and from real estate services such as Zillow and Redfin.

Climate change and disaster risk. Global warming translates to soaring costs. The cost of running air-conditioning in southern retirement meccas like Florida and Arizona may make these places not quite as appealing. As for costal locations, the rising cost of homeowner's insurance can pack a wallop year in and year out. The Federal Emergency Management Agency's National Risk Index for Natural Hazards calculates for every county in the nation a relative vulnerability measure for 18 natural hazards, including wildfires, heat, hurricanes, flooding, landslides, and earthquakes. These calculations also factor in a community's capacity to navigate those perils. Pollution and air quality metrics, which are tracked by the US Environmental Protection Agency, should also be part of your criteria.

Cost of living. Daily living costs swing from place to place. Moving to a smaller residence will instantly trim what you shell out on utilities and maintenance costs. Even in a larger home, energy bills may be reduced considerably from what you pay right now if you move from a place with cold winters and hot summers to somewhere more moderate year-round. Cost of living information is available from the US Bureau of Labor Statistics and services such as Best Places (bestplaces.nct).

Crime rate. For obvious reasons, safety rules. Each year, the FBI releases detailed data on over 14 million criminal offenses reported to the Uniform Crime Reporting (UCR) Program by participating law enforcement agencies. More than 16,000 state, county, city, university and college, and tribal agencies, covering a combined population of 94.3 percent inhabitants, submitted data to the UCR Program through the National Incident-Based Reporting System (NIBRS). This information can be found at the FBI's Crime Data Explorer website (cde.ucr.cjis.gov/LATEST/webapp/#/pages/home). Additional crime stats are tracked by services like NeighborhoodScout (neighborhoodscout.com), and, occasionally, official local chambers of commerce.

Health care accessibility and quality. How far away from your potential new home is a top-notch hospital? This matters, especially in old age, when your likelihood of needing medical care is greater. Do you want to be an hour's drive away if there's an emergency? You'll also want to get a bead on how many primary care physicians are in the region. Primary care doctor ratios on a county-wide basis can be found at the County Health Rankings & Roadmaps website (countyhealthrankings.org).

Medicare: Medicare premiums vary considerably by market. Each region of the country has its own blend of medical facilities and insurers. For the prices and terms of carriers that serve your future community, check the federal website for Medicare (medicare.gov) and the website of the state's department of insurance.

Taxes: Moving from a high-tax state to a low-tax state is strategic. Many people select a retirement home locale because there's no income tax. While income tax considerations in choosing a place to retire are imperative, you've got to account for state and local taxes in the new locale, which can vary, with some state and local sales taxes at 7 percent or more.

Florida, for example, imposes no state income tax, no taxes on Social Security, no inheritance tax, no estate tax, and no taxes on retirement income like pensions, IRAs, or 401(k)s, but it has significant sales taxes and property taxes. On the other hand, five states—Alaska, Delaware, Montana, New Hampshire, and Oregon—have no state-level sales tax.

Property taxes are typically the heftiest tax burden for homeowning retirees. According to the Tax Foundation, a think tank in Washington, DC, states with relatively low per capita real estate tax collections include Alabama, Arkansas, Louisiana, New Mexico, and Oklahoma, while those with high per capita real estate tax collections include Connecticut, New Hampshire, New Jersey, New York, and Wyoming.

Most states give breaks to residents over a certain age, and there may be property tax credits or homestead exemptions that limit the value of assessed property subject to tax. But it's generally up to a local assessor to set the total taxable value.

The bottom line is this: You should scrutinize the total tax picture of each of your possible destinations as part of a balanced assessment of the best place for you to live. Tax data can be found at the Tax Foundation website (taxfoundation.org) and at the websites of individual state tax agencies.

Recreation. Are there places to hike, bike, swim, ride horses—whatever moves you to, well, keep moving? Dig down to find out how walkable and bikeable a place is—both activities are big factors when you're seeking a healthy lifestyle. Are you moving, for instance, near a national or state park, a lake, or a waterfront?

Transportation. In addition to access to a good airport for visiting family and friends, before buying a retirement home, soon-to-be retirees and retirees should consider what their daily transportation needs will be when they are in their 70s and 80s. Is there reliable mass transit available to you? What does it cost? Are roadways crowded? Assessments of walkability (the ability to stroll easily to basic retail businesses and mass transit for everyday needs) and bikeability can be found at Walk Score (walkscore.com) and the League of American Bicyclists. You can also test out a location firsthand by exploring it on foot or bike.

Retiring in a Foreign Land

Opting to retire in another country isn't an out-of-left-field idea. Lots of retirees have taken this path. In fact, more than 450,000 retirees were receiving Social Security benefits outside the United States as of December 2023.[2]

There are plenty of reasons why it's appealing, and it can be a cost-saver in terms of housing and medical care. That said, there is a lot to consider before you make that choice. The US Department of State has resources to help you think things through. See the Retirement Abroad resource on Travel.State.Gov (https://travel.state.gov/content/travel/en/international-travel/while-abroad/retirement-abroad.html). In addition, here are some of our steps to get you started.

Research. *International Living* magazine publishes an annual global retirement index that ranks its World's Best Places to Retire. Its researchers crunch numbers on the cost of living, health care, housing, internet access, infrastructure factors such as international airports and, of course, weather. Also check out Expat Exchange (expatexchange.com), a popular website on living abroad.

Language. If you speak a foreign language, it can make sense to focus on places where it's spoken. If you want to work a bit in retirement, keep in mind that your English skills can open the door to a wide range of work that includes teaching English, interpreting, and guiding English-speaking tourists. You might land a job at a hotel, tourist-oriented art gallery, bistro, B&B, retail shop, or real estate agency.

Of course, you'll need to check out if the country allows foreigners to hold the kind of job you want and whether a work permit is required. Some countries make it difficult for immigrants to find legal work. Also, gauge competition for the job you're seeking; supply and demand applies everywhere. If a country has a high unemployment rate, it will likely be harder for you to find work.

You don't have to pick a place to live based on the job market there, though. Turn what you've done your entire career into a virtual consulting or project assignment-based business that you can do online. It's the ultimate remote job, provided you have a good internet connection.

Visit. Before settling on a place, spend a couple of months there to see if you really fit in. Befriend local expats and learn what brought them there and what kind of jobs they might have. Do your own sleuthing by talking to local business people.

Pay attention to taxes. If you're going to earn even a small salary, consult with someone who knows international tax issues. Both the United States and your new country of residence could try to tax the money you earn. Your foreign bank accounts might require that you file a disclosure form with the US Treasury Department. As a US citizen or resident alien, you are taxed by the United States on your worldwide income. That means you're required to file an annual tax return with the IRS. However, you may be eligible for the foreign earned income exclusion, which in 2024 exempted $126,500 of income per person from US taxes.[3]

Friends and Family. A major reason cited for moving in retirement is to be closer to friends and family, especially children and grandchildren. According to a report from the Transamerica Center for Retirement Studies, more than half of workers said spending more time with friends and family was a major retirement goal. However, although being closer to family can be rewarding, it might not meet all your expectations, as family members may have their own busy schedules. Talk to your family before you move about expectations in terms of getting together and helping out with childcare.

Jobs. For many retirees, working is also part of a retirement plan, so moving to a town with plenty of retiree jobs is something to keep in mind. College towns in particular are great places to live and work in retirement. They generally have entertainment and sports venues that offer a range of part-time and seasonal jobs. These communities tend to be recession-resistant, because each year a new class of students moves into and out of the area, which keeps the economy buzzing. Plus, many such towns are situated in regions with leading health care centers that are also a source of jobs for experienced workers.

AARP has partnered with several universities to support workers over 50. These universities include Clemson University in Clemson, South Carolina; Cornell University in Ithaca, New York; James Madison University in Harrisonburg, Virginia; West Virginia University in Morgantown, West Virginia; and Virginia Commonwealth University in Richmond, Virginia. You can find out more at AARP's Employer Pledge Program (aarp.org/work/employer-pledge-companies).

MORE SOURCES FOR RESEARCH

Lot of resources are out there to help you research locales. Some are published annually, from *Bankrate* to *Forbes* to *Travel and Leisure*, *International Living*, and *U.S. News & World Report*. *The Wall Street Journal* also has a guide to the best places to retire in rural America. Best Places (bestplaces.net) dissects the cost of living in various cities and more.

And they're fun to peruse. We admit the *Forbes* list is a favorite of ours. In recent years, William P. Barrett, the brains behind the list, and his team have compared roughly 800 locales in America, on everything from housing costs and taxes to health care, air quality, climate change, and natural hazard risk. They also measure the strength of the local economy with an eye toward helping those who aim to continue working, which is key in our view.

These best city beauty pageants are positioned as retirement locales, but we propose that you think of them as places for your next act, locales where you can reinvigorate yourself, recharge your creativity, and ramp up your learning curve as you meet new people and explore new places. Use these resources as a jumping off point to get your imagination going about what you might value in a new place to live, and to get some facts and figures about cost of living and other financial concerns.

YOUR TO-DO LIST

- Take your time to deliberately figure your priorities for where you would like to live, with considerations like your social network, your hobbies, sports opportunities, geographic beauty, and more.
- Make a list of your top five retirement locations.
- After you do your research, go for a visit, and then if you decide you like it, go back to rent for a few months, if possible, to get a deeper sense of the place beyond a tourist drop-in.
- Talk to your financial planner and accountant to get an overall view of what's possible for you.

In the next chapter, we explore how you can find and work with a professional financial planner and adviser who can help you map out a holistic picture of your overall wealth, run various future scenarios, and be someone you can trust to lean on as you create your own pathway to a rich retirement.

12

WHO CAN YOU TALK TO?

I love money. I love money more than the things it can buy. There's only one thing I love more than money. You know what that is? Other people's money.

—Larry Garfield

Other People's Money, 1991

For Rachel Cohen, turning 50 in 2024 made her focus on creating what she wants her next chapter to be. "My friends and I are all having the same conversations right now. Everybody is like, 'Okay, so are we going to be able to retire?' 'What is it going to look like?' 'How long do I have to work?' I have got to nail this down," the Pine, Colorado, resident told us.

"The stress for me is not knowing what the reality looks like on the other side," she said. "It's this mishmash of 'I have a path,' and then 'I'm afraid that the path is going to go away.' It's not going to be real."

And that's precisely why we wrote this book—to provide a valuable resource to see the reality on the other side—but nothing beats someone who knows your individual situation, or who can stay up-to-date on changes to tax code and the best investments for your unique situation as the economy tosses and turns. In this chapter, we review where a financial adviser can lend a hand and how to find one that works for you.

Cohen and her husband, Peter, work with a financial planner and that helps ease her nerves. "I see the numbers on the paper, and it says, we're solid," she said. "We're going to be fine to retire at 60 as long as we stay on the trajectory we're on and both continue making the money that we're making right now and continue our investments." Cohen, who runs her own consulting business designing age-friendly initiatives and intergenerational programs for foundations, community-based organizations, and academic institutions, added: "It's amazing to say that out loud."

THE UPSIDE OF HAVING A FINANCIAL ADVISER ON YOUR TEAM

A trustworthy financial adviser, as Cohen has discovered, is your guide to building wealth and avoiding making foolish money mistakes, say, when you freak out if the market swings madly or you have an unexpected expense, job loss, and more. They're a professional you can lean into for a sense of calm and confidence and direction.

They provide you with basic investment advice, such as when and how to periodically rebalance your investment portfolio, or to find what mix of stocks and bonds match your risk tolerance and goals. They can help you determine your retirement plan withdrawal rate when you get to that point.

Their mission should be to hold your financial hand as you navigate a wide range of decisions from home buying and selling, paying kids' college tuitions, and picking up the tab for your aging parents' care. If you're struggling to pay down debt, or trying to get a bead on budgeting, or have retirement savings, investments, and other banking accounts scattered far and wide that you have trouble keeping track of, an adviser can lead the way to making sense of it all. They can also keep you on track for investing in a way that will give you the best returns at the level of risk you're comfortable with taking on.

What we love about an adviser, too, is that he or she can push you to pay attention to your money and make those decisions that make you freeze or feel overwhelmed because you aren't comfortable at all with saving and investing. They can help answer your questions and lend a sharp eye to your overall financial picture. Their strategic role and relationship can lend expertise not only to your overall retirement plan but also to today's taxes, your insurance needs—life to homeowner and automobile—and your estate plan, including writing or updating your will.

If you die without a will, for example, there's no guarantee who will inherit your assets. What's more, your estate will go into probate, which is a costly, slow-moving legal process. Your will includes a durable power of attorney form that gives someone the ability to make financial decisions for you if you can't. It also includes your end-of-life instructions, such as a living will and health care power of attorney. (More on this in Chapter 13.)

Your adviser will be able to connect you with an estate lawyer to draft your will; if your assets are in the six figures or higher, you probably ought to have a trust as well, to help minimize estate taxes and avoid probate. A trust also offers you greater control over when and how your assets will be distributed. If your listed beneficiaries are out-of-date, when you die, your assets could go to the wrong person—your ex-spouse, for example.

While your adviser doesn't execute many of those final documents, they can connect you with trusted professionals, from an accountant to a lawyer, who can step in and work alongside you. Your adviser can also be a valuable resource for your heirs after you're gone.

GEN X WOMEN AND MONEY

While seven in 10 women now invest in the stock market outside their employer-provided retirement accounts, according to a report from Fidelity Investments, "Women are nearly two times more likely than men to describe their level of investing knowledge as 'nonexistent,'" Lorna Kapusta, head of women and engagement at Fidelity, told us.[1]

Women are also more likely than men to feel overwhelmed and intimidated by investing and managing their day-to-day finances and less likely to see themselves as investors, she said. Just 64 percent of women who invest consider themselves "an investor," compared to 76 percent of men who invest.

"Financial confidence varies significantly across generations—with anxiety peaking among Gen X women who can see their own retirement on the horizon," Andrea K. Williams, a Chicago-based wealth management adviser at Northwestern Mutual, told us.

Gen X women are the gloomiest. That could be because they have $95,000 on average saved for retirement and they believe they will need more than $2 million to retire comfortably, more than any other generation of women, according to a Northwestern Mutual survey.[2] Perhaps unsurprisingly, given the gap between their current reality and expectations, about four in 10 Gen X women described themselves as financially insecure.

Many women tend to push financial issues from investing to planning out of mind with justifications like "I'm not good with math" or "It bores me," which has absolutely no currency here. Insecurity can lead to taking a more conservative approach to finances, but being too conservative with your money has serious and lasting repercussions. It can mean you won't have enough to live on in retirement, especially when you consider that many older women are solely responsible for their finances at some point in retirement, due to divorce or the death of a spouse.

"Life is busy, and sometimes the best thing we can do is pause, think about what we want in life, build a plan, and then get back to living," Williams said. "Many women who I work with don't feel like they have the time or expertise to build a thoughtful financial plan that will work for them."

Jennifer Reingold, a former *Fortune* magazine reporter, who lives in New York City, has lived this scenario. (Reingold's favorite TV show in her youth: *The Bionic Woman*. For music: The Pretenders, The Cars, Devo.) "My financial journey started with a lot of ignorance," Reingold told us. "I graduated from the University of Pennsylvania in 1989, and I had to pay for a lot of it myself with student loans. I really didn't know much about managing money. I was used to living hand to mouth. I had grown up that way and just didn't understand the value of being thoughtful."

"At around 30, somehow I clued into the fact that everyone else was putting money into a 401(k)," she said. "So I understood what I was missing, but I still couldn't do it, and I didn't really have a sense of where I stood or the context for retirement."

After marrying in 2002, raising two daughters, and then a subsequent divorce in 2021, she was faced with the stark facts. "I really had zero understanding and had never had a financial adviser. Everything was all over the place. I had different jobs, so I had different 401(k)s. Nothing was consolidated. I had to separate from my husband to find out how much money I actually had."

That's about the time she connected with Stephanie McCullough, founder and chief executive of Sofia Financial, through her professional network and things began to come together. "She has a psychological approach to looking at people's values around money," Reingold said. "People's attitudes about money really are shaped by how they grew up. And I grew up with some level of financial insecurity, and it made me afraid and conservative."

McCullough's approach made Reingold realize a lot of her money choices were not rational. "They're emotional," she said. "It was really significant for me to see that."

The other thing McCullough did was help her bring everything together. "We ran different scenarios, say, living to 100 and if I am able to make a certain income, what is possible, and then all the things I might want to do between now and then like take my kids on trips, have money for their wedding, live in Manhattan. I don't care as much about other things like luxury goods and things that other people want to spend money on. That's just not my thing."

The work they did together was a lifesaver for Reingold. "It was incredibly helpful to take away some of the anxiety and say, okay, you know, chances are I'm going to be fine," she said. "She eased some of my emotional issues around money and brought that kind of discipline. I needed someone to help me get my act together and consolidate all my stuff in one place."

Reingold still has a nagging fear. "We Gen Xers have always had this threat of Social Security not being there for us," she said. "For my parents, it's essential to them. I actually assume that I'm not going to have it, which is terrifying, especially as a single woman now running my own advisory business. I know I'm fine, but I panic when I think about it. Then I call Stephanie."

The main thing to remember is that you don't have to do financial planning on your own. There are professionals who can help you to unpack your messy financial life, organize it, and get you on the path to financial security.

Rachel Cohen, too, has a healthy appreciation for her financial adviser. "I feel like Gen X is at this weird point," she said. "We're starting to see our parents' age, and there is this overload of caregiving worries, and then you start thinking, what the hell's gonna happen to me? My anxiety comes from all the unknowns," she observed. "You can do all the planning you want, and then life happens. And we see that in Technicolor. We're an experimental generation in terms of retirement. Our adviser is probably really tired of me at this point. I bring up a lot of things, like did you take into account the potential decrease in Social Security? Have you taken into account the massive increases in property taxes and homeowners insurance?" He has, of course.

"I can't wave a magic wand and make $10 million appear, but if we can reduce the money stress because they have a plan, and they feel confident in the plan we are working, then they can move forward with more confidence in the other areas of their life," McCullough said.

SELECTING A FINANCIAL ADVISER

Cohen realizes that she can be a hot mess when she's talking to her adviser, but her ability to focus and be self-aware is a plus. Like Cohen, it's important that you do some self-reflection so that you can be clear on what kind of help you want from your financial adviser. Do you want help in determining how much money you need to finance your retirement and when you could stop working, if you choose to do so? Do you want help with deciding what to do with a rollover from a 401(k) account at a former employer, or how to invest savings outside of an employer's retirement plan, or when to claim Social Security? The adviser your neighbor works with, or your cousin's best friend, or your sister's adviser who she loves might not be right for you because the odds are your friends are looking for different help than you are.

There are scores of people out there who call themselves financial advisers. It's a broad term to say the least. These include financial consultants, financial planners, and wealth managers, among many others. We've got to say the monikers surrounding the profession of financial adviser all point to similar services. They are virtually synonymous, with some minor points of differentiation.

Financial advisers, regardless of what they call themselves, typically have studied and attained a variety of licenses and certifications, but there's not one single certification that is required to call yourself a financial adviser. That makes it super important for you to do your vetting of the person you want to work with so that you can be sure they are really knowledgeable and equipped for the task at hand.

A first step is to make sure you understand the various types of advisers, what they can do for you, and what you will pay for their services. Here's a down and dirty breakdown.

In general, we're fans of unbiased advice from **fee-only financial planners**. These advisers typically charge an up-front fee for their advice. It can be a percentage of your assets and type of planning you need (say, 1 percent to 2 percent), a per-hour charge, or a basic fee per planning session. An overall strategy with ongoing asset management, for example, would be pricier than a one-time estate planning session. They don't, however, make any commissions from the investments they recommend. To find one, start by visiting the websites for the National Association of Personal Financial Advisors, or NAPFA (napfa.org); the Certified Financial Planner Board of Standards, or CFP Board (letsmakeaplan.org); and the Financial Planning Association (financialplanningassociation.org), which allow you to search for a financial planner in your geographic area, although, in reality, location is not as essential as it once was, thanks to virtual meetings.

Another type of planner is a **fee-plus-commission planner**. These planners typically bill you a set fee and earn commissions on some of the investments they recommend. Then there are **commission-only planners**. They are similar to stockbrokers and insurance agents in that they earn a commission on the investments you buy through them. Their employer pays them to sell the product to you.

This is not necessarily bad, but it does pose the question of whether there is a conflict of interest. Are they just telling you to buy something so they can land a commission, or is it really a good product for you? If the investment turns out to be a solid performer, it hardly matters if they get paid for their advice that way. But if it goes sour, it could leave you with a bad taste in your mouth.

A **financial consultant** is similar to a financial planner and often has studied and passed an exam to use the chartered financial consultant (ChFC) designation, which is issued by the American College of Financial Services (theamericancollege.edu). ChFCs are required to complete a series of financial planning coursework and exams and agree to follow the American College code of ethics.

Another source of financial advice is the Association for Financial Counseling and Education (afcpe.org). An **accredited financial counselor** (AFC) can address your immediate money challenges and help you create a plan to achieve your goals. You can search by location and area of expertise. Fees typically start around $200 an hour, but vary. Virtual sessions are possible.

A **wealth manager** is, generally speaking, a financial adviser who specializes in high-net-worth clients, with investable assets that start around $1 million. Though there's no one credential needed to become a wealth manager or wealth adviser, many hold multiple designations such as certified financial planner (CFP), certified public accountant (CPA), registered life planner (RLP), certified financial transitionist (CeFT), who is someone trained to help clients navigate through major life events and the financial transitions that accompany them, or chartered financial analyst (CFA).

SHOPPING FOR YOUR ADVISER

Shop for an adviser who will sign an agreement to act as a *fiduciary*, which means that he or she agrees to act solely in your best interest when giving advice or recommending investments for your retirement accounts. Not all advisers are fiduciaries, so it's up to you to make sure that your financial adviser is one. Hiring a fiduciary doesn't guarantee that you'll get the perfect plan, but this designation is the basic prerequisite for a relationship built on trust.

It's important, in our opinion, to also seek an adviser or planner who has Certified Financial Planner (CFP) accreditation through the CFP Board. Such an adviser is a professional who has completed a rigorous series of courses and exams in financial planning and undergoes hours of continuing education each year. To access a database of these planners, go to the website for the CFP Board (cfp.net). As part of their certification, a CFP professional commits to act as a fiduciary—which means they agree to act in the best interests of the client at all times when providing financial advice and financial planning.

Once you find a handful of advisers who seem to be possible matches, do a quick background check: Visit the websites BrokerCheck (brokercheck.finra.org) and Investment Adviser Public Disclosure (adviserinfo.sec.gov) to see whether they have any complaints against them in their disciplinary history. Look up the advisers *and* their firms. If someone has a lot of short stints at different firms, he or she may not be the right person for you. Stability is the name of the game.

That said, if your adviser moves to a new firm, and you love your adviser and have a great relationship, you can move your accounts over with them once they're settled. Kerry did that a handful of times to stay with her adviser. The upside is your relationship of trust remains in place and they handle the move for you, but you will have documents to sign to authorize all of it. The biggest downside is you may get hit with one-time transfer fees to a new platform, and may experience higher costs and fees from that new one, but that's not a given and shouldn't be a concern if you're happy with your adviser and how they work with you and your money.

Some state securities regulators offer reports that provide a fuller picture of an adviser's record, but the availability of these reports varies widely. The national organization Public Investors Arbitration Bar Association, or PIABA (piaba.org), has such a list and provides contact information for the state agencies.

If you're looking to do a deeper investigation into a potential financial planner, visit the website Investment Adviser Public Disclosure (adviserinfo.sec.gov), search for the name of the person or firm, and download their Form ADV Part 2 brochure. Then search the downloaded document for frequent use of key terms such as "annuities" and "private funds."

Annuities, as we discussed in Chapter 8, are insurance contracts that are designed to produce income over time after an up-front purchase. They have a reputation for being rife with swollen fees, and for carrying commissions up to 10 percent, along with annual fees and expenses that can add up to 3 percent. Some advisers do prudently recommend these investments, but do your research and eye these with caution.

Private funds are pricey and, generally speaking, financial advisers who offer you "proprietary" private funds have a tendency not to recommend other investments, even if droves of other choices are more suitable for you. Again, this comes down to how they can make money, not necessarily how you make money.

Choosing the right money adviser for you takes legwork, and you have to follow your own instincts about the individual. This is a business decision. It's not personal. Your adviser doesn't have to be your confidant, but he or she does have to be someone you can talk to face-to-face and not someone who talks down to you or is condescending in any fashion. There are no dumb questions for you to ask when it comes to your money, and don't let anyone make you feel that there are. After all, you're the customer. You deserve that respect. You're the employer, hiring someone to work for you—not the other way around.

What makes the partnership succeed is your own involvement and understanding of the decisions you are making that will affect you and your family for years to come. "You want to find someone you feel comfortable getting financially naked with," McCullough told us. "Talking about money makes you feel vulnerable. You don't want to feel judged or shamed by an adviser—you should feel seen and supported."

One sidenote: Many women we have talked to have felt disrespected by male advisers, although this is improving, and more women are entering the field as certified financial planners. The real roadblock for women, regarding money and working with financial advisers, is being comfortable with asking questions to financial professionals. Plain language, not arcane investment lingo, rules the day as does mutual respect.

Not long after Kerry and her husband, Cliff, got married, he asked her to join him for a meeting with his financial adviser. Cliff had invested and worked with this adviser for about a decade and Cliff was happy with the results. So she went along—and sheesh. As the adviser and Cliff bantered about his portfolio's returns, she felt invisible. When she asked why he wanted Cliff to buy stock in a particular company, the adviser glanced in her direction—never directly in her eyes—and replied in a tone that she translated as, "Seriously, you don't have a clue what you're talking about."

If the adviser had paid attention when she told him what she did for a living, he would have known that she knew a little about analyzing a company's potential. She returned for subsequent meetings because Cliff valued her opinions, but she vowed not to give the adviser a dime of her money. And she never did. Before long, the two found a female adviser that clicked for both of them.

Her experience is, unfortunately, anything but unique. Of course, many male financial advisers treat women clients well and deliver excellent service, and there are undoubtedly some difficult female financial advisers. But the bottom line is this: If a relationship with your adviser doesn't make you feel like you are being well-served, do something about it.

Your relationship with your adviser should involve more than investments and also include a holistic financial and retirement plan. Most people our age are going to an adviser to find out if they will have enough money to retire and when. "Retirement means different things to different people, and they may really be thinking of leaving the corporate job and doing something that they are really passionate about and maybe still make money," McCullough said.

QUESTIONS TO ANSWER

Once you identify a few financial pros to interview, get up the gumption to ask some key questions. It can feel uncomfortable, but if they get upset or defensive, or say it doesn't matter, that's a sign to move on to someone else. Your pro needs to be someone who gets you. If you're recently widowed or divorced, for example, it might be helpful to work with someone who has other clients who fall into that category.

You will know in the first 10 minutes if someone really understands you or only wants to talk about your investments. If all the questions are about how much money you have and how much you earn, you should look for another adviser because they are probably more focused on just the financials and not your overall financial plan and future goals.

QUESTIONS FOR YOU TO ASK

It is important that you get a solid understanding of an adviser's background and credentials, what their area of expertise is, and how they like to work with their clients.

Does the adviser take a holistic approach like McCullough's, one that leans into your hopes and dreams and ideal vision to help you live a life without regrets? Does the adviser provide purely by-the-numbers straight advice about your investments and how they are allocated for your risk tolerance and your potential retirement end game? These are things you should find out before you do business with them. We realize the following are a lot of questions, and certainly not all of them may be applicable to your situation. That said, we recommend you ask:

- How long have you been an adviser/planner?
- Do you focus mainly on investment management, or do you also advise on taxes, estates and retirement, budgeting, debt management, or insurance?
- How many years have you worked for this firm?
- Can you tell me some details about the firm's history and the areas you specialize in?
- What are your qualifications?
- What professional groups do you belong to?
- Do you take part in any continuing education programs? How often?
- How big are your clients' portfolios on average?
- How are you paid? Do you earn fees to advise a private fund or other investments you may recommend to clients? Are your fees negotiable, and will you charge by the hour or by the service, rather than on assets under management?
- What is your area of strength from an investment perspective?
- What is your money philosophy?
- Are you registered with the Securities and Exchange Commission?
- Can you give me three references?
- What was your worst investment last year?
- What was your best investment in the past 12 months?
- What can I expect from you in the way of services?
- How often will we meet?
- How do your contracts work? Are they written or oral?

- Are there any restrictions on terminating your services?
- Based on what you know about my financial situation and objectives, what types of investments do you think would be appropriate, and over what time horizon?

QUESTIONS A PROFESSIONAL SHOULD ASK YOU

In addition to the questions you have for a potential adviser, you should expect an adviser to probe your motivations and goals for hiring him or her. Someone who is eager to get to know you and wants to make sure the two of you will be simpatico should have the following kinds of questions for you to answer. Take time ahead of a meeting to make sure you have these answers in your pocket to help determine if this is going to be a good match for both of you.

- How old are you?
- Do you have any dependents?
- What are your assets?
- What are your liabilities?
- What is your total income?
- Do you rent or own your home?
- What is the current value of your home?
- What are your housing costs each month?
- What are your total expenses each month?
- What are your goals and objectives?
- Do you have a will in place?
- Do you have life insurance?
- What other insurance coverage do you have—health, automobile, homeowner's?
- What is your money philosophy?
- Are you a conservative investor or are you willing to tolerate some risk?
- Are you savvy about investing?
- How much money management can you handle by yourself?

- What will you need a professional to help you with?
- What benefits does your employer provide?
- How much have you saved in retirement accounts?
- Will you inherit money one day?

THE ROLE OF ROBO-ADVISERS

Many major brokerages offer robo-adviser services. One upside to using these services is that they're often significantly cheaper than the cost of hiring a human.

One task these automated services can tackle for you is rebalancing your retirement account regularly, which is a strategy for returning your investment portfolio to the mix of stocks and bonds that matches your risk tolerance and goals.

Your 401(k) plan may offer an auto-rebalancing option already, particularly if you are invested in a target-date fund. If that's all you are looking for right now, then you might consider using a robo-adviser such as Wealthfront (wealthfront.com), Betterment (betterment.com), or Vanguard Digital Advisor (investor.vanguard.com/advice/robo-advisor).

Robo-advisers are provided by firms that manage your investments via a computer algorithm, and they often charge significantly less than a human adviser would charge. That's because there's not a human in the middle making the decisions. A standard fee for a robo-adviser is 0.25 percent of assets or less; some firms offer computer supervision with the help of a human financial adviser and so charge a bit more. Management fees will be listed on their websites.

When you open an account with a firm to engage a robo-adviser, you usually fill out a questionnaire that asks your age, expected retirement date, risk tolerance, and income needs. The software then creates a blend of investments for you.

Although these online money management platforms do make it inexpensive and easy to buy and sell stocks and mutual funds, there's a drawback for retirement savers. If, for example, your nest egg begins collapsing because the stock market went haywire and you don't know which way to turn, you'll have no one to help navigate your way through it. Contrast this to a human financial adviser who knows you and your goals and is there to help you.

We suspect that if you are reading this chapter, your preference is to receive financial services through an independent adviser whom you can talk to on a regular basis. Robo-advisers were developed with the goal of making personalized financial planning available on the cheap, and that's a good thing. That said, an algorithm isn't going to pick up the phone and say, "How can I be of service to you?" in a kind and reassuring way.

Kerry, for instance, received an email from Vanguard (she is a client) touting its "suite of advisory services" offering "a range of support to prepare a future for your beneficiaries, from tax-efficient strategies and portfolio management to retirement planning and advice tailored to you."

She was curious enough to explore her options, whether she wanted automated investment management or an adviser who could serve as her "personalized sounding board."

She discovered she could pay an annual advisory fee of $15 for every $10,000 she had invested at Vanguard to have access to a robo-advisor or $30 for every $10,000 invested as long as she had at least $50,000 in Vanguard accounts for a hybrid personal adviser and robo-helper.

If she had $500,000 or more invested with the firm, she'd shell out no more than $30 per $10,000 invested to work directly with a certified financial planner and get a personalized plan. Not bad.

AI ADVICE AND RETIREMENT PLANNING

Some financial pros use artificial intelligence to run computer-generated spread sheets to do investment research and run future portfolio scenarios and potential returns for retirement plans in their everyday work, but that doesn't mean it's ready for us . . . yet.

We decided to put ChatGPT, the renowned generative AI chatbot, to the test and then get input from experts on how generative AI can help—or hurt—the average person's retirement planning.

When we started noodling around with ChatGPT to learn how it could help us manage our retirement planning and saving, we were surprised by the amount of information it tossed out and how straightforward the answers were. It correctly answered our three initial queries, namely how much of Kerry's retirement savings should be invested in stocks, what a target-date fund is, and when she should start taking Social Security. The answers came quickly and had some depth.

For the stock holdings query, for instance, the answer was: "The percentage of your portfolio that should be invested in stocks during retirement depends on several factors, including your risk tolerance, retirement goals, and overall financial situation. However, a common rule of thumb is the "Rule of 100," which suggests subtracting your age from 100 to determine the percentage of your portfolio that should be invested in stocks with the remaining in more conservative investments like bonds or cash. However, this is just a general guideline, and your specific situation might warrant a different allocation."

We personally recommend 110 (which can shift up to 120, depending on your risk tolerance) minus your age, but this is pretty standard feedback and not wrong. The reply also covered what else we need to consider: "If you're comfortable with market volatility and have a long-term perspective, you might choose to hold more stocks. If you're risk-averse, a more conservative approach might be better. If you rely heavily on your portfolio for income, you might want to be more conservative to avoid having to sell stocks in a downturn."

It added this: "If you have other sources of income such as Social Security, pensions, or rental income, you might be able to take on more risk with your investments." Smartly, it also suggested we consider our health and expected lifespan. "If you expect a longer retirement, having more in stocks could help ensure your savings last."

Finally, we were pleased to read the final guidance from our ChatGPT test. "Given the importance of this decision, consulting a financial adviser who can tailor advice to your specific situation might be a good idea."

This basic information using ChatGPT was free, and for someone looking for some guardrails and guidance, it's a good start. Don't expect, however, personalized recommendations like specific investments to buy.

We asked ChatGPT to figure out how much a 50-year-old Gen Xer would need to save each year to reach $1 million by the time they turned 65, provided they currently have $178,500 saved. The answer: "To reach $1 million by age 65, given your current savings of $178,500, you would need to save approximately $27,757 each year for the next 15 years, assuming a 5 percent annual return on your investments."

And it added a dollop of encouragement: "This savings goal might be achievable through a combination of consistent contributions and sound investment choices. If you'd like to explore different return rates or strategies, feel free to ask!"

To get a deeper perspective on AI and retirement planning, we reached out to some experts for their take on the pros and cons right now. "AI could be good for identifying investor blind spots with respect to some financial knowledge, but not specific asset and fund recommendations," Mark Johnson, an investments and portfolio management fellow and professor at Wake Forest University, told us.

"For example, if you use ChatGPT and ask it 'attributes of a good mutual fund,' it will provide some good suggestions for items to look out for," he said. "But there are many limitations to relying on AI for investment management because 'one size fits all' fits no one." Money is emotional and personal, Johnson added, and AI doesn't understand that. "AI cannot provide specific advice given all of our unique financial situations, objectives, and constraints. So I would not exclusively rely on AI to manage a retirement account, but as a supplement to gathering information and general high-level investment advice," he said.

"AI is excellent at simplicity and directness and at doing initial explorations," Dan Egan, Betterment's vice president of behavioral finance and investing, told us. "For now, it's a good advice accessory, and it doesn't judge you for asking stupid questions. But you want to have an accountability partner, an actual person, who's going to be a copilot for you."

For example, you might want to use AI to go over the definition of what catch-up retirement contributions are, or what the differences are between a Roth IRA and a traditional one so that you don't have to cover these matters with your financial adviser. "You want to spend time with her doing the most meaty stuff possible," Egan told us.

Because AI can analyze huge amounts of data, it can provide input on market dynamics, according to a new report from BlackRock, "potentially leading to more tailored and resilient portfolios capable of adapting to varying conditions."

That doesn't mean AI is ready to advise you on specific investments for your account. "If you want to use AI to do something like help you brainstorm ways to budget, then go for it," LendingTree senior economist Jacob Channel told us. "You probably shouldn't be using it to do much more than that. AI can make a lot of mistakes, and it might lead you down a path that doesn't end where you'd like to go."

Meanwhile, "AI often sucks at math," he said. "So if you're trying to use one to figure out how much you need to save in order to retire comfortably, you could easily be led astray."

"There's a good chance that what it tells you won't be even close to correct," said Channel. "We've got a long way to go before a machine will be able to provide you with the same level of nuanced expertise that a competent human can."

To be fair, there is a disclaimer in pale type at the bottom of the ChatGPT screen page: "ChatGPT can make mistakes. Check important information." Accuracy matters when it comes to critical life choices and investments. The last thing you want to do is base your retirement plans on incomplete or inaccurate information. Good retirement planning goes well beyond generic answers. Interest rates change, markets swoon, and laws change.

Also, there's no substitute for a relationship between two people where you can dream about your goals, what you might regret if you didn't do it, what you value, and what kind of retirement lifestyle you envision.

"Artificial intelligence is not designed to be a counselor and partner in retirement," Bradley Schurman, author of *The Super Age*, told us. "AI offers a great starting point, but it doesn't have the emotional intelligence needed to assist individuals in the long run."

YOUR TO-DO LIST

- Reflect on what services you need from a financial adviser.
- Research to find a handful of planners to contact, and understand what they charge for their services and how available they will be for you.
- Reach out and interview your top choices using the questions provided in this chapter.

In the next chapter, we show you why having a proper estate plan in place matters in terms of protecting your wealth and creating a legacy. Creating such a plan includes writing a will and assigning a power of attorney to someone you trust, and it's supported by making sure you have the proper insurance coverage. All are key to your retirement.

13

PASSING YOUR WEALTH ALONG

Do you have life insurance, Phil? Because if you do, you could always use a little more, right? I mean, who couldn't? But you wanna know something? I got the feeling... you ain't got any. Am I right or am I right? Or am I right? Am I right?

—Ned Ryerson

Groundhog Day, 1993

You spend your life earning and accumulating wealth and creating a family and household that matches your values. Now, how do you protect what's important to you and create a legacy that lasts after you've left this world? There are a number of ways.

To make sure your assets are distributed the way you want and that your children are taken care of in the manner that you desire requires a process called estate planning. Unfortunately, just 25 percent of folks in the 35 to 54 age range have put together a plan.[1]

To provide extra support for your family after you die (or if you become disabled) requires insuring against those circumstances. A good chunk of Gen Xers—45 percent—say they need life insurance or need more of it, so it's something on our minds.[2] We'll cover both of these concerns in this chapter, starting with estate planning.

ESTATE PLANNING

At its very core, estate planning is putting together a plan for what happens and who makes your decisions if you become incapacitated or if you pass away. When you're incapacitated, the documents that are part of your estate plan name who can make health care decisions for you and who can have access to your medical information. The plan also dictates who can make your legal and financial decisions when you aren't able.

Let's talk about incapacity for a minute. This is a legal ruling, and in some cases it's more obvious than others. When a person is in a coma or severely injured to the extent they cannot make decisions for themselves, their incapacitation seems obvious. Incapacity becomes harder to determine when a person is in some form of cognitive decline. A physician is the first person to help determine incapacity, and more than one doctor's professional opinion may be needed, depending on state laws. If there are conflicting opinions about whether a person is incapacitated or not, a judge may be asked to rule on the matter.

The biggest reason to go through the estate planning process, according to the estate planning attorneys we spoke to, is to prevent the wrong person from being in charge of your health, wealth, and children. Each state has its own statutes determining who would be the best person to step in to be your child's guardian, for example, and by law, it could be the exact person you do not want in that role, such as an ex-spouse rather than your parents. An estate plan keeps that from happening. For those with higher net worths, the estate plan also covers how to protect your assets during your life and how to minimize taxes on your estate.

If you own a business with employees, having a plan in place is especially important. Otherwise, an emergency petition would need to be filed, because no one would be in charge or have access to the company's bank accounts right away.

Monique Lavender Greenberg, an estate planning attorney in Miami, explains what can go wrong if there isn't an estate plan in place ahead of time: "I have to go to court to make payroll for a company... make sure people get paid for the holidays."

So there are a lot of good reasons to get started with estate planning, even if the conversations around it are at first uncomfortable. Let's begin with health care decisions.

HEALTH CARE DECISIONS

Most people don't like to dwell on what could happen if you end up incapacitated. But unfortunately, accidents and major illnesses do occur. And you'd much rather that your family is prepared to respond in those times of crises rather than scrambling—and frankly, possibly infighting—during such a crucial time. Fortunately, a few documents are available that can alleviate that process as much as possible and allow your loved ones to make the best decision for you when you can't. As a group, these documents are called your advance directives.

The first document is a **health care proxy**, but it has many other names, depending on your state, such as health care surrogate, health care power of attorney, and medical proxy. No matter the name, this document dictates who has the right to make your health care decisions if you can't do it yourself. To keep your bases covered, it's smart to name a primary person—often a spouse or partner—and two alternates in case the primary is not able to carry out those decisions because they, too, are incapacitated, have passed away, or are out of the state or country.

To help the health care proxy make medical decisions that align with your values, you should also have a **living will**. This document prescribes what kind of medical interventions you want or don't want if you're in a condition where you have no reasonable probability of recovery, according to more than one doctor. Those interventions can include cardiac resuscitation, a breathing machine, a feeding tube, or antibiotics.

"What that does is it prevents the Terri Schiavo type of battle, [when] someone wants to pull the plug and someone wants to keep that individual alive when they're on life support," Greenberg said. "So if someone has very clear wishes, it's important to sign a living will."

If you have dependent children—either minors or adult children with special needs—you also should declare a **standby guardian designation**—called a **pre-need nomination of guardian** in some states—which goes into effect if there is only one surviving parent and they are incapacitated. You need to name a primary agent along with two alternates.

While you want one person to make your medical decisions, you may want other family members to be involved in your medical care, and this requires a **HIPAA authorization or consent form**. HIPAA releases allow those named on the form to be able to talk to the doctors or obtain a medical record on behalf of the health care proxy.

"Maybe one child is the decision maker, but you want all of your kids to be able to ask the doctor, 'How's Mom doing today?'" Greenberg said.

Another aspect of estate planning that can be helpful to your loved ones are **body considerations**. If you're interested in being an organ donor, the best thing to do is register through your state. Often this can be done at your local DMV office or with the Health Resources and Services Administration via the website organdonor.gov. Let your health care proxies know that you've registered. You can also leave your wishes regarding organ donation in your living will.

If you're interested in donating your body to science, you must register in advance. Some states have an online body donation form you can download. Just google your state's name and the phrase "body donation form." You can also choose the medical university or research center where you want to donate your body. These institutions often have their own donation form you need to fill out ahead of time.

You can also name an **agent to control disposition of remains** to fulfill your cremation or burial wishes. Most states honor these requests; otherwise, the responsibility will automatically fall to your next of kin. Again, name a primary representative, likely your spouse or partner, plus two alternates. Make sure to include information about body donations, or about a family plot if you have one. You can find state-specific information related to this issue via the website of the

Funeral Consumers Alliance (funerals.org). The relevant page is titled "State by State: Assigning an Agent to Control Disposition."

FINANCIAL DECISIONS

A host of other documents need to be filled out to determine who controls your finances if you become incapacitated or if you pass away. Just like with the health care documents, these forms can help your family avoid strife and cumbersome court processes during an emotionally fragile time. It's a last gift that you can provide your loved ones. Here's what to know.

First is a **durable power of attorney**, which stipulates who can act on your behalf when it comes to legal and financial decisions. Just like with the health care proxy, it's smart to name a primary power of attorney, plus two alternates. Depending on the state, this document can be effective immediately, so whoever you appoint as the primary "has a lot of power right from the beginning," Greenberg said. Other states allow a springing durable power of attorney, which becomes effective only when you become incapacitated. But often a judge needs to determine that a person is incapacitated before it can go into effect, creating roadblocks and delays, and so having a springing power of attorney may not be worth it. Your estate planning attorney can offer insight. Of course, you want to choose someone who you trust won't try to make decisions when you're not incapacitated.

The second document you need is your **last will and testament**. This is probably the most familiar financial decision document to folks. It lays out how your assets should be distributed after your death, and it can include instructions for who will take care of your children, financial interests, and account management. It also names an executor, or your representative, to carry out the wishes outlined in the will. Without a will, the state will distribute assets and determine guardianship for minor and/or special needs children according to state law.

Your estate planning attorney should ask you to name what's called disaster scenario beneficiaries, which goes into effect in the very unlikely case where you pass away, your partner or spouse passes away, and there are no descendants. Where do you want your wealth to go? Possible beneficiaries include one or more charities, extended family, friends, or some combination of these.

When divvying up assets, it's best to think in terms of percentages of your assets or a certain dollar amount. Let's say, for example, you have two bank accounts that each have similar amounts in them when you write your will. Then let's say you name one child to get the money in Bank Account A and another child to get what's in Bank Account B. Great. But what happens if you end up draining Bank Account B later for an emergency and nothing's left in it? That child would get nothing if you passed away soon after.

Executing a will is often a public process called probate, which can be time-consuming or costly, depending on the state. To avoid that process, and for myriad other reasons, many families choose to create a **revocable trust**, or "your alter ego," as Greenberg puts it. At the most basic, a revocable trust allows you to control your financial assets and property while you're still alive and to dictate who should receive your estate after you pass away. In some states, it's called a living trust.

A good way to understand a revocable trust is by envisioning the trust as a business. Let's say, for example, you create a trust called Smith LLC. This trust owns assets, real estate, rental property, and bank and investment accounts. Smith LLC also has a manager that oversees those assets for the benefit of the owners of the LLC, who receive the profits of the business.

"A trust is just like that, except on a more personal level," said April Wise, a partner at estate planning firm Balch & Bingham LLP in Alabama. With a living trust, says Wise, "the Smith family trust owns all the assets and the trustee is like the manager of those assets for the beneficiaries that get the distributions."

In this case, while you're alive and competent, you serve as both trustee and beneficiary of your trust. But if you become incapacitated, your named successor trustee steps in, often your partner or spouse, if you have one, to manage the trust on your behalf. Again, it's good to name two alternates. Spouses can have joint trusts or separate ones, depending on what fits their family's circumstances. With a revocable trust, you should also have what is called a **pour-over will** to transfer any assets with no designated beneficiary or joint owner not already in the trust after death.

If you have minor children or dependent adult children, the trust also should indicate a guardian trustee for them as beneficiaries of the trust if both parents are deceased or the only one living is incapacitated. Again, name a first backup and second one.

In addition to avoiding probate, a revocable trust provides other benefits. If you don't have a trusted family member or friend to serve as your successor trustee, you can name a professional or corporate entity to do this for a revocable trust. Similarly, this arrangement may be helpful for a couple where one spouse or partner isn't familiar with managing assets, so the corporate entity can do that on their behalf. Also, if you own property in more than one state, probate may be required in both states after your death. Having those properties in a revocable trust can avoid that ancillary probate.

Some accounts such as retirement accounts, life insurance policies, annuities, and other financial vehicles may already have named beneficiaries. If they do, it doesn't matter how you instruct who gets the assets in these accounts in your will or revocable trust. "Beneficiary designations are going to trump that. It doesn't matter what your will or trust says," Greenberg said.

The cost of estate planning varies widely depending on what documents you need and how complicated your situation is, based on your family structure and the amount and variety of assets you own. For instance, someone who is married with no children and whose main assets are a house and retirement accounts will have a more straightforward, and likely less expensive, estate-planning process than a small business owner who is married with children and stepchildren. So the process can range from $300 to $1,000 on the lower end to between $2,000 and $5,000, possibly even more, on the higher end.

But Greenberg points out: "It's often cheaper in the long run, even if it feels more expensive" to pay for estate planning in advance rather than have a probate court sort everything out after your death. "You could do [probate court], but your kids probably won't get together at Thanksgiving, so we're saving money and strife.'"

If your estate is very simple, you may be able to find the downloadable documents online from your state. But you may still want an estate planning attorney to review those documents to make sure they are executed according to state law. Otherwise, you risk having documents that are not enforceable.

Find an attorney who specializes in estate planning, rather than a jack-of-all-trades lawyer, especially if you have a more complex estate. Make sure they are accredited and board certified. And look for those who have LLMs in estate planning or tax planning, which is like a "masters of law" degree above their actual law degree, Greenberg said. Ask trusted family and friends if they would recommend someone they used for their own estate planning. You want to find someone you are comfortable with and who fits in your budget, Wise said.

"Come in and meet with me. Let's talk about it. I can then give you a good estimate at that point of what it's gonna cost," Wise said. "If you decide to engage me, great, you're charged for the meeting as part of that estimate. If you decide not to engage me, then we just write off the time."

As you're interviewing possible candidates, here are some red flags to watch out for:

- If your lawyer suggests naming them as your trustee or personal representative, that's a big no-no and could be an ethics violation depending on the state.
- If your lawyer is meeting with just you, but drafts documents for you and your spouse/partner without meeting with your spouse/partner, that's "a giant red flag," Greenberg said. Your spouse/partner needs to meet with the attorney themselves to make sure they are properly represented.
- If your lawyer wants to keep the original documents, so your representative or family has to come back after you

pass away, that's an extra step that can be avoided. It's not necessarily unethical behavior on the part of the lawyer, but you should have those documents after they're finalized.

The last word on estate planning is that it can be an ongoing process. You should review your documents every five to 10 years or after every major life event, whichever is sooner. Major life events include births in the family, deaths, divorce, when your children turn 18, and if you come into a major windfall. That way, the documents accurately reflect your circumstances and your continuing wishes.

LIFE INSURANCE

Life insurance is another way to equip your family's finances with some protection. In general, this kind of insurance provides a payout when the insured person passes, helping widowed spouses and children stay afloat financially. Choosing which life insurance policy to get depends on a number of factors: your age, budget, and how you want the policy to fit into your overall financial strategy. Let's go over the two main types of life insurance: term life insurance and permanent life insurance.

Under **term life insurance**, you enter into a contract for a period—that can be 10, 15, 20, or 30 years—with an insurance company, which agrees to provide a payout in the event of your death during the term, provided you make the monthly payments. At the end of the term, you can renew your coverage for the same face amount for the payout, but typically at a higher premium because you're older. Some companies may offer the option to convert your term life insurance policy into a permanent one. More on that type later. Overall, term life insurance is more affordable than a permanent one because you can get insured for a larger amount at a lower monthly premium.

"Term life insurance would be great to look into for parents who have children that maybe have gone off to college and you still have a mortgage balance, or you're responsible for your children's education," said Ebony Ruffin, founder of Ruffin Consulting Services, which provides life insurance solutions to families and businesses. "Term life insurance satisfies your need to make sure that the mortgage balance is satisfied as well as your children have money for education in the event that you pass away."

Employers often offer life insurance as one of their many benefits for employees. A typical way this works is that the employer pays for a certain coverage amount of life insurance—often equal to one year's salary—for free and provides the option for the employee to purchase more coverage for a group price. Aside from being convenient, the additional coverage typically doesn't require a thorough medical underwriting process. So if you have a medical condition, it can be more affordable than private policies. But if you're healthy, you may find better pricing with private policies, which also come with the added benefit of being portable if you switch jobs.

Permanent life insurance comes in different forms, but the goal with this type of life insurance is to provide you coverage for as long as you're living. To get that, you must pay a monthly premium. Permanent life insurance generally costs more than term life insurance. The best way to understand the cost difference is to request quotes for the same face amount for both types.

For example, let's get two quotes for Marty McFly, who would be 56 years old as of this writing. Given he's average weight and is not a tobacco user or doesn't engage in riskier activities like scuba diving or parachuting (hoverboarding doesn't count), a 10-year term life insurance policy for a $500,000 payout would run between $73 and $133 per month, Ruffin told us. A guaranteed universal life policy covering Marty until he's 121 years old for the same payout amount would cost $562 per month.

"Usually that is the 'aha' moment where consumers understand the huge difference between term and permanent life insurance," Ruffin said.

Cost aside, permanent life insurance features some benefits that are missing from term life insurance. Permanent policies provide a cash value account. When you make a monthly premium payment, a portion goes to your death benefit and another portion to a cash value account, which grows depending on the type of permanent life insurance. Typically after an initial 2- to 5-year period, you can use your cash account for withdrawals, loans, or premium payments, but your death benefit will go down. Furthermore, there are different types of policies to choose from:

- Whole life policies offer a guaranteed fixed cash value account that grows according to a set rate.
- Universal life policies grow their cash value accounts based on interest rates and investments.
- Variable life policies invest your cash value money in subaccounts, which are similar to mutual funds. These are riskier because your cash account can rise and fall in value.

You need to weigh this investment benefit against the increased cost of the monthly premium and decide if there are better ways to invest the difference in the long term. You may find that it makes more sense to buy term life insurance with cheaper premiums and invest the difference between the two premiums on your own.

Next up is a quick and easy calculation to determine the minimum amount of life insurance you need. You should get at least enough to pay off all of your debts and cover five years of your income. If your family can pay off all of their debts with the insurance money, that frees up a lot of cash flow for them. It also takes some financial strain off surviving family members who are also dealing with the emotional toll of loss. Still, this amount is only a starting point. It provides an adequate amount of coverage, but it's not ideal. It's not going to replace all the goals you have as a family indefinitely.

The next step is to use the acronym, L.I.F.E., to determine your comprehensive needs. It stands for **Liabilities**, amount of **Income** that needs to be replaced, **Final** expenses—such as funeral arrangements and medical costs—and **Extra** goals like future education costs or charitable giving. Use your cash flow analysis and net worth exercise from Chapter 3 to help with these. Add up the elements of L.I.F.E. to determine an amount that's much closer to your actual needs.

If the premiums for that amount of life insurance coverage are too expensive for you at first, think of it as a goal to grow into as time goes on and you earn more money. Also, look at your budget and find where you can make sacrifices to increase your coverage.

If one person in a couple doesn't work, that doesn't mean that person shouldn't have life insurance on themselves. What work that person provides may not bring in income, but chances are they make vital contributions to the household, such as childcare, meal preparation, and maintenance that would cost money to replace.

"This is where I try to convey the message of understanding your value in your household," Ruffin said. "So I always try to encourage a stay-at-home parent to just jot down a list of how they contribute to their household. Would someone have to be hired to perform those activities? And that helps them better understand why they do need life insurance, as well."

DISABILITY INSURANCE

Not to continue to be a Debbie Downer, but you're more likely to become disabled during your working years than to pass away. That's why it's critical to have disability insurance coverage. This type of policy replaces a certain percentage of your income for a specific period if you can't work because of an injury or illness. Disability insurance also comes in two flavors: short-term and long-term.

The rule of thumb is that short-term disability insurance usually covers lost income up to a year. Long-term disability can offer income replacement up to age 65 and tops off at around 60 percent of income. It also comes with something called an elimination period, which is a waiting period before benefits kick in. You'll need emergency funds of your own to cover that gap. The shorter the elimination period, the more expensive the coverage typically is and vice versa. In other words, the longer the waiting period, the more affordable the policy.

Figuring out your disability needs is a bit more complicated. You need to identify how much of your typical spending you absolutely need to cover versus how much of your spending you feel comfortable reducing in the event of an emergency.

You may also want to check what each working adult in your household would qualify for from Social Security. Visit the Social Security website, and begin with the page titled "What You Could Get from Disability" (ssa.gov/disability/amount). You qualify for Social Security Disability Insurance if your disability affects your ability to work for at least a year or will result in death. You also must have worked for at least five of the last 10 years to be eligible.

Disability insurance is used to fill in the gaps that your personal assets and Social Security, if your disability qualifies for it, can't cover. How do you determine your level of disability insurance coverage? By answering three main questions.

- **What do you need?** Look at your cash flow from the exercises in Chapter 3. Which ones are essential expenses and which ones are discretionary that could be cut out if needed? That gives you an idea of how much you need from your disability insurance, your savings, and Social Security to live securely.
- **What do you have already?** Count up emergency savings—ideally six months' worth of expenses—and add it to any disability policy—short-term or long-term—that your employer provides. What does that give you in the case of a disability event? For example, if you have an employer policy that pays out 25 percent of your income, but you need 60 percent of your income to live securely, then you need to fill the 35 percent gap. You can also add in your estimated Social Security disability payments by using the SSA's "Online Benefits Calculator."
- **What coverage is best for you?** This is where you're looking to close the gaps. For instance, if your employer offers

short-term disability but not long-term, then you may want to consider something that covers a life-altering injury.

Note that if your employer pays the premiums for disability insurance, then the income from the disability insurance will be taxable. Overall, disability insurance costs roughly 2 percent of the annual salary of whoever is insured. Like most insurance, the more favorable the conditions are to the policyholder, usually the more expensive the premium.

YOUR TO-DO LIST

- Sit down with your spouse or partner to talk about how you'd like your legacy to look after you pass away.
- Set up initial meetings with estate planning attorneys to start the process of getting the necessary documents in place.
- Calculate how much life insurance and disability coverage you need based on your savings and the policies offered at your workplace.
- Compare life and disability insurance policies that will fill in your coverage gaps.

Now you can rest a bit easier knowing that you have your family covered financially in the event of death or disability. You also have the comfort of knowing that you've laid out your wishes for your assets and children's care if the worst happens. By doing this, you've saved your family from added emotional trauma during what would be a very difficult time. You've also come a long way in getting ready for retirement and tackling the roadblocks in your way. Pat yourself on the back. The next chapter is for those of you who are business owners and outlines the special planning you may need to do. For everyone else, it's time for happy hour.

14

GEN X BUSINESS OWNERS

Are You Ready for Retirement?

DR. PETER VENKMAN: For whatever reasons, Ray—call it fate, call it luck, call it karma... I believe that everything happens for a reason. I believe that we were destined to get thrown out of this dump.
DR. RAYMOND STANTZ: For what purpose?
DR. PETER VENKMAN: To go into business for ourselves.

—*GHOSTBUSTERS*, 1984

Destiny Burns, now nearing 60, opened CLE Urban Winery, a boutique winery and tasting room in her hometown of Cleveland, in 2016. "My business *is* my retirement strategy," she told us.

"I've invested everything into it, like an idiot. I am beginning to work on plans for an exit/sale of the business within the next five years. It's going to take a ton of work and planning, but I need to get my life savings out of my business so I can safely 'retire' and do something else. It's a big undertaking."

Burns had initially retired after a two-decade military career as a Navy intelligence communications officer and then spent 13 years in business development positions for defense contractors such as General Dynamics and Northrop Grumman. In fact, she worked full-time as a defense contractor for a year as she built her business and then quit her job two weeks before she opened her doors.

For Burns, it was a series of major life events that shifted her mindset and gave her the catalyst to open her small business in midlife. Her marriage of more than 25 years had collapsed. Her daughter, Aimee, had graduated from college and moved out. So, for the first time in more than two decades, Burns, then living in northern Virginia, was on her own. "I had always dreamed of having my own business. I had a desire to do something different and to, well, feed my soul," Burns said. "It wasn't easy walking away from the income I was making working for a defense contractor, but I was drained."

Burns's business has been profitable, but now she's ready to move on as she prepares to enter her sixth decade. She has no one in mind to pass it on to. "I did not go into this to be a millionaire. Money was not a primary motivator," she said. "I measure my success in traditional ways like being able to pay all my bills, by being the best boss I can be for my staff, by receiving good customer reviews, and by there being more black ink on my business financials than red ink," she said.

Today, though, Burns is clearly eager to put her exit plan in place. While on one hand, she is fortunate because she has a pension from her years of military service, she hasn't been able to set aside retirement savings in years, and she had to dip into her IRA to keep the business afloat during the COVID-19 pandemic. "I have everything I need and my credit score is great," she said, "but it's tough running your own business at times. I worry that a serious illness or other major catastrophe could be my ruin."

If you're a small business owner, you get this. It's not that you haven't or don't want to save for retirement outside of your business. Your priority has probably been to plow earnings back into the business to keep it growing. Chances are, your business is fairly modest in terms of revenue, and so you rarely pay yourself a big salary or carve money out to set aside for your retirement. Don't beat yourself up over this. It sadly goes with the territory.

When it comes to their own retirement savings, 85 percent of self-employed/microbusiness owners know they should be saving more for retirement, according to Fidelity Investments. Two-thirds of them, however, aren't sure if they are saving enough, and 42 percent worry they will never be able to retire.[1]

When asked what's preventing them from saving more, the most common response is that they only earn enough to cover their expenses (42 percent). According to the report, three in 10 entrepreneurs running midsize companies with 10 to 49 employees are focused on providing more pay or benefits to employees, and four in 10 owners with 50 to 99 employees feel they need to invest their money back into their business.

The business *is* their retirement plan. The plan is that when they retire, they are either going to transfer the business to a family member in exchange for a share of future wealth or a buyout, or they are going to sell it off and turn that profit into cash.

At the heart of the lack of retirement savings is that much of their wealth has been trapped in their business for years, and in order to set money aside in other retirement savings accounts, they would have to pull funds from their business, and, in essence, remove some of the juice that keeps it rolling. They worry, probably for good reason, that taking money out would put the brakes on growth and potentially ding their business's cash flow.

Still, for small business owners in their 40s and early 50s, it's important they find ways to carve out even a small amount regularly, in a disciplined approach, to contribute to their retirement accounts. They must determine an amount that isn't going to make a difference for the business but, invested wisely, can turn into something meaningful. Ideally, they would automate these transactions from a checking account to a retirement account, such as a SEP-IRA or a solo 401(k).

Another reason small business owners aren't paying attention to their own retirement planning is that they are focused on running the business, and so they may not have time to think about much else. "The creator of the business is the CEO and chief dishwasher, so to speak," says Matt Hansen, executive director and financial adviser at Morgan Stanley, helping business owners grow and prepare for a strategic exit. (Hansen, who was born in 1979, loved watching *The A-Team* TV show so much that one season he named his childhood soccer team after it.) "They're doing all aspects of the business, so there's no real time or energy left to focus on that. And they could also be working on paying down debt, so it sort of pushes off the retirement plan and then real exit planning."

He adds: "If we have enough notice before someone wants to exit, we try to talk to them about setting some money aside and not plowing every dollar back into the business so that they can maintain the same level of growth while also taking a few chips off the table along the way to protect themselves and their families."

THE RANGE OF EXIT PLANS

"For Gen X business owners looking to sell their business in the next few years it is critical to begin to give some thought to what a sale looks like," Howard Hook, senior wealth adviser and certified financial planner with EKS Associates, a financial planning firm based in Princeton, New Jersey, told us. "Is it a sale to someone already working in the business such as a minority partner or key employee? Or will it be a sale to an outside third party?"

There are myriad ways to transition your business to provide owners with income for their retirement years. Here are a few of the top options:

- **Family succession** is when business owners transfer the ownership of the business to family members and receive payment either in a lump sum or over time.
- **Stepping down to retire, but holding on to ownership** is an exit strategy some small business owners opt for. This

generally requires hiring someone from outside the family to run the business while the owner remains on the payroll. At some stage, though, this short-term transition will segue to an eventual sale.

- **Selling the business** can be the toughest choice, but the owner gets a say in who the purchaser is, and after the sale receives a pool of funds to use for retirement living expenses.
- **Liquidation** is probably the last thing owners want to do. When there is not a buyer or family member to step up to take over, however, this option can provide cash to fund the owner's retirement.

PREPARING YOUR EXIT STRATEGY

Burns knows what she has to do and has given herself the runway to do so. If you're like her, and you are nearing a time when you plan to cash out to fund your retirement, you can't afford to ignore the essential steps to get your company primed for sale. According to a UBS report, three in 10 small business owners haven't completed a business valuation to get a sense of what they could expect financially from a sale.[2] A third of small business owners don't have strategies in place to minimize taxes when they do sell their companies, and four in 10 have not spoken to their heirs if the idea is to pass the business along to a family member. Moreover, of those looking to sell, more than 30 percent either don't have an estate plan or a plan for what to do with the proceeds.

Don't wait too long. Of those who have exited in recent years, nearly seven in 10 spent less than two years preparing for a sale. There are so many reasons to drag your feet on selling your business. But let's be honest, emotions are a huge stumbling block. The bulk of small business owners are concerned that a buyer won't treat employees well, or they personally won't have a sense of purpose when they no longer have their business, or they fret that they won't agree with the direction a buyer will take their business, per UBS.

Once they get going though, the upside is that owners say they look forward to new opportunities, such as traveling and spending time with friends and family, starting a new business venture, and giving back to community or charitable causes. A friend of Kerry's, Wendy Volhard, sold her pet food business, Volhard Dog Nutrition, when she retired a few years ago. It was a good deal for her and she stayed on as a consultant. Plus, her buyer was one she had carefully vetted to be sure they would continue to produce the products at her high standards and that her customers (and their four-legged pals) would be in good hands. And that has been the case. Kerry's Labrador retriever, Elly, dines on it daily, and has no complaints.

Volhard, a renowned dog trainer and author, developed the recipe for her natural dehydrated dog food, and its creation and success has been her legacy. Often, entrepreneurs like Volhard see their business as their identity, their passion, and their contribution to the world. Selling their "baby," so to speak, can be heartbreaking. But if done carefully and prudently, it can have a financial payoff. This may very well be the most critical financial decision you'll make to ensure that your financial future is secure.

A good exit plan can be made as many as five years in advance of selling or transitioning the business, Matt Hansen said. "At the very least, give yourself two years to make a plan. What we like to focus on for business owners contemplating a sale is, number one, getting a valuation of the business. Let's figure out what we think the business is worth. And then we couple that with the business owner's personal financial plan to try and determine, on a net after-tax basis, whether it will meet expectations and their retirement income needs for the rest of their lifetime."

If it doesn't, the extra lead time you get from holding on to your business can give you more time to save in your retirement accounts to shore up your nest egg.

Hansen's exit-planning strategy for his clients has three stages: discovery, preparation, and decision. "You need to assess not just the business itself. Your own personal goals and future financial picture are factors, because most small business owners have 80 to 90 percent of their assets tied up in their business," he said.

You have to ask yourself: What am I going to do with myself after I sell my business and retire? I have spent my entire life dedicated to creating this legacy, and so can I really walk away and move to the third stage of my life?

WHAT'S IT WORTH?

It can be difficult to determine the value of your business. To create a formal valuation, or what you might expect to sell your business for, you can use comparable sales in the industry and in your geographic location, Hansen said.

Hansen and his team dig through all the positives and negatives of the company, and then they try to fix things so that the valuation is more in line with the business owner's expectations. "By doing a deep analysis of the business, we can determine if anything is holding the company back from maximizing the most value upon its sale," he added. "What's out there that could reduce the potential sales price, and what are the ways we can fix those? Do you have too few customers? Are 80 percent of your revenues, for instance, generated by one or two buyers? If so, that poses a risk. We want to make business owners diversify their customer base and spread out the risk."

This is precisely why it's important to get a jump start on this process. You want to give yourself enough time to make any changes that will increase the valuation of your company before you hang out the for sale sign. "Everyone thinks their business is the best and should command a premium over other businesses in the same industry," Hook said. "This of course is not always true."

If the numbers look good, then it's time to start bringing in estate planning attorneys and investment banking folks to help prepare for the sale of the business and take it to market.

"Remember even if the purchase price is agreed upon, there likely could be other stumbling blocks needed to be tackled," Hook said.

"Timing of payments, how much involvement you'll have or be required to have after the sale, and whether you'll be paid a salary for that time are just a few common issues needed to be worked through."

Once your attorney and the buyer's attorney draft up the agreement, there could be surprise legal issues that need to be negotiated. A solution to preventing this could be in letting your attorney know ahead of time your firmness on certain issues, as well as your level of desire to get a deal done, Hook said. "This way the attorney can gauge how hard they need to go on certain issues—with certain issues being nonnegotiable."

For the business owners who don't have any liquid assets and everything is in the business, it's a very nerve-racking experience to go through a sale, because they need that number to be X or else they may run the risk of outliving their money, Hansen said.

PASSING IT ON

If your dream is to keep your business in the family and pass it on to one or more of your children, you want to make sure your kids have the same vision toward growing that business as you did, and you want to be positive they really are on board with that idea. While more than half of business owners' adult children work for their parents' business full- or part-time, few are interested in assuming ownership, according to UBS. In fact, the majority of heirs would rather have money from the sale of the business than inherit the business.

"Just because family works in the business does not mean they want to own the business," Hooks said. "If they do, an evaluation needs to be made to determine if you think they can indeed run the business. Many business owners would love to have their kids take over the business, but the kids sometimes are not capable of running it."

Another consideration to selling to a family member is that sometimes sales to family members can be done at a reduced price and/or on more favorable terms, such as a longer payment schedule or a lower interest rate. This may sound great and be extremely helpful to a family member, but it comes at a financial cost to the owner. Knowing ahead of time the reduction in a potential sales price can allow the owner to determine if the reduced sales price and longer payment schedule will still be financially viable for them before agreeing to sell the business to family.

"The value of the business needs to be looked at no differently than other liquid assets such as brokerage accounts and retirement accounts if the owner will need to realize value for the business upon sale to a buyer, in this case a family member," said Hook.

Among owners who are planning to give the business to family members, the top concerns include the future direction of the business, the successors' ability to run the business, and the potential for strain on family relationships, we have found.

Without a doubt, selling to a family member often adds additional emotion. A business owner who sells their company to an outside buyer may lose interest in its success after the sale. But this may not be the case if the business is sold to a family member. The original owner might still have a vested emotional interest in the business, and will be horrified to watch a family member cause that business to go belly up.

Although emotions can run high when selling to a family member, the transition of ownership can be smoothed out if an employee stock ownership plan (ESOP) is created to hold the stock of the family business.[3]

An ESOP is an employee benefit plan that enables employees to own part or all of the company they work for. ESOPs are most commonly used to smooth the way for succession planning, allowing a company owner to sell his or her shares to employees and transition out of the business. In many cases, a business owner's wealth largely comprises company stock. In an ESOP transaction, if you as the owner sell at least 30 percent of the company to the ESOP, and then reinvest those proceeds in qualified investments, you can defer capital gains taxes on your gain. You might even be able to eliminate capital gains taxes entirely, Hansen said. To a retiring business owner, an ESOP can offer major tax savings, and liquidity, as well as tax advantages to the business itself, per Hansen. The business can deduct the entire purchase price of the stock sold to the ESOP plus interest, and the company may then qualify to be a tax exempt entity indefinitely in certain types of ESOP structures.

ACTION STEPS FOR SMALL BUSINESS OWNERS

If you're a small business owner, all the observations and advice in this book are important, but there are certain areas you especially need to focus on right now.

Add up those numbers. How much will you need to live on in retirement, especially when the business isn't picking up the tab for some expenses? Just getting a sense of what your living costs might be when you quit working could be the retirement-savings wake-up call you need. Most major financial services firms, such as Fidelity, T. Rowe Price, TIAA, and Vanguard, offer free online retirement worksheets and calculators to help you get a bead on future expenses.

Seek out help. Consider hiring a financial adviser to jump-start your retirement plan and help you focus. We recommend one with the certified financial planner (CFP) designation. You can consult various searchable databases to find one who is right for you, such as the National Association of Personal Financial Advisors (www.napfa.org), the Garrett Planning Network (garrettplanningnetwork.com), the Financial Planning Association (financialplanningassociation.org), and the Certified Financial Planner Board of Standards (cfp.net).

Build a diversified retirement plan. It's never too late to crank up outside retirement accounts, which can help trim your tax bill now and grow tax-deferred until you make withdrawals in retirement.

Take a simple approach. When investing, go for a globally diverse mix of low-cost index funds (or exchange-traded funds, ETFs). You might buy three funds: an index fund that invests in the entire US stock market; one that owns developed foreign stock markets and a smattering of emerging stock markets; and an index fund that owns the broad US bond market.

Or you might opt to invest in a target-date fund that automatically adjusts the balance of your fixed-income (bond) investments and stocks based on your age. Select a target-date fund based on the year you expect to retire. The biggest target-date fund families are through Fidelity, T. Rowe Price, and Vanguard, though most financial institutions offer them, too.

Start a retirement plan for your employees. Depending on how many years you have until you want to retire and sell your business, it might make sense to look into ways to start a retirement plan for your business. Check out 401(k) plans targeted to small businesses. The website 401khelpcenter.com has a free directory of firms that sell retirement plans to small business owners.

Creating a retirement plan for employees doesn't have to be a heavy lift these days. That said, only one-third (34 percent) of small employers currently offer a retirement savings plan to employees, per Fidelity. Of those that do not offer a plan, almost half (48 percent) say they do not believe they can afford one. Other small business owners feel they are too busy running their company to focus on it (22 percent) and an equal number (21 percent) don't know how to start the process of offering a retirement plan. With nearly half of all US employees working for a small business, this could leave many individuals not ready for retirement, according to the report.

Those who are self-employed or are running microbusinesses (with fewer than 10 employees) are most likely to say they cannot afford to offer a retirement savings plan to employees.

"Self-employed individuals are carrying the entire weight of their business's success on their shoulders," according to Roger Morrissette, Fidelity's vice president of small business retirement products. "Understandably, many feel they do not have the time or resources to administer a retirement savings plan. The good news is there are many options available. Whether you have one employee or 100, there are affordable, flexible solutions for businesses of all sizes."

The four main options for small business retirement products are: SEP-IRA, SIMPLE IRA, solo 401(k), and SIMPLE 401(k). For all but SEP-IRAs, a business entity can be a sole proprietorship, a partnership, a limited liability company, or a corporation. A SEP-IRA is a tax-deductible retirement plan like a traditional IRA and great if you're the company's only employee. One caveat: If you have employees, you generally must also fund SEP-IRAs for them. A SIMPLE IRA is a retirement plan for owners with 100 or fewer employees. Contributions are pretax and taken directly out of employee paychecks, similar to a 401(k). A solo 401(k) is for self-employed people without employees (except perhaps a spouse).

YOUR TO-DO LIST

- Assess your own personal goals and future financial picture by running your numbers.
- Conduct a formal evaluation of the value of your business. You can determine what you might expect to sell your business for from comparable sales in the industry and in your geographic location.
- Ask yourself: Am I emotionally ready to exit? What am I going to do with myself after I sell my business and retire?
- Seek out guidance from your financial adviser and ultimately a team that includes your accountant and your attorney.
- What retirement assets do you have outside of your business? Can you build up these accounts?
- Research how you can start a retirement plan for your company.

AFTERWORD

The Generation X retirement reality doesn't have to bite.

That's the message we hope you've discovered as we guided you with practical steps to a new way of envisioning and embracing your financial future. This is your time to recognize and acknowledge the key threshold you're on, to take your time to appreciate it, and to take action to see what emerges.

While there's underlying evidence that some of us born between 1965 and 1980 are woefully behind in saving, we also know many of us are ramping up our retirement preparedness and debt management.

We're right alongside you. Our job has been to help you see the possibilities in a new light as you enter this next life stage. Retirement means something different to all of us. This book is dedicated to helping you take control of your money by making smart decisions and allowing you to imagine new beginnings and ways to stay challenged and relevant and prosperous as the years unfold.

As the poet and Gen Xer Matthew Zapruder wrote in his memoir *Story of a Poem*, we hope we have been "as simple and clear as possible, to reach out to you, without making things simpler and clearer than they actually are, which would be a deep betrayal."

After reading this book, we hope you clearly realize that you can't be complacent and not care. Planning for retirement is too important to put off. We know you will succeed. You have the ability and talent to navigate the messy world of money and make the choices that are right for you.

In that spirit, as you learn and build new ways toward your personal financial freedom, we wish you patience and power and a dollop of fun. Remember, saving for retirement truly means saving for a rich life in all its aspects.

A parting thought to hold on to from Douglas Coupland, in his book *Generation X: Tales for an Accelerated Culture*:

> After you're dead and buried and floating around whatever place we go to, what's going to be your best memory of earth? What one moment for you defines what it's like to be alive on this planet? What's your takeaway? Fake yuppie experiences that you had to spend money on, like white water rafting or elephant rides in Thailand, don't count. I want to hear some small moment from your life that proves you're really alive.

ACKNOWLEDGMENTS

FROM KERRY HANNON

Thank you first and foremost to our Hachette Book Group executive editor, Emily Taber, and agent, Linda Konner at the Linda Konner Literary Agency. It's the creative power of these two women that sparked this project.

They perceived the demand for a playbook to successfully guide Gen X to new financial acumen as they begin to enter their retirement phase of life. And Linda, Happy 10th book for the two of us! Working with you has been a highlight of my career.

John Marcom, our Yahoo Finance sage and pathfinder, your leadership set this endeavor in motion and moved it forward every step of the way through all the dance maneuvers necessary to navigate this publishing territory for Yahoo Finance. You instantly understood what this resource means to our Yahoo Finance Gen X audience and readers, and how it can help them take control of their financial lives. A mere thanks doesn't capture the essence of your behind-the-scenes footwork.

Myles Udland, head of news at Yahoo Finance, your keen interest in this book was the catalyst that launched the partnership between Yahoo Finance, Janna, and myself. Heartfelt appreciation for that vision.

Chris Noble, your editorial leadership and guidance took this book to the finish line with enthusiasm and grace.

To my Yahoo Finance editor, Molly Moorhead, a deep respect for your editorial chops week in and week out and gobs of gratitude for your support and encouragement.

Janna Herron, I'm delighted you agreed to join forces with me as coauthor of *Retirement Bites*. What a gift. Your clear editing, sharp writing, and keen storytelling abilities inspire me. Our teamwork, as the oft used saying goes, makes the dream work.

Michelle Welsh-Horst, senior manager of editorial production, you were an ace at making the process smooth, and the trains run on time. To Mike van Mantgem, thanks for the top-drawer copyediting. And a big shout-out to Jenny Lee, Jessica Breen, and Alcimary Pena—our superstar publicity and marketing team at Hachette.

A huge round of applause to the following experts who shared their insights with me: Marci Alboher, Nancy Ancowitz, Christine Benz, Jacob Channel, Catherine Collinson, Chip Conley, Ken Dychtwald, Dan Egan, Aja Evans, Ryan Frederick, Marc Freedman, Jordan Grumet, Matt Hansen, Howard Hook, Morgan Housel, Cindy Hounsell, David John, Mark Johnson, Laurence Kotlikoff, Robert Laura, Kelly LaVigne, Stephanie McCullough, Dorian Mintzer, Ramona Schindelheim, Bradley Schurman, John Scott, Ed Slott, Justin Smith, Emerson Sprick, and Gerri Walsh.

Thanks to my banjo-picking pal and font of retirement expertise, Mark Miller, for always taking my calls and teaching me the nuances of Social Security, Medicare, and more.

Chris Farrell, my colleague and friend along this path, has deeply reported this profound shift in the concept of "retirement" in our culture with his terrific books, *Purpose and a Paycheck* and *UnRetirement*, and is always there to bounce off ideas.

To the many people who shared their money stories with me, including Barbara Brooks, Destiny Burns, Mark Cappone, Rachel Cohen, David Conn, Sallie Cosgrove, Joyce Harman, Jennifer Reingold, and Reina and Don Weiner—thanks for opening the door into your journey for others to learn and be inspired.

Profound gratitude to Beverly Jones, my go-to executive coach, savvy career strategist, author of *Find Your Happy at Work: 50 Ways to Get Unstuck, Move Past Boredom, and Discover Fulfillment* and *Think Like an Entrepreneur, Act Like a CEO*...and fellow Labrador lover.

Richard Eisenberg, former managing editor of *Next Avenue* and former executive editor of *Money* magazine, has been an essential guide down this path of learning and discovery about all things retirement. Rich, you continue to show me how to tap curiosity and work to help people change their lives for a secure financial future.

Hank Gilman, one of the top editors I have had the pleasure to work with and now a dear pal. What can I say, you just get it. Thanks for the laughs and always sharp editorial acumen.

Heartfelt appreciation to my home team, the Bonney family: Paul, Pat, Christine, Mike, Caitlin, Shannon, Garrett Goon, Eileen Roach Bonney, Lindsay Corner Bonney, and Kodi; the Hannon family: Mike, Judy, Brendan (Max), Sean (Emily), Conor, and Brian; the Hersch family: Ginny, David, Corey, and Amy; and the Hackel family: Stu, Sue, Cassie, and Eric.

Deep gratitude to Peter Foley, whose wisdom, kindness, and love of horses gets me through many days with smiles. Thanks for helping me find my childhood joy again. Peter, your simple phrase, "Have fun," as I enter the show ring on Caparino Z, says it all.

To all my horse friends and, particularly, my ringside cheerleaders at Woodhall Farm in Aldie, Virginia, including Dale Crittenberger, Eladio, Laura Schroff Scaletti (my show manager), Roger Scaletti, Dennis and Brenda Schroff, Tracy Lyn Mathews, Sue Clark, Nancy Davidson, Kirsten Good, Martine Hartogensis, and Teralyn Carlson.

...and profound thanks to my sidekick who bakes the cake, Lydia Davidson. What a team.

To my horse of a lifetime, Caparino Z—from my heart to your heart. To Elmore "Elly," my Labrador retriever, who reminds me of the small moments of delight each and every day.

And saving the best for last, to my husband, Cliff Hackel, who has never wavered in his love and pride in what I do and makes the road a better one together. To paraphrase Bruce Springsteen, we walk together, come what may and should we lose our way, I'll wait for you, and should I fall behind, wait for me.

Note: The material you discovered here is gleaned from my own research and reporting. Some of the content initially was shared in my Yahoo Finance columns.

FROM JANNA HERRON

Of course, let's start with our incredible book editor and almost Gen Xer, Emily Taber, whose savvy insights and on-the-nose edits elevated this book to where it needed to be. Your pitch to us to "pump up the volume" sealed the deal for me.

To Linda Konner, our agent, and my very first, thank you for guiding me through the nerve-racking book-pitching process and calmly swatting away my anxiety early on when I asked, "What happens if no one picks up our book proposal?" You knew better.

A hearty thanks to John Marcom at Yahoo Finance, who championed this project from its earliest days. Without your navigation, we may never have left the ground floor.

To Molly Moorhead, my old editor at Yahoo Finance, who understood the time and effort writing this book would take and provided the required space for me to do it. She also knows the real writing doesn't begin until right before the deadline.

So much love and respect to my coauthor Kerry Hannon, who must have found a rip in the space-time continuum, because I've never met someone who could write so much so quickly and always with a smile on her face. I would never have finished writing this book—my first and your 15th!—without your experience, enthusiasm, optimism, and encouragement shepherding me through. Thank you so much for including me.

Major high fives to the experts who make me look smarter: Judith Brown, Paul Caylor, Benny Goodman, Jennifer Grant, Monique Lavender Greenberg, Bridget Grimes, David John, Carolyn McClanahan,

Judson Meinhart, Ebony Ruffin, Scott Sheldon, Matt Schulz, Jon Ulin, April Wise, and Adam Wojtkowski.

Huge shout-out to the folks who opened up their lives and shared their retirement worries, hopes, goals, and strategies: Christine Condry, Chuck and Dawn Hansberry, Laura Heller, and K. Sommer.

And on the childhood home front, to Mom, who taught me a good sale saves money, and to Dad, who taught me a good sale does not save money. Jokes aside, you both have always been my biggest supporters through life's ups and downs. There are not enough thank yous in the world.

To my brother Kim and sister Dawn, whose taste in music, clothes, and pop culture solidified my Gen X bona fides.

To Pennie, my constant purring companion as I wrote, except when doing zoomies out of the litter box.

And to the other two J's in my household. My son Jude, the reason I try to be a better person every single day and whose humor and hugs can brighten my worst moods. And to my husband Jeremy, who is my first go-to editor and can help me quash any writer's block I might have. Thank you for our wonderful J3 life.

ADDITIONAL RESOURCES

OVERVIEW AND RESEARCH

AARP, About PPI: aarp.org
Bipartisan Policy Center: bipartisanpolicy.org
CoGenerate: cogenerate.org
Employee Benefit Research Institute: ebri.org
FINRA Investor Education Foundation, Research Center: finrafoundation.org
Insurance Information Institute: iii.org
Second Act Stories podcast: secondactstories.org
Social Security Administration, Delayed Retirement Credits: ssa.gov
Transamerica Institute: transamericainstitute.org
WorkingNation: workingnation.com

RETIREMENT CALCULATORS

AARP, Retirement Nest Egg Calculator: aarp.org
Prudential, Retirement Income Calculator: prudential.com
Charles Schwab, Retirement Calculator: schwab.com

INVESTING

University of Missouri, Investment Risk Tolerance Assessment: cafnr.missouri.edu

SOCIAL SECURITY

Social Security Administration, Create Your Personal my Social Security Account: ssa.gov/myaccount

Carroll Advisory Group, Break Even Calculator for Social Security: carrolladvisory.com
Social Security Works: socialsecurityworks.org
Social Security Administration, Life Expectancy Calculator and Early or Late Retirement Calculator: ssa.gov
Consumer Financial Protection Bureau, Planning Your Social Security Claiming Age: consumerfinance.gov
AARP, Social Security Calculator: aarp.org
Maximize My Social Security: maximizemysocialsecurity.com
SSAnalyzer: ssanalyzer.com
Next Avenue, Where to Get Help to Claim Social Security Wisely: nextavenue.org
RSSA, National Association of Registered Social Security Analysts: narssa.org
National Social Security Advisors: nssapros.com
Social Security Administration, What You Could Get from Disability: ssa.gov

REAL ESTATE

US Department of Housing and Urban Development, Home Equity Conversion Mortgages for Seniors: hud.gov
AARP, HomeFit Guide: aarp.org

ESTATE PLANNING

AARP, Advance Directive Forms: aarp.org
Health Resources and Services Administration (HRSA): hrsa.gov
Funeral Consumers Alliance, State by State: Assigning an Agent to Control Disposition: funerals.org

CREDIT CARD DEBT

Yahoo Finance, Best Balance Transfer Credit Cards, and Best Personal Loan Rates: finance.yahoo.com

HEALTH CARE

HealthCare.gov, Health Savings Account (HSA): healthcare.gov
Medicare.gov: medicare.gov
Life Planning Partners: lifeplanningpartners.com

Fidelity, Retiree Health Care Cost Estimate as Americans Seek Clarity Around Medicare Selection: newsroom.fidelity.com

Employee Benefit Research Institute (EBRI), Projected Savings Medicare Beneficiaries Need for Health Expenses Increased Again in 2023: ebri.org

Genworth, Calculate the Cost of Long-Term Care Near You: genworth.com

TAXES

IRS, Self-Employed Individuals Tax Center, and How Small Business Owners Can Deduct Their Home Office from Their Taxes: irs.gov

CAREER COACHING

International Coaching Federation: coachingfederation.org

Life Planning Network: lifeplanningnetwork.org

Retirement Coaches Association (RCA): retirementcoachesassociation.org

JOB SEARCH AND JOB BOARDS

AARP Employer Pledge Program, Job Search, and Job Board: aarp.org

CareerBuilder: careerbuilder.com

Certified Age Friendly Employers: Retirementjobs.com

US Department of Labor's CareerOneStop: careeronestop.org

Indeed: indeed.com

Ladders: theladders.com

LinkedIn Jobs and LinkedIn Services: linkedin.com

Monster: monster.com

O*NET Resource Center, Career Exploration Tools: onetcenter.org

US Department of Labor Statistics, Occupational Outlook Handbook: bls.gov

ZipRecruiter: ziprecruiter.com

PAY AND SALARY

Glassdoor: glassdoor.com

Payscale: payscale.com

Salary.com: salary.com

FREELANCE/CONTRACT JOBS

Fiverr: fiverr.com
FlexJobs: flexjobs.com
FlexProfessionals: flexprofessionalsllc.com
Freelancer: freelancer.com
Freelancers Union: freelancersunion.org
GLG: glginsights.com
Rat Race Rebellion: ratracerebellion.com
SideHusl.com: sidehusl.com
TaskRabbit: taskrabbit.com
Upwork: upwork.com
Work-At-Home Vintage Experts: wahve.com

SMALL BUSINESS

AARP Small Business: aarp.org
Small Business Administration: sba.gov
SCORE: score.org
SBA, US Small Business: usa.gov

SELF-ASSESSMENT

Penn Authentic Happiness, Questionnaire Center: www.authentichappiness.sas.upenn.edu/testcenter
Gallup, CliftonStrengths: gallup.com
Myers-Briggs Type Indicator (MBTI): mbtionline.com

WHAT'S NEXT: EDUCATION PROGRAMS

Advanced Leadership Program—Harvard: advancedleadership.harvard.edu
Distinguished Career Institute—Stanford: dci.stanford.edu
Inspired Leadership Initiative—University of Notre Dame: ili.nd.edu
Experienced Leaders Initiative—Yale: som.yale.edu
Change Makers—University of Colorado Denver: ucdenver.edu
MEA: meawisdom.com

EDUCATION: IN-PERSON AND ONLINE CLASSES

GetSetUp: getsetup.io
Coursera: coursera.org
LinkedIn Learning: linkedin.com

MasterClass: masterclass.com
Oasis Institute: oasiseverywhere.org
Osher Institutes, US Lifelong Learning Institute Directory: sps.northwestern.edu
Udemy: udemy.com

RELOCATION/AGING IN PLACE

Here: here.life
Best Places: bestplaces.net
ExpatExchange: ExpatExchange.com
International Living, Best Places to Retire: internationalliving.com
US Department of State, International Travel, Retirement Abroad: travel.state.gov
Social Security Administration, Your Payments While You Are Outside the United States: ssa.gov

GETTING ADVICE

US Securities and Exchange Commission: adviserinfo.sec.gov
Certified Financial Planner Board of Standards: CFP.net
Financial Planning Association: onefpa.org
Certified Financial Planner Board of Standards: LetsMakeAPlan.org
The National Association of Personal Financial Advisors: napfa.org

BOOKS

The Encore Career Handbook: How to Make a Living and a Difference in the Second Half of Life by Marci Alboher

How to Retire: 20 Lessons For a Happy, Successful, and Wealthy Retirement by Christine Benz

The Little Book of Common Sense Investing: The Only Way to Guarantee Your Fair Share of Stock Market Returns by John C. Bogle

Learning to Love Midlife: 12 Reasons Why Life Gets Better with Age by Chip Conley

The New Retirement: The Ultimate Guide to the Rest of Your Life by Jan Cullinane

What Retirees Want: A Holistic View of Life's Third Age by Ken Dychtwald and Robert Morison

Feel-Good Finance: Untangle Your Relationship with Money for Better Mental, Emotional, and Financial Well-Being by Aja Evans

Purpose and a Paycheck: Finding Meaning, Money, and Happiness in the Second Half of Life and Unretirement: How Baby Boomers Are Changing the Way We Think About Work, Community, and the Good Life by Chris Farrell

Right Place, Right Time: The Ultimate Guide to Choosing a Home for the Second Half of Life by Ryan Frederick

How to Live Forever: The Enduring Power of Connecting the Generations by Marc Freedman

The Intelligent Investor, 3rd Ed.: The Definitive Book on Value Investing by Benjamin Graham and Jason Zweig

Taking Stock: A Hospice Doctor's Advice on Financial Independence, Building Wealth, and Living a Regret-Free Life and *The Purpose Code: How to Unlock Meaning, Maximize Happiness, and Leave a Lasting Legacy* by Dr. Jordan Grumet

In Control at 50+: How to Succeed in the New World of Work by Kerry Hannon

Same as Ever: A Guide to What Never Changes and *The Psychology of Money: Timeless Lessons on Wealth, Greed, and Happiness* by Morgan Housel

Find Your Happy at Work: 50 Ways to Get Unstuck, Move Past Boredom, and Discover Fulfillment and *Think Like an Entrepreneur, Act Like a CEO: 50 Indispensable Tips to Help You Stay Afloat, Bounce Back, and Get Ahead at Work* by Beverly Jones

The Price You Pay for College: An Entirely New Road Map for the Biggest Financial Decision Your Family Will Ever Make by Ron Lieber

Retirement Reboot: Commonsense Financial Strategies for Getting Back on Track by Mark Miller

Get What's Yours for Medicare—Revised and Updated: Maximize Your Coverage, Minimize Your Costs by Philip Moeller

Ask Questions, Save Money, Make More: How to Take Control of Your Financial Life by Matt Schulz

The Super Age: Decoding Our Demographic Destiny by Bradley Schurman

The Retirement Savings Time Bomb Ticks Louder: How to Avoid Unnecessary Tax Landmines, Defuse the Latest Threats to Your Retirement Savings, and Ignite Your Financial Freedom by Ed Slott

Boomer Reinvention: How to Create Your Dream Career Over 50 by John Tarnoff

The Second Fifty: Answers to the 7 Big Questions of Midlife and Beyond by Debra Whitman

NOTES

INTRODUCTION

1. Bond, Tyler, Celia Ringland, and Dr. Joelle Saad-Lessler. "The Forgotten Generation: Generation X Approaches Retirement." National Institute on Retirement Security, September 28, 2023. https://www.nirsonline.org/reports/genx/.
2. "2023 US RETIREMENT SURVEY: Generation X and Retirement Report." https://mybrand.schroders.com/m/641f99601ba5236e/original/Schroders_2023_US_Retirement_Survey_Gen_X_Rpt_FINAL.pdf.
3. "Two-Thirds of Americans Expect the United States to Enter Recession This Year; Most Are Taking Steps to Navigate Economic Uncertainty." Northwestern Mutual. Northwestern Mutual, May 15, 2023. https://news.northwesternmutual.com/2023-05-15-Two-Thirds-of-Americans-Expect-the-United-States-to-Enter-Recession-This-Year-Most-Are-Taking-Steps-to-Navigate-Economic-Uncertainty.
4. "Workers Expect Employers to Care About Their Lives At and Outside of Work Amid a State of Permacrisis." MetLife, May 18, 2024. https://www.metlife.com/about-us/newsroom/2024/march/workers-expect-employers-to-care-about-their-lives-at-and-outside-of-work-amid-a-state-of-permacrisis/.
5. Farrell, Kerry, and Joana Allamani. "1974–2024: Celebrating 50 Years of Protected Retirement Plans." U.S. Bureau of Labor Statistics, March 2024. https://www.bls.gov/spotlight/2024/celebrating-50-years-of-protected-retirement-plans/.
6. Costo, Stephanie L. "Trends in Retirement Plan Coverage over the Last Decade." U.S. Bureau of Labor Statistics, February 2006. https://www.bls.gov/opub/mlr/2006/02/art5full.pdf.
7. Farrell, Kerry, and Joana Allamani. "1974–2024: Celebrating 50 Years of Protected Retirement Plans." U.S. Bureau of Labor Statistics, March 2024. https://www.bls.gov/spotlight/2024/celebrating-50-years-of-protected-retirement-plans/.
8. Sabelhaus, John. "The Current State of U.S. Workplace Retirement Plan Coverage." The Pension Research Council of The Wharton School of the

University of Pennsylvania, March 2022. https://repository.upenn.edu/server/api/core/bitstreams/53f6523d-7c37-4052-add0-676774a6181a/content.

9. Butrica, Barbara A., Karen E. Smith, and Howard M. Iams. "This Is Not Your Parents' Retirement: Comparing Retirement Income Across Generations." Social Security Administration, 2012. https://www.ssa.gov/policy/docs/ssb/v72n1/v72n1p37.pdf.
10. Bond, Tyler, Celia Ringland, and Dr. Joelle Saad-Lessler. "The Forgotten Generation: Generation X Approaches Retirement." National Institute on Retirement Security, September 28, 2023. https://www.nirsonline.org/reports/genx/.
11. Holden, Sarah, Peter Brady, and Michael Hadley. "401(k) Plans: A 25-Year Retrospective." Investment Company Institute, November 2006. https://www.ici.org/doc-server/pdf:per12-02.pdf.
12. "Schwab Modern Wealth Survey 2024." Charles Schwab, June 12, 2024. https://www.aboutschwab.com/schwab-modern-wealth-survey-2024.
13. Collinson, Catherine, and Heidi Cho. "Post-Pandemic Realities: The Retirement Outlook of the Multigenerational Workforce." Transamerica Institute, July 2023. https://www.transamericainstitute.org/docs/default-source/research/post-pandemic-retirement-realities-multigenerational-workforce-report-july-2023.pdf.
14. Neuman, Tricia, and Anthony Damico. "Retiree Health Benefits: Going, Going, Nearly Gone?" KFF, April 12, 2024. https://www.kff.org/medicare/issue-brief/retiree-health-benefits-going-going-nearly-gone.
15. Yellen, Janet, Julie A. Su, Xavier Becerra, and Martin O'Malley. "Status of the Social Security and Medicare Programs: A Summary of the 2024 Annual Reports." Social Security, Trustees Report Summary, 2024. https://www.ssa.gov/OACT/TRSUM/index.html.
16. "Two-Thirds of Americans Expect the United States to Enter Recession This Year; Most Are Taking Steps to Navigate Economic Uncertainty." Northwestern Mutual. Northwestern Mutual, May 15, 2023. https://news.northwesternmutual.com/2023-05-15-Two-Thirds-of-Americans-Expect-the-United-States-to-Enter-Recession-This-Year-Most-Are-Taking-Steps-to-Navigate-Economic-Uncertainty.
17. Horymski, Chris. "Average Credit Card Debt by Age in 2024." *Experian* (blog). Experian, July 2, 2024. https://www.experian.com/blogs/ask-experian/research/credit-card-debt-by-age/.
18. Hanson, Melanie. "Student Loan Debt by Generation (2024)." Education Data Initiative. November 21, 2024. https://educationdata.org/student-loan-debt-by-generation.
19. Maguire, Brianna. "Overcoming the Sandwich Generation's Caregiving Challenges." *Carewell* (blog). Carewell, June 17, 2024. https://www.carewell.com/resources/blog/the-sandwich-generation/.
20. Maguire. "Overcoming the Sandwich Generation's Caregiving Challenges."
21. Fry, Richard. "Gen X Rebounds as the Only Generation to Recover the Wealth Lost after the Housing Crash." Pew Research Center, July 23, 2018. https://www.pewresearch.org/short-reads/2018/07/23/gen-x-rebounds-as-the-only-generation-to-recover-the-wealth-lost-after-the-housing-crash/.
22. Katz, Lily, and Sheharyar Bokhari. "Gen Z's Homeownership Rate Stagnated in 2023, but Millennials and Gen Xers Saw Gains." Redfin

Real Estate News, January 17, 2024. https:/www.redfin.com/news/homeownership-rate-by-generation-2023/.

23. "The Cerulli Report: U.S. High-Net-Worth and Ultra-High-Net-Worth Markets 2021." Cerulli Associates.
24. "Table 2602. Generation of Reference Person." U.S. Bureau of Labor Statistics, September 2023. https://www.bls.gov/cex/tables/calendar-year/mean-item-share-average-standard-error/reference-person-age-generation-2022.pdf.
25. "Archived: The History of Yahoo!—How It All Started..." Yahoo! Media Relations. Wayback Machine, 2005. https://web.archive.org/web/20130402073246/http://docs.yahoo.com/info/misc/history.html.

CHAPTER 1: YOUR MONEY MINDSET

1. Kelton, Katie. "Survey: Half of American Cardholders Now Carry Credit Card Debt." Edited by Brooklyn Lowery. Bankrate, January 2025. https://www.bankrate.com/credit-cards/news/credit-card-debt-survey.
2. Ko, K. Jeremy, Olivia Valdes, Ritta McLaughlin, and Gary R. Mottola. "How Gen X Compares Financially to Other Generations: Doing Alright but Feeling Bad." FINRA Foundation, October 2024. https://www.finrafoundation.org/sites/finrafoundation/files/2024-10/how-gen-x-compares-financially-to-other-generations-oct2024.pdf.
3. "Gen X: The Economy's Struggling Middle Child?" Bank of America Institute, September 26, 2024. https://institute.bankofamerica.com/content/dam/economic-insights/gen-x-economy.pdf.
4. "Planning: The Missing Link to Retirement Security: Retirement Survey & Insights Report 2024." Goldman Sachs Asset Management, September 2024. https://am.gs.com/en-us/institutions/insights/report-survey/retirement-survey.

CHAPTER 2: DESIGNING YOUR RETIREMENT VISION

1. Galambos, Nancy L., Harvey J. Krahn, Matthew D. Johnson, and Margie E. Lachman. "The U Shape of Happiness across the Life Course: Expanding the Discussion." *Perspectives on Psychological Science*, July 1, 2021. https://pmc.ncbi.nlm.nih.gov/articles/PMC7529452/.
2. "Thinking Positively About Aging Extends Life More than Exercise and Not Smoking." *Yale News*. Yale University, July 29, 2002. https://news.yale.edu/2002/07/29/thinking-positively-about-aging-extends-life-more-exercise-and-not-smoking.

CHAPTER 3: CREATING YOUR FINANCIAL PLAN

1. Collinson, Catherine, and Heidi Cho. "Post-Pandemic Realities: The Retirement Outlook of the Multigenerational Workforce." Transamerica Institute, July 2023. https://www.transamericainstitute.org/docs/default-source/research/post-pandemic-retirement-realities-multigenerational-workforce-report-july-2023.pdf.
2. "How Much Will You Spend in Retirement?" Fidelity, November 25, 2024. https://www.fidelity.com/viewpoints/retirement/spending-in-retirement.

3. Yakoboski, Paul J., Andrea Sticha, and Annamaria Lusardi. "An Unrecognized Barrier to Retirement Income Security: Poor Longevity Literacy." TIAA Institute, August 21, 2023. https://www.tiaa.org/public/institute/publication/2023/an-unrecognized-barrier-to-retirement-income-security-poor-longevity-literacy.
4. John Kho Consulting. "Investing in Peak Earning Years." ALEC Wealth Management, 2022. https://www.alecu.org/financial-well-being/financial-education/investing-in-peak-earning-years.
5. Guzman, Gloria, and Melissa Kollar. "Income in the United States: 2022." U.S. Census Bureau, September 2023. https://www.census.gov/content/dam/Census/library/publications/2023/demo/p60-279.pdf.
6. Bialik, Kristen, and Richard Fry. "Millennial Life: How Young Adulthood Today Compares with Prior Generations." Pew Research Center, February 14, 2019. https://www.pewresearch.org/social-trends/2019/02/14/millennial-life-how-young-adulthood-today-compares-with-prior-generations-2/.
7. "Wells Fargo: Younger Women Are Increasingly Earning the Title of 'Breadwinner.'" Wells Fargo, March 8, 2021. Wells Fargo. https://newsroom.wf.com/English/news-releases/news-release-details/2021/Wells-Fargo-Younger-Women-Are-Increasingly-Earning-the-Title-of-Breadwinner/default.aspx.
8. "DFA: Distributional Financial Accounts." The Fed—Table: Distribution of Household Wealth in the U.S. since 1989, September 20, 2024. https://www.federalreserve.gov/releases/z1/dataviz/dfa/distribute/table/#quarter:139;series:Net%20worth;demographic:generation;population:all;units:levels.
9. Aladangady, Aditya, Jesse Bricker, Andrew C. Chang, Sarena Goodman, Jacob Krimmel, Kevin B. Moore, Sarah Reber, Alice Henriques Volz, and Richard A. Windle. "Changes in U.S. Family Finances from 2019 to 2022: Evidence from the Survey of Consumer Finances." Washington: Board of Governors of the Federal Reserve System, October 2023. https://doi.org/10.17016/8799.
10. Gregory, Victoria, and Kevin Bloodworth. "Assets and Debt across Generations." Federal Reserve Bank of St. Louis, May 24, 2024. https://www.stlouisfed.org/on-the-economy/2024/may/assets-debt-generations.
11. Sattelmeyer, Sarah. "Borrowers' Student Loan Balances Are Growing over Time. And It's Not Just Because of the Interest Rate." *New America* (blog). New America, May 12, 2022. https://www.newamerica.org/education-policy/edcentral/borrowers-student-loan-balances-are-growing-over-time-and-its-not-just-because-of-the-interest-rate/.

CHAPTER 4: NUTS AND BOLTS OF RETIREMENT ACCOUNTS

1. "Retirement Security Across Generations Is Faltering in the Post-Pandemic Environment." Transamerica Center for Retirement Studies, July 6, 2023. https://www.transamericainstitute.org/research/publications/details/retirement-security-across-generations-is-faltering-in-the-post-pandemic-environment.
2. Clark, Jeffrey W. "How America Saves 2024." Vanguard, 2024. https://corporate.vanguard.com/content/dam/corp/research/pdf/how_america_saves_report_2024.pdf.

3. Clark, Jeffrey W., and Kevin D. Kukulka. "Generational Changes in 401(k) Behaviors." Vanguard, April 2023. https://institutional.vanguard.com/content/dam/inst/iig-transformation/insights/pdf/2023/generational-changes-in-401k-behaviors.pdf.
4. Clark and Kukulka. "Generational Changes in 401(k) Behaviors."
5. Collinson, Catherine, and Heidi Cho. "Post-Pandemic Realities: The Retirement Outlook of the Multigenerational Workforce." Transamerica Institute, July 2023. https://www.transamericainstitute.org/docs/default-source/research/post-pandemic-retirement-realities-multigenerational-workforce-report-july-2023.pdf.
6. "New AARP Research: Nearly Half of Americans Do Not Have Access to Retirement Plans at Work." AARP, July 13, 2022. https://press.aarp.org/2022-7-13-New-AARP-Research-Nearly-Half-Americans-Do-Not-Have-Access-to-Retirement-Plans-at-Work.
7. "State of Independence in America 2024." MBO Partners, 2024. https://www.mbopartners.com/state-of-independence/.
8. Collinson, Catherine, and Heidi Cho. "24 Facts About Women's Retirement Outlook." Transamerica Institute, October 2024. https://www.transamericainstitute.org/docs/research/gender-lgbtq/24-facts-women-retirement-survey-report-2024.pdf.
9. "State Programs 2025: Partnerships Continue to Expand and Several New Programs Will Launch," Center for Retirement Initiatives, January 2025. https://cri.georgetown.edu/states/.
10. "2024 Mid-Year Devenir HSA Research Report." Devenir, September, 25, 2024. https://www.devenir.com/research/2024-midyear-devenir-hsa-research-report/.
11. "Analysis of Health Savings Account Database with Over 13 Million Accounts Finds Accountholders Paying Health Care Expenses, Not Fully Taking Advantage of Tax Benefits." Employee Benefit Research Institute, March 1, 2023. https://www.ebri.org/docs/default-source/ebri-press-release/pr-1326-hsalong-1mar23.pdf. See also: "You Can Save $1 Million in Your Health Savings Account (HSA)." EBRI, January 23, 2025. https://www.ebri.org/content/you-can-save--1-million-in-your-health-savings-account-(hsa).

CHAPTER 5: HOW TO DIVVY UP YOUR INVESTMENTS

1. "Investment Risk Tolerance Assessment." College of Agriculture, Food and Natural Resources, University of Missouri, 2024. https://cafnr.missouri.edu/divisions/division-of-applied-social-sciences/research investment-risk-tolerance-assessment/.

CHAPTER 6: PLANNING FOR A LONGER WORK LIFE

1. Collinson, Catherine, and Heidi Cho. "Retiree Life in the Post-Pandemic Economy." Transamerica Institute, November 2024. https://www.transamericainstitute.org/docs/research/retirees/retiree-life-post-pandemic-economy-survey-report-2024.pdf.
2. Collinson, Catherine, and Heidi Cho. "Post-Pandemic Realities: The Retirement Outlook of the Multigenerational Workforce." Transamerica Institute, July 2023. https://www.transamericainstitute.org/docs/default-source/research

/post-pandemic-retirement-realities-multigenerational-workforce-report-july-2023.pdf.

3. "Amid Falling Confidence, 1 in 3 U.S. Employees Wants to Phase into Retirement." WTW, August 21, 2024. https://www.wtwco.com/en-us/news/2024/08/amid-falling-confidence-1-in-3-us-employees-wants-to-phase-into-retirement.
4. Lin, Luona, Juliana Menasce Horowitz, and Richard Fry. "Most Americans Feel Good about Their Job Security but Not Their Pay." Pew Research Center, December 10, 2024. https://www.pewresearch.org/social-trends/2024/12/10/most-americans-feel-good-about-their-job-security-but-not-their-pay/.
5. Dee, Jane E. "Becca Levy and the Fight against Ageism." Yale School of Public Health, Spring 2023. https://ysph.yale.edu/about-school-of-public-health/communications-public-relations/publications/public-health-magazine/article/becca-levy-and-the-fight-against-ageism/.
6. "How Small Business Owners Can Deduct Their Home Office from Their Taxes." Internal Revenue Service, October 15, 2024. https://www.irs.gov/newsroom/how-small-business-owners-can-deduct-their-home-office-from-their-taxes.
7. Collinson, Catherine, and Heidi Cho. "Workplace Transformations: Employer Business Practices and Benefit Offerings." Transamerica Institute, March 2024. https://www.transamericainstitute.org/docs/default-source/research/employers-benefit-offerings/workplace-transformations-employer-business-practices-and-benefit-offerings-report-march-2024.pdf.
8. Fry, Richard, and Dana Braga. "Older Workers Are Growing in Number and Earning Higher Wages." Pew Research Center, December 14, 2023. https://www.pewresearch.org/social-trends/2023/12/14/older-workers-are-growing-in-number-and-earning-higher-wages/.

CHAPTER 7: OPTIMIZING SOCIAL SECURITY

1. Hannon, Kerry. "What Employers Are Doing to Help Family Caregivers." Next Avenue, July 22, 2021. https://www.nextavenue.org/caregivers-what-employers-are-doing/.
2. "Social Security Credits." Social Security Administration. Accessed December 2024. https://www.ssa.gov/benefits/retirement/planner/credits.html.
3. "State and Local Government Workers Without Social Security Coverage." The National Conference of State Legislatures, September 22, 2022. https://www.ncsl.org/fiscal/state-and-local-government-workers-without-social-security-coverage.
4. "Social Security: If You Were Born between 1960 or Later, Your Full Retirement Age Is 67." Social Security Administration. Accessed December 2024. https://www.ssa.gov/benefits/retirement/planner/1960-delay.html.
5. "Social Security: Starting Your Retirement Benefits Early." Social Security Administration. Accessed December 2024. https://www.ssa.gov/benefits/retirement/planner/agereduction.html.
6. Li, Zhe. "Social Security and Older Workers." Congressional Research Service, October 16, 2024. https://crsreports.congress.gov/product/pdf/R/R48232.
7. "Social Security: Income Taxes and Your Social Security Benefit." Social Security Administration. Accessed December 2024. https://www-origin.ssa.gov/benefits/retirement/planner/taxes.html.

8. Stone, Gale Stallworth. "Audit Report: Higher Benefits for Dually Entitled Widow(er)s Had They Delayed Applying for Retirement Benefits." Office of the Inspector General: Social Security Administration, February 2018. https://oig-files.ssa.gov/audits/full/A-09-18-50559.pdf.
9. Yellen, Janet, Julie A. Su, Xavier Becerra, and Martin O'Malley. "Status of the Social Security and Medicare Programs: A Summary of the 2024 Annual Reports." Trustees Report Summary, 2024. https://www.ssa.gov/OACT/TRSUM/index.html.

CHAPTER 8: OTHER INCOME SOURCES

1. "Redfin Reports Gen Z's Homeownership Rate Stagnated in 2023, But Millennials and Gen X Saw Gains." Redfin, January 17, 2024. https://investors.redfin.com/news-events/press-releases/detail/1032/redfin-reports-gen-zs-homeownership-rate-stagnated-in.
2. Khater, Sam, Len Kiefer, Ajita Atreya, Rama Yanamandra, Penka Trentcheva, Genaro Villa, Song You, and Jessica Donadio. "U.S. Economic, Housing and Mortgage Market Outlook." Freddie Mac, May 2024. https://www.freddiemac.com/research/pdf/Freddie_Mac_Outlook_May_2024.pdf.
3. Cerulli Associates. "The Cerulli Report: U.S. High-Net-Worth and Ultra-High-Net-Worth Markets 2021."

CHAPTER 9: MANAGING COMPETING FINANCIAL PRIORITIES

1. Ratcliffe, Caroline, Brianna Middlewood, Melissa Knoll, Misha Davies, and Grant Guillory. "Emergency Savings and Financial Security: Insights from the Making Ends Meet Survey and Consumer Credit Panel." Consumer Financial Protection Bureau, March 2022. https://files.consumerfinance.gov/f/documents/cfpb_mem_emergency-savings-financial-security_report_2022-3.pdf.
2. Horymski, Chris. "Average Credit Card Debt by Age in 2024." *Experian* (blog). Experian, July 2, 2024. https://www.experian.com/blogs/ask-experian/research/credit-card-debt-by-age/.
3. Khater, Sam, Len Kiefer, Ajita Atreya, Rama Yanamandra, Penka Trentcheva, Genaro Villa, Song You, and Jessica Donadio. "US Economic, Housing and Mortgage Market Outlook." Freddie Mac, May 2024. https://www.freddiemac.com/research/pdf/Freddie_Mac_Outlook_May_2024.pdf.
4. Hanson, Melanie. "Student Loan Debt by Generation (2024)." EducationData.org, November 21, 2024. https://educationdata.org/student-loan-debt-by-generation.
5. Levine, Phillip. "How Much Should College Cost Students?" The Brookings Institution, September 6, 2023. https://www.brookings.edu/articles/how-much-should-college-cost-students/.

CHAPTER 10: PLANNING FOR FUTURE HEALTH CARE COSTS

1. "Fidelity Investments Releases 2024 Retiree Health Care Cost Estimate as Americans Seek Clarity Around Medicare Selection." Fidelity, August 8, 2024. Fidelity. https://newsroom.fidelity.com/pressreleases/fidelity-investments-releases-2024-retiree-health-care-cost-estimate-as-americans-seek-clarity-arou/s/7322cc17-0b90-46c4-ba49-38d6e91c3961.

2. Spiegel, Jake, and Paul Fronstin. "Projected Savings Medicare Beneficiaries Need for Health Expenses Increased Again in 2023—Some Couples Could Need as Much as $413,000 in Savings." EBRI, January 18, 2024. https://www.ebri.org/publications/research-publications/issue-briefs/content/projected-savings-medicare-beneficiaries-need-for-health-expenses-increased-again-in-2023.
3. Zheng, Hui, and Paola Echave. "Are Recent Cohorts Getting Worse? Trends in US Adult Physiological Status, Mental Health, and Health Behaviors across a Century of Birth Cohorts." *American Journal of Epidemiology*, November 2021. https://academic.oup.com/aje/article/190/11/2242/6178413.
4. Rosenberg, Philip S., and Adalberto Miranda-Filho. "Cancer Incidence Trends in Successive Social Generations in the US." JAMA Network, June 10, 2024. https://jamanetwork.com/journals/jamanetworkopen/fullarticle/2819747.
5. "New Research Report Finds Projected Savings Medicare Beneficiaries Need for Health Expenses Increased Again in 2023." EBRI, January 29, 2024. https://www.ebri.org/content/new-research-report-finds-projected-savings-medicare-beneficiaries-need-for-health-expenses-increased-again-in-2023.
6. Samuels, Claire. "How Much Does In-Home Care Cost in 2024? A State-by-State Guide." *A Place for Mom* (blog), May 2, 2024. https://www.aplaceformom.com/caregiver-resources/articles/in-home-care-costs.
7. "Risk Factors for Dementia." Alzheimer's Society, June 2021. https://www.alzheimers.org.uk/sites/default/files/pdf/factsheet_risk_factors_for_dementia.pdf.
8. "2024 Long-Term Care Insurance Facts, Data, Prices and Statistics—2024 Reports." American Association for Long-Term Care Insurance. Accessed December 2024. https://www.aaltci.org/long-term-care-insurance/learning-center/ltcfacts-2024.php.
9. Hamel, Liz, and Alex Montero. "The Affordability of Long-Term Care and Support Services: Findings from a KFF Survey." KFF, November 14, 2023. https://www.kff.org/health-costs/poll-finding/the-affordability-of-long-term-care-and-support-services/.
10. Yellen, Janet, Julie A. Su, Xavier Becerra, Martin O'Malley, and Chiquita Brooks-LaSure. "2024 Annual Report of the Boards of Trustees of the Federal Hospital Insurance and Federal Supplementary Medical Insurance Trust Funds." Centers for Medicare & Medicaid Services, May 6, 2024. https://www.cms.gov/oact/tr/2024.
11. eHealth Inc., "Gen Xers and Millennials Worry Medicare Won't Be There for Them and Are Willing to Pay More to Keep It, eHealth Report Finds." *PR Newswire*, May 22, 2024. https://www.prnewswire.com/news-releasesgen-xers-and-millennials-worry-medicare-wont-be-there-for-them-and-are-willing-to-pay-more-to-keep-it-ehealth-report-finds-302152370.html.

CHAPTER 11: RELOCATING IN RETIREMENT

1. "Welcome to the Peak 65 Zone—A New Chapter in America's Retirement Landscape." Protected Lifetime Income: Alliance for Lifetime Income. Accessed December 2024. https://www.protectedincome.org/peak65.
2. "Social Security: Annual Statistical Supplement, 2024." Social Security Administration, 2024. https://www.ssa.gov/policy/docs/statcomps/supplement/2024/5j.html.

3. "Foreign Earned Income Exclusion." Internal Revenue Service, August 22, 2024. https://www.irs.gov/individuals/international-taxpayers/foreign-earned-income-exclusion.

CHAPTER 12: WHO CAN YOU TALK TO?

1. "Fidelity Investments: 2024 Women & Investing Study." The News Market, 2024. https://preview.thenewsmarket.com/Previews/FINP/DocumentAssets/678330.pdf.
2. "The 2024 Planning & Progress Study." Northwestern Mutual, Newsroom, 2024. https://news.northwesternmutual.com/planning-and-progress-study-2024.

CHAPTER 13: PASSING YOUR WEALTH ALONG

1. Lustbader, Rachel. "2025 Wills and Estate Planning Study." *Caring* (blog), February 21, 2025. https://www.caring.com/caregivers/estate-planning/wills-survey/2024-survey/.
2. "Securing the Future—2024 Insurance Barometer." LIMRA, 2024. https://www.limra.com/siteassets/research/research-abstracts-shared/2024/securing-the-future/2024-insurance-barometer-securing-the-future-infographic pdf.

CHAPTER 14: GEN X BUSINESS OWNERS

1. "Fidelity Study: Despite Concerns About the Future, Two-Thirds of Small Businesses Do Not Currently Offer Retirement Savings Benefits." Fidelity, May 11, 2023. https://newsroom.fidelity.com/pressreleases/fidelity-study—despite-concerns-about-the-future—two-thirds-of-small-businesses-do-not-currently-o/s/72432825-233e-4a33-a470-3bed305b2f04.
2. "Selling a Business." UBS Wealth Management USA, 2023. https://www.ubs.com/us/en/wealth-management/who-we-serve/specialized-advice/business-owners/planning-a-business-sale.html.
3. "Employee Stock Ownership Plans (ESOPs)." Internal Revenue Service, August 20, 2024. https://www.irs.gov/retirement-plans/employee-stock-ownership-plans-esops.

INDEX

Credit: Elizabeth Dranitzke, Photopia

KERRY HANNON is a leading authority and strategist on retirement, jobs, career transitions, entrepreneurship, leadership, and personal finance. She is a senior columnist and on-air expert at Yahoo Finance and the award-winning author of fourteen books, including *Great Jobs for Everyone 50+*. She lives in Washington, DC.

Credit: Gino DePinto, Yahoo Finance

JANNA HERRON is an award-winning reporter and editor with twenty years of expertise in personal finance, retirement, taxes, and real estate. Before becoming a freelance journalist, she was a senior columnist and on-air expert at Yahoo Finance. She lives in New York.

RAISING READERS

Books Build Bright Futures

Thank you for reading this book and for being a reader of books in general. As an author, I am so grateful to share being part of a community of readers with you and I hope you will join me in passing our love of books on to the next generation of readers.

Did you know that reading for enjoyment is the single biggest predictor of a child's future happiness and success?

More than family circumstances, parents' educational background, or income reading impacts a child's future academic performance, emotional well-being communication skills, economic security, ambition, and happiness.

Studies show that kids reading for enjoyment in the US is in rapid decline:

- In 2012, 53% of 9-year-olds read almost every day. Just 10 years later, in 2022, the number had fallen to 39%.
- In 2012, 27% of 13-year-olds read for fun daily. By 2023, that number was just 14%.

Together, we can commit to **Raising Readers** and change this trend. How?

- Read to children in your life daily.
- Model reading as a fun activity.
- Reduce screen time.
- Start a family, school, or community book club.
- Visit bookstores and libraries regularly.
- Listen to audiobooks.
- Read the book before you see the movie.
- Encourage your child to read aloud to a pet or stuffed animal.
- Give books as gifts.
- Donate books to families and communities in need.

BOB1217

Books build bright futures, and **Raising Readers** is our shared responsibility.

For more information, visit **JoinRaisingReaders.com**

Sources: National Endowment for the Arts, National Assessment of Educational Progress, WorldBookDay.org, Nielsen BookData's 2023 "Understanding the Children's Book Consumer"